A GREAT SONG

A GREAT SONG

URSULA WEIGERT

Pacific Press®
Publishing Association

Nampa, Idaho | Oshawa, Ontario, Canada
www.pacificpress.com

Cover design by Gerald Lee Monks
Cover image by Martin U. K. Lengemann
Inside design by Aaron Troia
Inside photos by Wilma Björling, Walter Boberg, Bullocks, Matthias Creutziger, Erwin Döring, René Larsson, Martin U.K. Lengemann, Kerstin Schindelhauer, Paul Yates.

Originally published as *Ein großer Gesang: Der Dirigent Herbert Blomstedt als Mensch und Musiker* (Leipzig: Henschel, 2013).

The author assumes full responsibility for the accuracy of all facts and quotations as cited in this book.

Unless otherwise noted, all Scripture references are from the New King James Version®. Copyright © 1982 by Thomas Nelson. Used by permission. All rights reserved.

Additional copies of this book are available by calling toll-free 1-800-765-6955 or by visiting http://www.AdventistBookCenter.com.

Library of Congress Cataloging-in-Publication Data
Names: Blomstedt, Herbert, 1927- author. | Weigert, Ursula.
Title: A great song : a biography of Herbert Blomstedt, world-renowned conductor of the San Francisco Symphony Orchestra / Herbert Blomstedt as told to Ursula Weigert.
Description: Nampa : Pacific Press Publishing, 2017. | Includes bibliographical references.
Identifiers: LCCN 2016047153 | ISBN 9780816362479 (pbk.)
Subjects: LCSH: Blomstedt, Herbert, 1927- | Conductors (Music)—United States —Biography. | LCGFT: Autobiographies.
Classification: LCC ML422.B56 A3 2017 | DDC 784.2092 [B] —dc23 LC record available at https://lccn.loc.gov/2016047153

January 2017

Acknowledgments

E VERY BOOK HAS ITS own story, so it is said. On the one hand, there is the "historical data" from 2006 to 2013 when this book was written. On the other hand, the writing of this book has also been marked by hope and fear and has undergone much development—including some trial and error. But gradually, it gained a large number of collaborators and supporters who, in manifold ways, contributed to make this project a reality. Now it is time to thank those people.

My first thanks goes to Joachim Lippert, radio journalist at Hope Channel: the idea for a biography of Herbert Blomstedt was born during a conversation with him. Mr. Lippert not only encouraged me enthusiastically and established contact with Maestro Blomstedt, but over the years has made invaluable contributions to the development of the biography with many ideas, interest, and his own research and practical support—not the least of which was translating relevant documents from Swedish. Thanks also to his wife, Beate, who patiently answered my numerous phone calls and questions.

I thank all the contributors: those who were willing to do interviews (mostly with prolonged correspondence afterward for clarification and additional information), and those who wrote their own contributions. It was an enriching experience to see that they all shared enthusiasm and appreciation for Herbert Blomstedt's personality and life's work.

I thank Christiane and Lothar Frauenlob, Beate and Joachim Lippert, Cecilia Blomstedt, Anja Schäbe, Bonnie and Bill Blythe, Dr. Johannes and Christiane Wilde, Waltraud and Gerd Christiansen, Rita and Frederick Goerke, and Dr. Fridrun and Harald Hantke for the hospitality shown me during my research.

Thanks also to everyone who provided background information and helped and supported me: the team at the KünstlerSekretariat am Gasteig artist agency in Munich, especially Eva Oswalt and Hanne Bast; also Dr. Ildiko Gal, Dr. Renate Herklotz, Lillian Blomstedt, Martina and Jürgen Diedrichsen, Yvonne Löfgren, Reinhard Rupp, Dr. Johannes and Ruth Wilde, Markus Metz, the secretariat of St. Catherine's Church in Hamburg, Gull and Per-Ove Ohlson, Kerry McDaniel, Kurt and Elisabeth Wiklander, Achim Dobschall and Volker Donandt for material from the archives of the Norddeutscher Rundfunk (NDR) Symphony Orchestra, Marie Theres Pless from the Leipzig Gewandhaus for myriad support, and the secretariats of the Bamberg Symphony Orchestra and the Staatskapelle Dresden for information and material; and finally, Alicia Gutjahr for translating the French reviews.

While working on the manuscript, it was helpful to count on the frequent support of the copy editor Andrea Cramer. I'm indebted to Gerd Christiansen for reviewing the finished manuscript and his many invaluable comments. Special thanks to my daughter, Katrin Weigert, for all her support and encouragement during the whole process of writing.

But most of all my thanks goes to Maestro Herbert Blomstedt, who through his life and by his consent made this biography possible. SDG: *Soli Deo Gloria*! To God be all Glory!

Ursula Weigert
Neufahrn bei Freising, November 2013

Contents

My Life—a Great Song

I'm circling around God, around the ancient tower,
and I circle for millennia;
and I do not know: am I a falcon, a storm,
or a great song.[1]

I FOUND THESE WONDERFUL words from Rainer Maria Rilke in an artistic, well-designed calendar that I received for my eightieth birthday at Ekebyholm Castle in Sweden. These words originate from a time when the young poet was still at the beginning of his lifelong search for meaning and purpose. Looking back, I find myself in Rilke's *I* again: although no one lives for thousands of years, the poet represents each artist and every human being who thinks about their existence.

Nobody can escape God; yet He does not always reveal Himself to us by that name. For some people, He is "the Beginning," "the Lord," "the Absolute," "the Judge," or "the Father"—all at once or at different moments in life. For others, He is just an obstacle along the road; something one has to pass by or pass over. But God, like a tower, cannot be ignored.

For a long time, a tower was a symbol of protest against God. The infamous Tower of Babel was supposed to show that humanity was independent of God: no more would He be able to inundate humankind with floods. We would provide our own salvation.

In Rilke's poem, however, the tower is a symbol of God Himself. As the nest is to the falcon, so do we find safety and security in the tower. As we grow and mature, we want to learn to fly for ourselves and appreciate the updrafts around the tower that aid in our flight. And frequently there are storms—rebellion against the old, the conventional. We need to train our muscles to their full strength. The storm is good. We need activity and drama.

We also need beauty. We long for grandeur and eternity. The tower

9

is also a symbol of these things. It has given us everything. We did not build the tower ourselves. And so, out of gratitude, we can only sing "a great song."

That's why I chose this title for my biography. As a musician, I was also driven by the basic needs for security, meaningful activity, and beauty. Sometimes one need took precedence over the others; sometimes I felt all these needs at once. I was always looking for the perfect balance between rest and activity. But the one constant, the cantus firmus, the ultimate goal is "a great song." As Ludwig van Beethoven expressed it so touchingly and beautifully in the String Quartet in A Minor, written two years before his death: "A holy song of thanksgiving of a convalescent to the Deity."

Herbert Blomstedt
Bengtstorp, Sweden, August 2013

---

1. Rainer Maria Rilke, "Ich lebe mein Leben in wachsenden Ringen," in *Das Stunden-Buch* [The book of hours] (Leipzig: Insel-Verlag, 1905), bk. 1, poem 2.

A Cosmopolitan Childhood

The past is never dead. It's not even past.
—William Faulkner

T HE CALL CAME AS if it were marching orders: Pastor Adolf Blomstedt, who had immigrated to the United States as a fourteen-year-old Swedish orphan, should return to his homeland to train future pastors at the Adventist missionary school in Nyhyttan, along with his wife, Alida, and their two sons, Norman and Herbert.

The family went to visit Alida's parents one last time and say good-bye. They covered nearly two thousand miles on their journey from Springfield, Massachusetts, one of the oldest and largest towns in New England, to the small town of Golden, Colorado.

Almost forty years earlier, Olof and Maria Thorson had immigrated to the United States and settled on a farm near Denver. It was very difficult for them to deal with the fact that their only daughter, who had been born in the United States, was now returning to their homeland. Everyone knew that a trip between the Old and the New World in the late 1920s was extremely complex and expensive. They wondered whether they would ever see each other again. Little did they know that this move would be the first of many to come in the subsequent years for the Blomstedts.

Decades later, Herbert Blomstedt met another world-renowned conductor at the Vienna airport and commented, "We are gypsies." He added, as his colleague looked at him questioningly, "For here we have no continuing city," quoting Hebrews 13:14, a Bible text that Johannes Brahms set to music in his *German Requiem*. Constant travel and never lingering too long in one place—these are things Herbert became familiar with during his childhood.

Part of our interest in someone's life story is in knowing the things that have molded him and where his unique traits and characteristics come from. In childhood lie the roots of a life; this is where the foundation is laid for the person's future résumé. If the life story is about an artist, our curiosity about his early years is great. How exactly did it all begin? Were there early indications of an exceptional talent? Was the person perhaps a child prodigy? Was his childhood very serious, overshadowed by long hours of practicing, which left too little time to play?

Measured by such conjectures and compared with many other biographies, Herbert Blomstedt's early years were rather unspectacular. One can indeed speak of him as a happy child.

His mother, Alida, was a trained concert pianist and had worked as a piano teacher at Broadview College and Theological Seminary near Chicago before she got married. Even before Herbert was born, she played Frédéric Chopin and Franz Liszt for him. She told him later that, as a young boy, he had sometimes refused to go to bed until she had played yet another Chopin prelude for him. For many years, his favorite place was the rug in front of the piano in the living room while his mother played the piano.

Herbert's brother, Norman, had a gentle, quiet nature. He kindly endured the sometimes-rambunctious behavior of his younger siblings. He was a real big brother in the best sense of the word. "I could not have wished for a better one," Herbert said after his brother's death in 2005, also saying that Norman was his best friend.

Herbert's younger sister, Marita, remembers the loving atmosphere in their home, where a strong sense of companionship prevailed: there were always loving arms in which one could hide. Their parents were caring Christians with strong beliefs in God; these beliefs naturally included times for daily prayer and worship. In a letter to the author, Marita wrote, "Our home was characterized by warmth, hospitality, lots of good conversations, and generosity. It was at the same time permeated by discipline and genuine piety. These are traits that Herbert has acquired and developed further. He is a strong and godly man. He taught me to stand up for what I believe in, to live out my faith, to form my own opinions and investigate to find my own answers, and not to judge people, but to be an example."

Because Herbert and Norman were born to Swedish parents in the United States, they received both Swedish and American citizenship at birth. In the 1920s, this was considered to be something like winning a jackpot. Norman was born on April 30, 1924, in Hartford, Connecticut, and Herbert was born on July 11, 1927, in Springfield, Massachusetts.

There was possibly something special about July 1927, because two other world-renowned conductors were born that month: Kurt Masur on July 18, and Michael Gielen on July 20. However, Herbert sees his talent—on the rare occasions that he thinks about it—exclusively as a gift from God that comes with an enormous responsibility: to work hard and to strive with all his strength to do his work as well as possible. Hence, throughout his life, he has always been convinced of the fact that it's not appropriate to be proud of one's own talent and skill, thereby following entirely in the footsteps of his great role model, Johann Sebastian Bach, who reputedly said, "Talent is hard work, nothing else."

Moving to a new culture

Originally from Värmland, a remote area in Sweden that was predominantly a farming community, Olof and Maria Thorson were both enthusiastic and talented hobbyist musicians. If young people in that area during the late nineteenth century wanted to listen to music, they had to play it for themselves. Rural minstrels typically memorized up to 150 ballads, earning some extra money at family celebrations such as weddings and baptisms.

Olof Thorson was an exceptionally talented guitar player and played "upscale" music, greatly simplified arrangements of popular classical pieces for guitar. "My grandfather would sit in the Nordic forests with his ten-stringed guitar and struggle to play the *William Tell* Overture in half time with his thick farmer's fingers," Herbert remarked after conducting a charity concert in aid of the United Nations Children's Fund, in which the well-known piece by Rossini was performed at the Leipzig Gewandhaus.[1] Now some of Olof's music and his guitar are in the possession of his grandson Herbert.

Grandmother Maria also played guitar—a normal six-stringed one—at dance events or as an accompanist in church services. She was a strikingly beautiful woman, but in particular she was smart and capable, as her grandson reflected, "both on the dance floor as well as at home and at school. As devout and spiritual as she was, she always had a funny remark up her sleeve. Sometimes she was mischievous, and she loved adventure. No, she even looked for it!"[2] Later in life, she loved to have Herbert play her favorite piece of music on the violin, the Sicilienne in E-flat Major.

Olof Thorson's father had been a well-known folk music fiddler for dances, weddings, funerals, and other events. He carried the title of *Riksspelman* (minstrel of the kingdom)—a special honor that was given to farmers with exceptional musical ability.

A Great Song

Later, when their grandparents moved back to Sweden, Herbert and Norman spent many weeks with them every summer, working hard to help out with the farm chores. One can still see that Herbert's hands are used to manual labor. Even though his childlike imagination tended to exaggerate and was not always completely logical, the fact that there was no shortage of fun on the farm is made evident in the following school essay, which Herbert wrote when he was eleven.

When I Once Had to Help a Farmer

During the summer, I was on Öland. I was actually not there on summer vacation but to "work." Naturally, my brother was also there. Since we had to work every day, I had no time to collect plants for my herbarium at school. But the good thing was, I had collected some before we left. On the summer day that we arrived on Öland, I had to ride a bicycle to a sugar beet field, which was over one mile away from the farm. And I had to hoe sugar beets. That was worse than I thought. My back hurt. It felt as if it would break. But that was not the worst. . . . The field had to be covered with manure. My shoes got covered with it as well. My nose was filled with the most disgusting smell I had ever known. Yes, it was terrible. That was my first time, then I got used to it. It was almost as good a fragrance as 4711 [a German cologne]. There is a saying that fertilizer is the gold of farmers. I also had to do other things besides hoe sugar beets and stand in fertilizer. I milked cows, used the harrow, plowed, and more. During harvesttime, I often drove the combine. I could see the whole rye field from my elevated seat on the combine. I do not remember exactly how big it was, but definitely six to seven "Doppelmorgen."[3] But I did not always get to sit comfortably up there; I had to stand a lot and tie bales by hand.

By the time fall harvest came around, I knew what I was doing. Once when we had such a large hay load that I had to walk, I ran ahead and climbed up a tree by the roadside, waiting for the load. As they drove below the tree on which I was sitting, I jumped down and landed with a thud on the hay. No one realized that I had hitched a ride until we were almost at the farm. Just as we drove into the farmyard, I swung myself on a tree branch. They looked for me but could not find me. When I showed up shortly afterwards, they were completely bowled over.

For one long day, I had to weed out the carrot field. That was terrible. . . . Five-sixths of the field was covered with weeds that were very troublesome. Some weeds were up to one and a half feet high.

On our next to the last day on Öland, we just lazed around. We had to ride home to Jönköping on our bicycles. That took three days. In Emmaboda, we met Karl-Otto Nilsson [a childhood friend], who had been in Ronneby and had worked just as we had. On August 11, we were happy to be home again in Jönköping. After a month of "work" on Öland.[4]

In Sweden, the Thorson grandparents had been members of the state church, but in America they came into contact with and joined the Seventh-day Adventist Church.[5] Herbert remembers them as "avid believers."

On the other hand, Adolf's parents had passed away many years before. His father, Carl-Otto Blomstedt, who had worked as an insurance agent, died of tuberculosis at the young age of forty-three. Just two years earlier, Adolf's mother, Greta Sophia, was buried. She had died of stomach cancer. So Adolf became an orphan when he was thirteen years old; his sister Alyse was only nine. Later, in Adolf's sermons, when he shared his personal conversion experience, he would enjoy telling the congregation that back then he was a real street urchin and a ruffian. Because he had a strong and robust physique, he used to love impressing his friends and also some girls with the fact that he was able to walk around an entire city block on his hands. Herbert is convinced that he inherited the physical constitution of his father, who up until a very old age still had lots of energy and vigor.

An uncle, who had immigrated to the United States many years before, took Adolf and Alyse in and made sure that they received a good education.

In November 2006, during a guest performance in Liverpool, England, Herbert sought out the famous Albert Dock.

I wanted to experience some of the atmosphere that my father Adolf witnessed in 1912 when he emigrated from Liverpool to New York. The waterfront of the river Mersey, which is here over one thousand yards wide, still flaunts the magnificent and imposing white buildings of the Cunard Line and other shipping companies, which were built in the late nineteenth century and gave a foretaste of the wealth of the great country in the west. Here my father embarked early September 1912 on the luxury liner *Mauretania* with its four powerful black funnels. At that time, it was the fastest steamer in the world. With its revolutionary steam-turbine technology, it made the crossing in less than five days. The steamship captured the Blue Riband for the fastest transatlantic crossing on its maiden voyage and then retained it for twenty-two years until the German ship [Bremen] won the title in 1929. The furnishings in first class were fit for a king. But Adolf traveled third class, in a six-bed cabin without a window. There was a sink in each cabin, which is something my grandmother Maria Gustafsdotter and her fiancé Olof Tholsson, who traveled a few months after her, could only dream about twenty years before. My father arrived in New York on September 9.[6]

The experience of losing loved ones early on in life and the lack of safety and security, together with all the ensuing potential risks, made deep impressions on Adolf. Rigor, discipline, and strict limits were important principles for him, which he tried to pass on to his children while raising them. Many who knew him described him as "remarkable" and having authority but also as rather distant and unapproachable. Adolf's granddaughters Cecilia and Maria remember that he was fond of children and could be warm with them. He took his faith very seriously, and he lived out what he preached. His enormous diligence, coupled with a high sense of duty, and his Swedish language skills were the reasons why he was considered an appropriate candidate for the education of students at the Nyhyttan seminary in Sweden, and so the family was relocated there.

After the family had traveled by boat to Gothenburg, the journey continued by train. The memory of their last train journey through the endless prairies of America stood in sharp contrast with the train ride from Gothenburg to Hultafors. The children felt as though they were driving through a green tunnel.

The family rested from their travels for a few days at the Hultafors Sanitarium. Soon word got out that Alida was a pianist, and she was asked to give a piano concert on one evening. On the designated evening, as she was about to open the door to enter the room and sit down at the piano, Sister Asta, the sanitarium's manager, stopped her, "Please wait, Mrs. Blomstedt. You cannot go in yet."

"Why not?"

"You have no rings."

"I've never worn rings. Why do I need to wear rings?"

Sister Asta pointed to Herbert and Norman. They would be considered illegitimate children if their parents did not wear wedding rings. In haste, the manager found a few curtain rings and put them on Alida. But, alas, the rings were too large and rattled on the piano keys. There was a short pause, and then the piano music continued—without the rings.[7]

A visit to a goldsmith shortly afterwards ensured that Adolf and Alida were recognized as a married couple. They had entered another culture and tried to conform to it as best they could.

"Next stop, Järnboås!" The driver of the steam engine put on the brakes, and the screeching train arrived at the small station of a mining town, just over twelve miles from Nora. They drove in a rental car to Nyhyttan, which would be home to the Blomstedts for the next three years. They lived on the second floor of one of about a dozen houses that were scattered on the property of an old mine.

Alida worked thirty hours a week teaching piano at the seminary to prospective pastors. Often in small communities, pastors themselves had to accompany the church while singing. The young mother was already showing the early signs of arthritis, and it soon became apparent that she would not be able to pursue a career as a concert pianist.

Nyhyttan was a wonderful place for Norman and Herbert. There was a lot of space to play and explore, with nature all around them. During this time, they developed friendships that have lasted a lifetime.

Summer in Vienna

In the summer of 1932, Alida traveled with her sons to Vienna. From her modest earnings, she had steadfastly saved up enough money to take advanced piano classes from Hedwig Rosenthal. Hedwig was married to Moriz Rosenthal, who was one of the best pianists at the time and had received part of his instruction from Franz Liszt. Carin Gille traveled with them to take care of the two boys.

The foursome took the train to Trelleborg, crossed over to Sassnitz by ferry, and then traveled again by train to Berlin. Alida was enchanted by Berlin; it reminded her of America. There the small traveling company visited the Waldfriede clinic, which was directed by Dr. L. E. Conradi, son of the German Seventh-day Adventist Church founder Ludwig R. Conradi.

From Berlin, they journeyed to Prague and then to Vienna. They stayed in a small house in the Schubertgasse (Schubert Alley) belonging to a woman by the name of Mrs. Teckel. They all slept in one room with two beds, and the kitchen was shared with the landlady. Norman describes in his family chronicle how he shuddered at the sight of a wobbling calf brain, which Mrs. Teckel sliced into thin pieces and then fried in a pan. Another less-than-pleasant experience was the many lice and fleas that climbed up the exterior walls and came in through the cracks in the drafty windows.

The excursions to Schönbrunn Palace and the Prater amusement park became unforgettable experiences for the Blomstedt boys.

The brothers were also deeply impressed by a visit to St. Stephen's Cathedral and its catacombs. When Herbert once again conducted the Vienna Symphony in 2006, he noted in his diary, "I was just at St. Stephen's. I thought back to my visit there in 1932—I'll never forget how I shuddered at the sight of a skull in the catacombs under the church."[8]

Carin Gille often took the children to one of the bigger parks that had a playground. War veterans were begging at the park entrances—many had lost arms or legs—a terrible reminder of the madness of the First World War.

Norman writes in "Minnen" (Memories) of an evening orchestral concert that took place in front of the illuminated facade of a castlelike building: "The audience sat on benches in the park facing the structure. There, for the first time, I became fascinated by symphonic music."

The years in Finland

After working in Nyhyttan for three years, Adolf became president of the Swedish-speaking Seventh-day Adventist churches in Finland. Another move lay ahead for the family.

This was a difficult time, right after the Great Depression in 1932. Finland was poor and had been independent for only fifteen years. Swedes could live quite inexpensively in Finland with their own currency, the Swedish krona, but Adolf was paid in the local currency—Finnish markka. At first, the family lived in a beautiful villa in the suburb of Grankulla (today Kauniainen, west of Helsinki). After one year, the family left the villa and moved to Helsinki.

Ascetic or a pleasure seeker?

Herbert's lifestyle, especially his eating habits, are an inexhaustible topic of discussion for many who know him. Even journalists, who have gathered a little information prior to their interviews, are repeatedly intrigued by this issue. In his diary, Herbert Blomstedt describes how after an interview, the journalist Christiane Irrgang from Norddeutscher Rundfunk (Northern German Broadcasting) accompanied him to his taxi and wanted to know more about his religion:

"Adventists are known for their ascetic way of life: they do not smoke, they do not drink, and so on."

I hear this so often and answered—perhaps in a slightly irritated tone, "This is not asceticism. It is common sense, you know that yourself! I am not an ascetic but a gourmet and an epicurean."

She did not contradict me but confirmed, "Yes, nonsmokers can taste their food so much better; they can detect many subtle nuances."[9]

There are even cartoons on this subject. One of them shows Herbert in a plain monk's robe with a cord around his waist and a raised baton. The caption reads, "The conductor with the spiritual baton." It was released in the *Financial Times*, during the period in which he bade farewell to the San Francisco Symphony. Despite his great sense of humor, he felt that he was incorrectly depicted in that instance.

On the opposite side of the globe, in Tokyo, a cartoon was once published of a mosquito dripping with blood and just flying away from the conductor. A violinist enters from the right in a great hurry, her skirts billowing and her instrument under her arm. She runs towards the mosquito, wanting to catch it and get a blood sample to finally discover the mysterious substance Herbert Blomstedt has in his veins that, in spite of a vegetarian diet, makes him so agile and full of vigor. This amused him!

A Russian violinist even asked Herbert whether he really had four daughters. When the violinist was asked why he doubted this, the man stated, a little surprised and embarrassed, that it was because the maestro did not eat meat.

Even as a child everything had to be aesthetically prepared for Herbert, and the food on his plate needed to be clearly recognizable. He never touched an indefinable mass. "I'd rather grab a carrot that looked like one or tomatoes that were in season only from August to October and were prepared by my mother in every possible way."

Later psychological and ethical issues about eating meat came up: "How can one eat one's friends? To kill an animal in order to eat it is a reminder of cannibalism. I believe that the aversion to killing animals is a natural and healthy instinct, which is almost totally desensitized by cultural conventions. Actually, I don't see it as all quite that dramatic. Long ago I accepted it when my best friends and closest family members ate meat. They are not worse people for it."[10]

The Early Years

Near the villa in Grankulla, there was a Swedish elementary school where

Norman was enrolled in the third grade. At the time, Helsinki had about 250,000 inhabitants, a quarter of which were Swedish speaking. There was distinct hostility between the two language groups, especially among the children. As a very sensitive child, Norman suffered because of this. Herbert was of a more robust nature and later on could cope better with the situation.

Adolf's office was downtown, on 7 Annegatan (Anne Street). In addition to his administrative tasks, he also conducted evangelistic meetings where his wife played some piano pieces as a prelude. Adolf's secretary, Lydia Sandholm, quickly became Herbert's favorite aunt. "She was so loving, often gave us sweets and stamps and could invent an infinite number of small games. . . . And she could tell stories! . . . She was the ideal aunt for someone like me."[11]

While Norman attended the new Swedish school, Herbert, at five and a half years of age, entered the second grade in the *Svenska folkskolan* (Swedish elementary school) at the upper end of Anne Street. "It was decided that I should skip the first grade. I could already read, and they feared boredom and perhaps worse." This fear seemed to be substantiated, as young Herbert told his mother after she scolded him yet again, "One cannot live totally without pranks." Today he knows the full truth: "As a child, I was very headstrong and a bit dangerous in my parents' eyes. I would attack my older brother when something did not suit me. I hit him and bit him. He had strict orders that he was not allowed to strike 'the little one.' This was certainly not easy for him. Only my father was allowed to discipline us."[12]

As a second-grader, he proved to be very eager to learn and, in his own words, could not get enough of all school subjects.

Bobrikov's piano workshop

The apartment building where the Blomstedts lived still stands today as Herbert remembers it.

> Yes, I still know our old home by heart. We lived in Arcadia, and it was actually a pretty elegant residential area. . . . I'm truly amazed today that we lived so well. Perhaps the church officials in Finland had a particular respect for the new man from Sweden, who had received his college education in America and whose wife was an artist. Maybe my father asked for some consideration because his wife was already suffering from rheumatism and had some special needs.
>
> We even had a nanny, Edja, who would help in the house when

"Mutchi," as we called our mom, was playing piano at Father's lectures. Edja made up a very special game with my brother and me: Bobrikov's piano workshop. At bedtime, she poked us with a hairpin between the ribs. It did not tickle or hurt, but we shouted loudly, and Edja then decided that the piano was not tuned properly. More twists of the needle, and then the sound was tested again. We found it incredibly funny and almost died laughing. This was probably our first game that involved music. What we didn't know at the time, however, was that Edja had not invented the name *Bobrikov*.[13]

Nikolai Ivanovich Bobrikov was the hated former Russian governor-general of Finland. Equipped with dictatorial authority by Tsar Nicholas II, he immediately arrested all opponents of his attempts to Russianize the then-Russian autonomous Grand Duchy of Finland. In 1904, a patriot finally killed him. Unfortunately, Edja never told us why the funny game was named after the dreaded governor; perhaps because he had pestered the Finns so?

Edja also introduced the pastor's family in war games. "Under the table, we hung rugs to create a castle cave. We then fired at each other with folded paper balls that got real momentum from taut rubber bands. Or we settled down on the top shelf of the wardrobe and threw pillows at each other from there. Meanwhile our parents proclaimed, in words and music, the gospel of peace and love in the Sibelius Academy."[14]

A special encounter

One day in Helsinki, seven-year-old Herbert went with his father to visit the famous scientist Henning Karström in his villa on the island of Lauttasaari. Pastor Blomstedt gave some pastoral counseling to the brilliant biochemist who was tormented by difficult inner struggles. Herbert later wrote, "I held my breath in admiration when he and my father talked about profound things that I did not understand about God and the fathomless nature created by Him." Herbert remembers, "After we ate, Karström played 'Haydn's Serenade' on the violin. I have never forgotten this music. It was the first time that I heard music like that."[15]

Karström, who at that time lectured at the university and directed the laboratory of Professor Artturi Virtanen—later a Nobel Prize winner—was finally able to find inner peace and affirmation. In later years, he served as the rector of Finnish and Swedish Seventh-day Adventist schools and published numerous articles about healthy nutrition and natural remedies until he was very old.

First love

During this time, Wilhelm Sucksdorff and his family lived near St. John's Church in Helsinki. He was a popular physician with a private practice in Helsinki and was a leader in his church. Dr. Sucksdorff, also called "Sucken," was small in stature, had a sanguine temperament, often laughed loudly, and spoke with a slightly hoarse voice. He was a consulting physician for a medical institute where Alida was being treated for the rapidly spreading rheumatism in her limbs. Mrs. Sucksdorff was a quiet little lady. She was always well dressed; in winter, she wore a fur coat, so she made an almost aristocratic impression. The Sucksdorffs had three daughters: Hellin, Maj-Lis, and Ulla.

Hellin was then about thirteen years old and had long yellow-blond hair and lots of freckles in a round face. Herbert was only half her age but fell violently in love with her.

> I dreamed of her. And once luck was on my side, for a public lecture that my father gave at the Sibelius Academy, where my mother played a few Chopin pieces as a prelude to the lecture, I was simply taken with [the Sucksdorffs] since the nanny, Edja, was not available, and I was allowed to sit on the second balcony, next to Hellin. Oh, what bliss; what joy! Hellin took my hand—and I was in paradise. I can still feel that endless happiness today. Emotions, even to the smallest details, etch themselves firmly in my memory, while memories of external circumstances quickly fade. Just this one experience was in every respect unique. Never again did Hellin take my hand. She later studied medicine and gave her hand and heart in marriage to Leo Hirvonen, who was a professor of physiology at the University of Oulu and later also in Helsinki.[16]

First music lessons

When Herbert was six years old, he received his first official music lessons. "Aunt Aina," one of his mothers' friends, was his teacher. Aina Holm taught at a preschool of the Sibelius Academy and had a grand piano at home, which impressed her students immensely. Herbert has little recollection of the actual lessons as he writes in his diary entry. However, he very clearly remembers the embarrassing feeling as he walked the long road "to piano lessons at Aunt Aina on 13B Michelingatan [Michelin Street]. The lesson itself was not the bad part but having to carry my sheet music in the old black, worn leather case that belonged to my father; that was a disgrace. I was so ashamed and just hoped that I would not run into any of my playmates on Runebergsgatan [Runebergs Street]."[17] Even the "embarrassing and shameful feelings" when he learned how to ice-skate and "fell on the ice, which today are dark echoes in [his] memory," were, in comparison, a minor embarrassment.

Otherwise, there are only good things to say.

> I could borrow sheet music from Aunt Aina, with her personal bookplate on it: a small yellow piece of paper, and on it was a pianist wearing a full skirt sitting at the piano, below which was written "Aina Holms Book." Later on she gave me music from her collection, which is now scattered about in my own library. . . . She was very pleased with the musical career of her little pupil, and we corresponded a number of times. I still saw Aunt Aina in the 1970s when I was invited as a guest conductor to Helsinki. However, when I visited Helsinki in 1983 with the Staatskapelle Dresden, Aunt Aina was no longer living. I received a small photo of Aunt Aina from my brother's estate; in [the photo], she is sitting under a large oil painting in her apartment on Michelin Street.[18]

The singing saw

Once during the Finland years, when Herbert accompanied his father on a pastoral visit, he met a coffin maker named Färm. Herbert remembers that

> he was a very unique and educated man. He played music on a saw, which impressed me immensely. He held the handle between his knees and produced the sound with a violin bow, which he played almost perpendicular to the straight edge of the saw. He varied the pitch by bending the upper part of the saw. He played with great vibrato—perhaps it was not possible to play it otherwise. The combination of coffins, saw, Färm, and music fascinated me in an unforgettable way. *Färm* means something like "firm," "determined," and it seems like it may have a deeper significance that five years later, the name of my esteemed violin teacher in Gothenburg was precisely Fermæus.[19]

In 1935, the family moved to Turku, a town of sixty thousand inhabitants, where Swedish was the mother tongue of one in six people. There, the Blomstedts bought their first wireless set, a crystal radio receiver. They listened regularly to broadcasts of classical instrumental music. If opera, operetta, or even pop songs were played, it was turned off—one couldn't do much with that kind of music.

During the Finland years, the family spent their summers at the grandparents' farm in Värmland. The grandparents sold their house in Golden, Colorado, and moved back to Sweden in order to be closer to their only daughter and her family. They moved into a small house called Lyckan—meaning "happiness"—in the village of Kortlanda in the forests of Eda, in western Värmland. Eda, which is where the family originally came from and many of their relatives lived, borders on Köla and Skillingmark.

The grandparents owned a radio from the earliest of times. They also listened only to classical music, and when Herbert was about twelve years old, he experienced a key moment in his life. A German radio station broadcast a concert with the Staatskapelle Dresden, conducted by Karl Böhm, performing Variations and Fugue on a Theme of Mozart by Max Reger. The boy was, by his own confession, spellbound, and this orchestra remained for him "simply the epitome of harmonic sound." He had no idea at the time that almost exactly thirty years later he himself would perform with the Staatskapelle Dresden.

In Sweden again

When Herbert was ten years old, his family moved for the fifth time. After working for five years in Finland, Adolf was elected president of the South Swedish Conference of Seventh-day Adventists. The family moved into an apartment with three rooms and a kitchen on the southernmost tip of Jönköping. The town in the province of Småland is situated on the southern shores of Lake Vättern.

Adolf's office was located in Gothenburg, but he was also the pastor in Jönköping at the same time. The Blomstedts soon made friends with several families in the city, including the Nilssons, whose daughter Brita and son Karl-Otto, Herbert's classmate, became lifelong friends with the Blomstedt boys.

Karl-Otto remembers that he noticed Herbert right away. "He was so different from the others, somehow living in his own world. Everyone in the class noticed that he was a member of a different church than the usual Church of Sweden since he did not come to school on Saturdays. He also knew an unusually large amount about music. Somehow I became interested in him. I soon discovered that he had a great sense of humor."

The two boys also shared a common passion: soccer. Almost every day they spent several hours on the soccer field. Karl-Otto remembers well how Adolf Blomstedt would sometimes come and fetch them from the soccer field while chiding, "What will become of you two one day if you waste so much time here?" "But then," the now-retired doctor adds with a grin, "he sometimes did join us and played with us for a while."

The maestro still played soccer up until a few years ago but only with his grandsons and as the goalkeeper, where he once almost sprained his right wrist. "My grandson Oscar shot so hard! I could barely hold the ball. They are already talented [soccer] players, these boys. If they didn't have such good grades in school, I would be seriously worried as to what would become of them one day."

The "Butcher quartet"

In Jönköping, Herbert and Norman finally had the opportunity to study stringed instruments at the General Institute of Higher Learning. Norman chose the cello and Herbert the violin. But the instrument wasn't a good one, and the teacher was not very motivating. Herbert continued his piano studies with moderate enthusiasm under Enok Nilsson, the music director for the A6 artillery regiment, which was stationed in Jönköping. Nilsson was an excellent cellist, a good pianist, and at the same time, the conductor of the symphony orchestra of the city. After a while, Herbert took lessons from another teacher, who was also not ideal for him. Only in their third year in Jönköping did he meet an excellent teacher, an old German, named Boysen.

When the family moved to Gothenburg three years later, Herbert received violin lessons from the assistant concertmaster of the symphony orchestra, Lars Fermæus.[20] However, the lessons were expensive—the cost was about ten krona per lesson. Herbert had to explain to him that his parents couldn't possibly afford that. So they finally agreed upon three krona per lesson. Herbert cherished his teacher very much and practiced three to four hours every day, in addition to his daily homework. Soccer was forgotten! Herbert wrote in his diary in 2008: "How I secretly rejoiced when my father looked up from his books to watch his son playing music. He liked the fact that I exerted myself to learn. This sense of acceptance and appreciation meant a lot to me."

Fermæus advised his gifted pupil to complete his secondary education at all costs because he could not become a comprehensively educated musician otherwise. The maestro commented on this from his current perspective:

That was what I did.

I am very grateful to him for that kind of advice. It is one thing to train your fingers and your musicianship, and another thing to develop as a complete person. In the long run, that defines what you can do with the music. I think all important musicians I know are deeply cultivated and spiritual persons. It's not enough to know all the symphonies and string quartets and operas, or whatever. You have to know also about the painting and literature of the period, and so on, to make a more complete view.[21]

Playing music at home was a given in the Blomstedt family. Despite her severe rheumatoid polyarthritis, Alida still proved herself a good musician. Adolf was an excellent tenor; his voice reverberated not only at family worships but also at church events. Daughter Marita recalls as if it were yesterday, "the evenings at our house. The evening prayer was said and then the lamp put out, as my mother went over to my brothers to play with them. Mama sat at the piano, Herbert played the violin and Norman the cello. I could fall asleep to live music. When he was not out of town, Papa mostly sat completely absorbed with a spiritual book in his hand."

Brother Norman proved to be a gifted cellist. The family played trios and sonatas, concertos and other solo pieces together. On Sundays, violinist friends from Fermæus's music school came to play quartet music. With Herbert on the viola, they played all the quartets they could find. Norman reported in "Minnen," "We butchered one quartet after another, and we therefore called ourselves the 'Butcher Quartet.'" The maestro commented, "And that as a vegetarian!"

It is good, to engage with chamber music very early on. There is no deeper, more expressive music than the string quartets of Haydn, Beethoven, Schubert, and Mozart. Even after a strenuous concert, I know of no better way to relax than playing in a quartet. There I could still continue making music.

Quartet playing is also a good school because you have to listen to each other and you can hear each other. One must not only express oneself, but must be able to be stimulated by the others. As a conductor, I also have to listen; I may not only lead and put myself in the scene.

While they lived in Gothenburg, the two brothers—now thirteen and sixteen years old—went at least twice a week to concerts. Norman, as a member of the orchestral school of the symphony, received free tickets, and Herbert was able to acquire cheap student tickets. He earned the money by selling newspapers. Thus, over the years, they had the opportunity to get to know many conductors and instrumentalists with a large repertoire in the excellent concert hall. Herbert loves to tell how they "drank in" the music and how on the way home they talked as drunkards, raving over individual musicians and enthusiastically singing to each other the passages of music that they particularly liked. They spoke all the jargon and distributed praise and censure for individual musicians in the orchestra, the conductor, and the compositions. Once they heard the Piano Concerto No. 1 by Franz Liszt. On their way home, they disclosed their displeasure with the music and agreed with youthful impetuosity that this was truly "an emetic." Though Liszt still remains one of Herbert's least favorite composers, he learned to appreciate Liszt over the years and performed several works by him; however, when he thinks back to this episode, he has to smile over the arrogance of his adolescent judgment.

Herbert had quite a different experience with Anton Bruckner in those days. After hearing his Symphony No. 4 for the first time, he was "as if bewitched by this music. On the way home through a park, my brother and I tried to sing or whistle the melodies. At home, I then tried (with only partial success, of course) to write the melodies down, so as not to forget them. This music spoke to me immediately."

Sometimes the brothers even took little Marita with them to the concerts, which for her, in retrospect, was the highlight of her childhood.

Every morning at eight o'clock in Herbert's junior high school, a brief worship was held for everyone. A chorale was also sung, accompanied by a student on the organ. When this particular student graduated from high school, the music teacher, a virtuoso organist himself, asked the now fifteen-year-old Herbert whether he would like to learn to play the organ. Would he ever! In addition to the violin, the organ would become a favorite instrument. Even today, when his tour schedule allows it, he still accompanies the congregational singing at his church in Lucerne.

Already in high school Johann Sebastian Bach's music was to me like a musical guiding star on which I oriented myself. Like someone possessed, I played all six of his solo sonatas for violin, from memory. As an organist, I was passionate about Bach. Becoming a conductor was something that fell into my lap later on, but initially I dreamed of performing a Bach cantata on the organ balcony of a beautiful church every Sunday. Nothing came of it, but in my debut with the Stockholm Philharmonic Orchestra the first piece that we performed was the Suite No. 2 in B Minor by Bach. With my first orchestra of thirty musicians, I naturally played much baroque and thus also Bach. With increasing orchestra sizes, Bach was gradually passed by. . . . But I always again returned to my "first love."[22]

During the middle of World War II, Wilhelm Furtwängler's performance as guest conductor was a very special event for the brothers. On this occasion, Herbert plucked up all his courage and asked the world-renowned conductor for his autograph—an unforgettable moment for Herbert and the only autograph he has ever asked for! For many years now, an autographed portrait of the revered conductor, colleague, and predecessor has hung in the office of the musical director of the Gewandhaus in Lucerne.

In school, Herbert was very active in sports. He enjoyed sports a lot, was athletically built, and achieved exceptional accomplishments in sports earlier on than in music. The first newspaper reports about him told of his remarkable success in high-jumping, long-jumping, and sprinting. He always won first place. Otherwise Herbert was rather a loner, who loved to spend time with individual friends but didn't feel as comfortable in a group.

The church congregation as a family

The Blomstedts' home was always open to others. However, there were few artists and musicians among the never-ending stream of visitors. Primarily, the guests, who came from all over Sweden and abroad, were members of the Seventh-day Adventist Church and came to attend meetings together with Adolf. The sons liked that in this way they could get a glimpse of what was going on in the world. For Alida, however, this meant that the various responsibilities of the church and those at home left her little time for music, especially since their third child, the youngest Marita, was born in Jönköping. Marita said in retrospect, "Mama's patience and positive outlook on life caused all who met her to love her. And there were many. We always had guests in our home, and there was always something good to eat, even though we were relatively poor. A pastor's salary did not go very far for a large family in the '40s and '50s in Sweden. But I always felt rich."

Their local church, writes Norman, was just like one big family where everyone got along, young and old alike. The Blomstedt boys were happy going to church, whether for the worship service or other events. Soon they participated by playing music in church. In addition, it was one of the tasks of the younger children to recite a poem or read something during the worship service once in a while. On several occasions, when it was his turn to read, young Herbert experienced his father calling out from the last row of chairs, "Louder, please!" Adolf was known for his powerful voice, which he used effectively in lectures and sermons. Herbert, who was equipped with an equally good voice, did not find that he spoke too softly. Inwardly, he made up his mind: *One day when my father is up front, preaching away loudly, I'll also call out and interrupt. But I'll shout, "Quieter please!"*

To this day, Herbert still especially loves the quiet—in music as well as in his demeanor. As a conductor and orchestral trainer, he places great importance on the orchestra being able to produce not only as loud a sound as possible but also as quiet a sound as possible.

Although he became more independent from his father and gradually began to establish his own identity, Herbert's interest in religion during his teenage years remained strong, and it even grew. A few years ago while reading through old letters and essays of that time, he noted, "My religious zeal is very apparent and also a heritage from my parents, especially from my father."[23] He found the Bible "incredibly interesting" and helped himself to his father's extensive library to read about whatever was of interest to him. In 1940, he joined his father's baptismal class.

> Overall I was a very sensitive child. My sensitivity soon included music and emotions. I was totally enthused by music that spoke to me. Music that I did not like, I shunned and strictly refused to listen to or play. Such an attitude can easily lead to willfulness. However, since this was also connected with an awakening sense of quality and judgment, my parents did not really want to curtail it. Surely, it was also sometimes difficult, because I was overconfident. During adolescence, I became aware of this willfulness and stubbornness and how hideous it was. I realized that I had sometimes hurt other people, and I was terribly sorry. I realized at that time that I really needed to change. . . . I used to be very irritable, hot-tempered, and violent and tended to exaggerate. I had developed little social feeling or interest in other people, except for the very closest of friends and family. If someone else suffered, it rarely touched me. My interest in other people was only awakened later on and is still growing today. In the meantime, I find every person interesting, whether they have something to do with me or not. When I meet some listeners after a concert, I'm so curious about them that I sometimes have to stop myself.

A Great Song

Herbert did not, to use his own words, "have a miraculous conversion experience":

> But the inner change was very noticeable for me, and my hitherto pronounced tendency to be hot-tempered disappeared. I really feel that this is a miracle of God. One could also explain it as a maturing process that progresses little by little, even at times jerkily. Suddenly one no longer feels the old temptations but begins to think more about others and is no longer so self-centered. That was probably the beginning of a maturation process that everyone goes through in life, but it can be very individual due to different circumstances.
>
> For me, it happened simultaneously with a significant maturation in the religious, intellectual, and musical spheres. I suddenly became aware of how much there was to learn and see in the world and how fantastic it all was. Gradually, I also began to take an interest in the people that formed part of my expanding world. Before I would only notice an amusing teacher or someone who had unusual looks. For example, one boy we called "piglet" because he had such small eyes and a very pink skin—these were boys' pranks and typical for our ages. Now, Jesus' example gave me direction for my life. He was the great Maestro.

The contents of a letter, which Herbert received a few years ago, show that as a student he was able to empathize with others, or at least he tried to. A former schoolmate, Pelle Flodman, gave the letter to one of the orchestra members before a concert in Gothenburg. As Herbert read it, the story slowly came back to his mind: Pelle was an orphan and not very diligent at school. The class teacher had scolded him repeatedly because his homework was not done neatly. But that did little good. As a last resort to apply pressure to the boy, the teacher told him in front of the whole class to let his father know that the teacher wanted to speak with him. "But I have no father," Pelle said.

"Then tell your mother."

"But I have no mother."

"Then tell your sister."

Pelle Flodman wrote in his letter that on that day Herbert came to him on the playground during recess, put his arm around his shoulder, and asked him, "How does it feel to have no parents?" Pelle had never forgotten this, and throughout his life, he followed the musical career of his former classmate with interest.

Herbert was baptized in June 1941 and became a member of the Seventh-day Adventist Church in Gothenburg. Today he still has the Bible that he received at that time. It is very much used, full of notes and comments, and has had to be repaired several times.

As a schoolboy, young Herbert was already confronted with the challenge of having to appeal for an exemption of the regulations because of his Sabbath observance, as this newspaper article "High School Exam at Dusk" from the year 1942 shows:

> The school board has notified that a Seventh-day Adventist student from the local secondary school in Gothenburg, is allowed to write his Swedish essay exam (on Saturday) after "sunset." He should arrive at the same time as the other students at the school, but will only take the exam after 19:45 pm. Prior to that, he will be under the required supervision of a teacher.[24]

No time for girls

When Herbert was in the sixth grade, a girl began to slip little pieces of paper with small rhyming poems into his jacket hanging in the hallway. He had an inkling of who it might be. In any case, one day this is what was on the note:

Att älska en Blomstedt	To love a Blomstedt—oh my dear,
är inte lätt—	It is not easy—hear!
på många vis och sätt.[25]	Sometimes it even brings a tear.[25]

In fact, he who was then so admired by girls "had on the whole no time for them. Of course, I had my crushes at school but only from a distance, just fleeting daydreams. I was far too interested in music and school subjects." After all, he was following in his father's footsteps—"a great moralist, in the best sense of the word, but sometimes also in a slightly worse sense." As a man in a position of leadership, he admonished *his* pastors when they, in his opinion, showed too little commitment to their work and wasted time. In retrospect, Herbert finds that this was not really an issue at home: "In this way, we had a clear idea of what was acceptable and what was not. One should be thankful that boundaries were set. When one is a bit more mature, then one can modify these standards; but for a starting point, it was very good that no one wasted their time."

Adolf had a pet phrase: "eternal value." Even in one's free time, one should only choose to do activities that had "eternal value."

Of course, my father was not alone in this somewhat lofty requirement of "eternal value"—which may sound a little peculiar or crazy for modern ears—but it was a short rule by which one could judge, a kind of a compass. In 1942, I received a book by the Danish composer Rudolph Simonsen as a gift for graduating from junior high school. The title was *Sub Specie Aeternitatis*, and it contained musical essays considered from the element of eternity and inspired by Baruch Spinoza. I think it is good to put this notion above one's passing emotions, even if perhaps, at times, different things had eternal value for my father than for me. It boils down to the fundamental perspective, which is very well emphasized for Christians in two ways: belief in creation tells us that we are not a coincidence. And then the second coming of Jesus gives us hope and directs our thoughts toward the future! We live this pronouncedly exciting life in the middle of this very broad range: big tasks as well as little ones that become large enough, if we take them seriously. I am firmly convinced that we can undertake them better if we have a clear perspective.

Music as a career?

Herbert finished his *Abitur* (final secondary-school exams) at the high school in Gothenburg at the age of seventeen; he was two years younger than his classmates. For a long time, he had been thinking about what career to choose and had even written a school essay a year and a half before on the topic "The Future—Hopes and Fears." He is convinced of one thing: those who want to achieve great things must set a goal early on and then with "incontestable energy" strive to achieve it. In the essay, he confesses that his own goal is still not entirely clear, but he would like to learn as much as possible in school because knowledge is power. He writes about the fact that he started to love music in a very special way when he was five or six years old. One does not detect a sentimental tone here, but one of sober consideration as he asks whether he has a future as a musician. And he states, "In this profession, there is terrible competition." He is acutely aware of the fact that only very hard work— practicing daily for many long hours—"by the sweat of his brow," will bring about the possibility of being good enough. "Well, I am not afraid of work. It's fun to practice, although it can be very draining, both physically and intellectually. If one has not played for a few days, you naturally get out of practice . . . and then one finds virtually no pleasure in playing a very simple piece, because you feel that it sounds so bad. One can then only sit down and play some small important passages over and over again until one is satisfied. That is what practice means."

> I had found my old writing compositions . . . and also some letters to my parents as a teenager. . . . They show how my feelings about "good and bad" in music were formed at an early age. The tendency to make moral statements is precocious. Much of it seems of course "secondhand," almost ridiculously taken over from what I had heard from my father in his sermons and lectures. My religious zeal is very apparent and also a heritage from my parents, especially from my father. On the other hand, the sense of humor, which is also omnipresent, I think is something I got from my mother, and even more from my maternal grandmother, Mary Thorson.[26]

In his essay, Herbert sees rather slim chances for career opportunities as a musician:

> One or two centuries ago, the need for musicians was significantly greater than it is today. Not only the important but also the less important nobility had their own, often quite large, orchestras. For example, Louis XIV had 128 salaried musicians at his court in Versailles. Even a small count had a small paid orchestra. The great Joseph Haydn was the musical director for Count Esterházy in Austria. Now things have changed. The interest in really good and artistic music has decreased over the last half a century. Nowadays the demand for music, in whatever form, can partially be satisfied by the radio. . . . That's why only a few select musicians will be able to make a living from their music.

At this time, in the fall of 1943, the Second World War raged all about peaceful Sweden. As in many other educated, middle-class Swedish families, the Blomstedts held fast to the almost romantic ideal of the "old Germany" with its high culture of poets and thinkers. Many Swedes could not see the dark side of the Nazi regime even after the war was over.

In his essay, quoted above, the young Herbert worries about the impact of the war on society and culture, which "could possibly be devastating." An economic issue preoccupied him as well: can one make a living from music? "That of course depends on how good the musician is. If he is talented enough to give his own concerts, then he can potentially earn himself a fortune. Even as a member of a symphony orchestra, he can at least make ends meet, maybe better than many others."

It is clear to him that the training and education are very expensive. But he also knows that "scholarships have become a great help. How many world-famous musicians have by means of scholarships received the opportunities to develop their talents!"

He states his most important thought in the conclusion of the essay— a love of music is crucial! "One's existence is boring if one just makes music to earn a living. No, one makes music for the sake of music itself and in order to give pleasure to and edify other people; something that noble music has always provided."

A champion of high culture

Young Herbert's views on music did not always fall on understanding ears among his peers. He remembers that some may well have perceived him as quite peculiar. He was the boy who never came to class on Saturday, constantly practiced the violin, and unilaterally advocated for classical music! In retrospect, Herbert feels that having to stand alone was a good lesson for him: "That was very good for me. It helped me many times in future years—a kind of schooling, just as the cubs of animals get used to fighting to develop their muscles and hunting instincts, so I had to get used to frictions. . . . I never really had any problem with my comrades, but I always felt I was kind of a loner, and I think that developed some spiritual muscles." For him, this meant not simply following the masses, but deciding for himself. He admits freely, "Perhaps, also, out of protest—that's a little bit in my nature."[27]

Even among the young people in his church, Herbert was part of a minority because of his high demands in music. To this day, he dislikes the sentimental hymns that originated and were popular in the nineteenth century: "It does not bring glory to God when we deal mainly with our own feelings and revel in them."

When he was about sixteen years old, Herbert got so upset at a youth camp over some of his opinions about kitschy songs that he made a bet about being able to compose a song of this simplistic nature on the spot in order to demonstrate its worthlessness. He composed a song in a very short time but not with the desired result: the people loved it!

Gösta Wiklander, now a retired pastor, recalled a campout when he proudly presented Herbert with his new accordion: "Herbert was at first quite opposed to it. This instrument did not fit his understanding of cultured music. So I played some music on it for him, and he gradually became curious. Finally, he even took the accordion in his hands and tried it himself. I had the impression that he no longer thought it was so bad." Much later, in his early thirties, the now-tenured conductor set out to sift through a hymnbook with several hundred choruses and evaluate each piece. Since it just happened to be mushroom season, he chose the classification from a mushroom book:

Symbol	Mushrooms	Music
* * *	delicious	very valuable
* *	good	good
*	edible	sentimental or worthless—even if a favorite
+	poisonous	kitsch or otherwise distasteful
+ +	deadly	blasphemy, openly or covertly

He laughs now when he speaks of this type of classification. Yet this splash of humor, which he added to a serious evaluation, has remained one of his typical characteristics: one has to take things seriously, but one doesn't have to be grim about it. Herbert's daughter Cecilia later wrote, "My father has a very specific view about what constitutes 'good' music. As far as church music is concerned, the matter is even more complicated. My father says that over the years he has become more tolerant—and this is a good thing. Otherwise he would not be able to endure some church services today."

---

1. On November 28, 1999.

2. These and other unmarked quotations by Herbert Blomstedt are taken from conversations between Herbert Blomstedt and Ursula Weigert (UW) from 2006 to 2012.

3. Between seventy-five and eighty-six hectares (185 and 213 acres).

4. Herbert Blomstedt, "When I Once Had to Help a Farmer" (grade school essay, November 5, 1938).

5. Holger Teubert, the editor of the Adventistischer Pressedienst (APD), the Adventist news service of the Seventh-day Adventist Church in Germany, explains that the Seventh-day Adventist Church was founded in the United States in 1863, and today has about

eighteen million members worldwide. The church emphasizes the separation between church and state and supports religious liberty. Its name highlights the second coming of Jesus and the observance of the Sabbath, the seventh day of the week, as a day of rest. The Sabbath is observed from sundown on Friday to sundown on Saturday.

6. Herbert Blomstedt, diary entry, November 13, 2006. In the United States, Olof Tholsson changed his last name to Thorson and started a family under this new name.

7. In American Seventh-day Adventist culture at that time, jewelry of any kind, even a wedding band, was seen as a sign of worldliness and vanity. This episode was taken from Norman Blomstedt's unpublished family chronicles, "Minnen" (Memories). Translation of the excerpts from Swedish to German by Joachim Lippert.

8. Herbert Blomstedt, diary entry, May 4, 2006.

9. Herbert Blomstedt, diary entry, May 11, 2006.

10. Herbert Blomstedt, diary entry, July 8, 2006.

11. Herbert Blomstedt, diary entry, January 7, 2007.

12. Ibid.

13. Ibid.

14. Ibid.

15. Herbert Blomstedt to UW, personal communication, January 22, 2012.

16. Blomstedt, diary entry, January 7, 2007.

17. Ibid.

18. Ibid.

19. Ibid.

20. A *concertmaster* is "a musician who is the leading violin player and the assistant conductor of an orchestra." *Merriam-Webster Online Dictionary*, s.v. "concertmaster," accessed October 17, 2016, http://www.merriam-webster.com/dictionary/concertmaster.

21. Herbert Blomstedt, quoted in Roy Branson, "The Song Is a Sermon: An Interview With Herbert Blomstedt," *Spectrum* 29, no. 3 (Summer 2001): 19.

22. Herbert Blomstedt to Lord Mayor of Leipzig, Burkhard Jung, thank-you letter, October 31, 2010, after receiving the notification of being awarded the Bach Medal of the city of Leipzig.

23. Herbert Blomstedt, diary entry, March 8, 2007; originally written in English.

24. Translated from Swedish into German by Joachim Lippert.

25. Translated from Swedish into German by Herbert Blomstedt.

26. Herbert Blomstedt, diary entry March 8, 2007; originally in English.

27. Branson, "The Song Is a Sermon."

The Foundations Are Laid

That which you inherit from your fathers,
you must earn in order to possess.
—Johann Wolfgang von Goethe

D URING THE SUMMER HOLIDAYS of 1946 at Hultafors Sanitarium, Herbert saw for the first time that one can at least earn some money with music. This is where, seventeen years earlier, the family had stopped to rest on their long journey from the United States to Nyhyttan, Sweden, and Alida had given a piano recital. Herbert and Norman not only served food in the dining room but also entertained the guests with music in the lounge. Gunhild Abrahamsson, the manager, was a good singer and played the piano for them.

Working was nothing new for Herbert. Besides helping on his grandparents' farm during the summers, he earned money in a completely different field for several years. During the summer of 1942, he sold Christian literature door-to-door with a friend in southern Sweden. At that time, vendors were nothing unusual, especially in the sparsely populated areas; however, a salesman of Herbert's young age was uncommon. In the rural area in which he chose to work, there were only scattered farmsteads; one bought food directly from the farmer. Herbert, however, had to first earn this money to buy food. Two days before his fifteenth birthday, he wrote a letter to his parents that gives an indication of how hard this work must have been:

Mörarp, Thursday, July 9, 1942.
Dear Parents! Two minutes ago I came home after the day's work. I should probably wait with writing this letter until Sunday, but I have experienced so much that I'm afraid I won't remember everything until then. . . . I started on Monday with the goal of

getting four orders per day. The week before, however, I had not even reached a significant number of sales, but I was sure to get help from up above. All day I had no success. The people were so outrageous that I almost fainted. Wherever I went, I met with insults. Almost all of them thought that it was all a load of "nonsense" and that I should "go to h—." "All right," I said with a friendly smile, bid them good-bye, and left. That's how it went all day, until in the evening I got an order for a book in bonded leather. The result of that day: discouragement, depression, tears, and fifteen crowns. So now Wednesday approached. I started the day with many joyful expectations. But, as usual, the terrible chastisement began again. They told me that religion, the book, and even I myself were completely worthless. There were horrible, nasty people. For example, I came by a farm worker who was busy transporting sugar beets. After a few minutes of talking with him, a fat older man came along the road on a bicycle. He turned to us, stopped, and shouted, "What's going on here?" I briefly explained. "I will not tolerate this impertinence, standing around here and talking nonsense! Get out!" "All right, I'm on my way," I said and went.

On Sabbath, as usual we cycled to Hälsingborg. There we met Norman. He had brought my violin, so now she is at home with me in Mörarp. Wonderful! I've been sick with longing for her.[1]

Seventy years later the former bookseller comments on his letter of that time as follows:

> The writing style is very much like that of my father. Nonetheless, the experience at the time was a good school for me. Early on, I had to learn to endure difficulty. This helped me later in life. Many things in the orchestral world are also very challenging. One has to learn to take criticism—even malicious criticism.[2]

Herbert now studied at the Royal College of Music in Stockholm. The road to get there was not an easy one for him. For many years, Adolf was of the opinion that his sons should follow in his footsteps regarding their profession. Although Herbert could imagine becoming a pastor, music drew him powerfully. Yet, the decision was not an easy one for him. He soon made a proposal to his father: because he had completed high school so early, he could use the two years gained to first study music.

Then there would still be an opportunity to see whether this way was the right one for him. Pastor Blomstedt liked this clear plan, and despite persistent doubts, he gave his consent.

Music, music, music

Herbert had applied to take three subjects at the Royal College of Music: music education, organ, and choral conducting. After meeting all the entrance requirements, he was accepted. He now studied violin and piano, organ, conducting, and the usual minors. Alongside his studies, he gave music lessons. He did not need a lot of money because he was very frugal and could still live at home because his father had been transferred again in 1945, and so the family had moved to Stockholm.

Because Adolf worked at times in very rural areas, his wife, their sons, and their daughter lived in a small apartment in the southern suburb of Älvsjö. Even though Sweden was spared the hostilities of war, there was a great housing shortage. One was happy about what one could find, even if the apartment was cold and cramped. Mother Alida slept on the sofa in the living room, Marita in the kitchen, and the two brothers in narrow guest beds that doubled as seating for the dining room table in the narrow hallway. For financial reasons, the Blomstedts rented the small bedroom to a student at the technical college. There was a toilet in the unheated stairwell, and a communal bathroom in the basement.

From the first day, Herbert enjoyed studying. Everything interested him: "I found life very exciting—and still do. One never stops learning."[3]

He soon served as the concertmaster for the college orchestra. For half a semester, choral singing was part of the curriculum. It was not something that fascinated him, especially all the opera literature! To him, this music sounded artificial and unnatural. But he quickly realized that there is wonderful vocal music that is equal to the great symphonies and sonatas. Paul Britten Austin and Alan Blair, two young Britons who had not lived for very long in Stockholm, presently got him to be the choirmaster in a small Anglican church. "There we sung a lot of William Byrd, Orlando Gibbons, and Thomas Tallis—magnificent music."

At that time, there was a death in the English royal family. Because of the royal family's close relationship with the Swedish monarchy, a funeral service was scheduled in Stockholm, for which the music had to be organized somewhat quickly. The college choir had just rehearsed the *German Requiem* by Johannes Brahms, and Herbert was asked to conduct two movements of it in the Hedvig Eleonora Church. In the absence of an orchestra, an organ accompanied the choir, which proved to be a good substitute. "That was quite an experience for me to be able to do that! It was a wonderful choir with my friends and fellow students, and it sounded magnificent!"

As a student in Gothenburg, I owned only a very cheap violin. During my student days in Stockholm, I could buy a better instrument, a Johannes Cuypers, built in 1798 in The Hague. I gave it to my daughter Cecilia in 1980. In Copenhagen, I later bought two valuable violins: a Giovanni Battista Guadagnini, Milan 1758, and a Nicolas Lupot, Paris 1812. I mainly played the Lupot; the Guadagnini was mostly left in my safe. During my time in Dresden, I bought several newly built instruments and bows, partly for my children, partly for rental to befriended young people—all very decent instruments worth one thousand to five thousand East German marks. I also bought two grand pianos and a piano, which I gave to my children and the Adventist Church in Stockholm. When I arrived at the Leipzig Gewandhaus Orchestra and realized that even prominent members of the orchestra were playing bad instruments, I thought to myself, *My instruments are lying unused at my home. Why should they not embellish the sound of my orchestra and be an inspiration to the excellent artists?* And so it is, that now seven of my best instruments reside with the Gewandhaus Orchestra. The remaining approximately twenty-five instruments are stored in the Gewandhaus and are available to students of the University of Music and Theater "Felix Mendelssohn Bartholdy," Leipzig. Ten simpler instruments can be borrowed by children who receive instruction at the Music School "Johann Sebastian Bach" in Leipzig.[4]

In Professor Tor Mann's conducting class, there was a young composer and music director named Gunno Södersten who was employed by the then Mission Covenant Church of Sweden—Sweden's largest Reformed free church. The two young men quickly became friends.

As a student, Herbert began to visit the opera once in a while. A couple of times he took his sister Marita with him so as to introduce her to the world of the arts. Among other things, they went to *The Magic Flute*, *Lohengrin*, and *Wozzeck* and also the ballets *Swan Lake* and *The Rite of Spring*. Although the opera was not his first love, "yet it is glorious music and simply part of one's general education," he comments from today's perspective.

Herbert did his best to get his father to go to a concert at least once.

His father was of the opinion that going to a concert was quite secular, and it took some time until he was persuaded to do so. Igor Markevitch, from whom Herbert had taken a master's class, was the conductor. Even today Herbert vividly remembers how his father, already gasping for oxygen in the foyer, clearly showed his displeasure over the smoke-filled air. When they went to their seats in the concert hall, it turned out that his father sat next to a lady wearing an extremely low-cut dress. Another affront! While Herbert studied the concert program to prepare himself for the concert, his father pulled out a church publication from his jacket pocket and began to read in order to use his time effectively.

A choice with weighty consequences

In 1948, Herbert came of age, and because the Swedish parliamentary elections took place in that same year, as a responsible resident, he cast his vote. When the American embassy in Stockholm learned of this, they immediately issued him with a certificate of loss of American citizenship and sent it to him. The young man, already a "committed European" in his heart, calmly accepted the notice. He had no idea then how many times he would have to apply for visas to the United States to take part in future performances.

Woe to him who needs a visa—an experience from 2006

I spent a lot of time with the visa application for the United States. For safety reasons, the Americans are now making it very difficult for visitors. One can book an appointment with the embassy by invitation only. And one can only get the date of the appointment by calling from a special domestic line that costs 2.5 Swiss francs per minute. The application form is available only on the Internet. And visa fees are constantly rising; currently, they are at 130 Swiss francs. This amount needs to be paid in advance; without the receipt, one will not be admitted. The fee is also not refundable under any circumstance—not even if one cannot travel, or the visa is not granted. For someone like me, who is constantly traveling, it is very difficult to find a suitable date for the appointment. On Monday, I had the hard-won appointment. It was already terribly hot at ten o'clock. In front of the embassy, the road was blocked off, only pedestrians were allowed to pass through a small opening. Although I had an appointment at eleven o'clock and it was already half past ten, I had to join the queue on the street. A lady checked our papers, and if everything was in order, one was given a number. Whoever was up next was then allowed to proceed through the high gate and past a security guard who could require one to leave one's bag—with another number as one's receipt. At the next security control point, one had to hand over any metal objects and pass through a metal detector—like the security check at an airport. Then one entered a waiting room, where there were already about twenty people of all ages and races awaiting their fate. One was called by name to one of six counters. My patience was severely tested. I had left a Gustav Mahler score in my bag and tried to continue studying it from memory. But it was difficult to concentrate in this environment. At last, it was my turn; it was already 11:45. A young lady at counter number one said my papers were all in order. She even returned one passport photo—even though they had asked for two. I should sit down again and wait for an employee who would ask me more questions. This time it was a young man. He was very friendly and asked me which orchestra I would conduct when in America. When I mentioned the Boston Symphony Orchestra, as well as the Chicago Symphony Orchestra and the Los Angeles Philharmonic, his eyes grew bigger and bigger, and he said that he was an enthusiastic violinist who practiced every day. So I had found a friend. Now I had to have fingerprints made—both index fingers. Then he wanted to know why I was not an American citizen, although I was born in America. This seems to be an unfathomable riddle to the Americans. How can one freely give away the greatest gift one could receive—American citizenship? One is easily suspected of being a criminal who has betrayed America and consequently has been expelled from paradise. Having learned through past experience, I had a copy of the clarifying notice ready: Certificate of Loss of Nationality of the United States, which the American embassy in Stockholm had issued to me in 1948 after I had voluntarily cast my vote in the Swedish parliamentary election. This heinous act was classified as a "hostile act against the United States" during the McCarthy era. Since then, I'm a Swedish citizen only and quite satisfied with that. Also the friendly violinist at the counter was happy, even slightly amused, and promised that I would be issued a work visa for the next three years within a few days by mail. All's well that ends well.[5]

Finally in Germany

In the summer of 1949, Herbert experienced a double first: it was the first time he attended summer school for professional musicians, and his first trip exclusively to Germany, which for him was the land of high culture, where some of the greatest composers of all time came from. As early as 1947, he traveled by train on the way to a youth congress in London via Hamburg and found it unforgettably tragic to see the ruins and the starving, begging children.

Margarethe Undritz, a former teacher of biblical languages, recalled in an interview how she first met the young student:

It was not long after the war. Germany still lay in ruins. Darmstadt, Germany, was about 80 percent destroyed. Now it happened that the Kranichstein Music Institute, directed by Wolfgang Steinecke, head of cultural affairs and of the Department of Culture for the city of Darmstadt, was searching for an appropriate venue for the institute's international summer school courses in New Music [twentieth-century period classical music]. Our Adventist seminary, Marienhöhe, in Darmstadt, which is located on the outskirts of the city and had remained undamaged, presented itself as an ideal venue with its large and small classrooms. The leadership of the school was more than willing to make it available for the event.

Among the international participants was a young music student from Sweden. Since I speak Swedish, we quickly became acquainted. We met on the school premises and also in the church services. I was then living in the main building, where there was a large hall. When Herbert Blomstedt saw that a piece I particularly loved was going to be played—for example, the Concerto for Two Violins by J. S. Bach—then he would come and get me, and I was allowed to listen.

The misery of bombed Germany touched him deeply, especially since he came from rich and intact Sweden. Shortly after his return to Sweden, he wrote me a letter in which he said that the thirty days in Germany had made the greatest impression upon him: "In a way, it was good to leave the Americanized Sweden behind me and to find at least one remainder of the *German* Germany. The cultural and spiritual ideals are available to everyone, while in Sweden they are reserved for an intellectual minority. Last fall, Germany had a remarkable Volkswagen exhibition in Stockholm, which was highly acclaimed. One hears almost daily of new revolutionary inventions that will be registered in the reestablished German patent office. German scientists hold guest lectures at Swedish universities. One gets an inkling of new German literature and music. German newspapers provide food for thought, far above the level of what one is accustomed to in other Western countries."

For us as Germans, this euphoria was almost strange so soon after the war. Maybe it was because of the good relationship with me and with other newfound German friends that he had a perhaps overly optimistic idea of post-war Germans and their country.

When he returned home after his first visit to Germany, we accompanied him to the train station and said good-bye on the platform. I felt a bit sad that he didn't turn around once on his way to the train to wave good-bye. Could it be that he wanted to hide a sudden surge of emotion? I had noticed earlier that he was struggling to keep his composure.[6]

Introduction to New Music

The Kranichstein Music Institute had an excellent reputation. It especially promoted New Music, which is often difficult to play and listen to. Herbert says from his current perspective, "It was often a hyperintellectual music style, which would later 'avenge' itself. Twenty to thirty years later, there would be a huge revolution, because it was recognized that these cerebral music experiments had gone too far. It was said that 'we need to make music again, which comes directly from the heart.' This comes and goes in waves and is part of music history. As a young student, one is part of it." As a more conservative Christian, he felt by no means out of place. "It especially suited me. Christians should be at the forefront of cultural development and not just go along with it out of necessity, thinking in their hearts that this is beneath their dignity."

According to Blomstedt, in that summer school, "Paul Hindemith was the big name. He had left Germany during the Nazi regime after his music was prohibited. Although not a Jew, he was too modern for the Nazis. In the United States, he taught for several years at Yale University. In post-war Germany, there was an urgent need to catch up on knowledge of his works and those of other composers with a similar fate. Very prominent composers such as Wolfgang Fortner and Ernst Krenek were there and held lectures on contemporary music. Several works from Fortner were performed." Herbert took chamber music courses led by Maurits Frank, "a wonderful elderly gentleman" who had played as cellist in the Amar Quartet alongside Hindemith, a violist. He taught Hindemith's chamber music, of which he had witnessed premiere performances and knew the exact style.

Ingvar Lidholm, a young Swedish composer, made the journey

to Darmstadt especially to conduct one of his earlier works of 1944, *Toccata e Canto*, which sounded very modern at the time. Later Blomstedt frequently performed it with his various orchestras, and the two men became longtime companions and lifelong friends. Herbert also maintained his friendship with Margarethe Undritz. Besides the letters containing concert information and the occasional free tickets, the help Herbert provided could also be very practical, as the language teacher once noted in her diary: "My clavichord was delighted to be tuned by an expert hand. When Herbert was recently invited to dinner with us, he asked whether we had anything else that needed repairing. Yes, our hanging lamp needed some fixing. He stood on a chair, and in a moment, the job was done."

Again in Darmstadt

In 1956, Herbert had been in his first permanent position as a conductor for more than a year when he went for a second time to the Kranichstein summer school in Darmstadt and found "that the foundations were already being laid differently there. Because music is constantly evolving, many composers see it as their goal in life to be at the forefront of developments. One has to learn and practice the latest techniques. Traditional methods are uninteresting, because everyone knows them already. One must have already mastered writing a sonata or a symphony. It's all about the latest that has happened and what the newest trends are."

This time the most interesting speaker for Herbert was John Cage—an American born in 1912 and one of the most important composers of the twentieth century. Cage and others initiated aleatoric, or chance, music in which the deliberate design of the composer is seen as a barrier needing to be broken down in order to rediscover the possibilities of each note and sound.

> It was also a response to the exaggerated intellectualization of music. Arnold Schoenberg had already begun this when he assigned a number to each note in the scale and then followed mathematical rules in his compositions. For example, he would compose a melody with the odd notes 1-3-5-7-9 and then the next tune with the even notes 2-4-6, and so on. Then every fifth note and then every fifth note backward—very elaborate. The intention was not to find a new musical language but to open the imagination to new possibilities without being bound by the traditional conventions. These rules one wanted to do away with—not out of nihilism but simply to

discover where all this would lead to when one forgot the old and could start something completely new. This was furthered through contact with other musical cultures.

After the war, one could at last travel again! Indian music now played an important role. The very advanced Indian folk music uses quarter tones, which at that time were barely known in Europe. It was a wonderful time—it was an invigorating time! New ideas came from all parts of the world.

John Cage once gave a presentation using a radio. As he read from a manuscript, he did not pause in his reading where it would have been appropriate but instead spoke to the rhythm of a mathematical series. After fifteen seconds, he paused for two seconds; after a further thirty seconds, he paused for half a second; and after forty-seven seconds, he made a five second pause—just as in a musical score. He used a stopwatch, and when he paused, music came from the radio until the seconds that he had predetermined were over. Then he continued reading. The whole thing was completely fragmented and did not follow the meaning of the lecture, but instead that of a mathematical pattern that lay outside of its meaning. The audience found it strange and unmusical, but Cage remained undeterred and thereby demonstrated a possibility to open one's senses to new pathways in music.

Herbert met the American composer one day while strolling in the Odenwald forest. He was searching for mushrooms and wanted to relax a bit in this way. It turned out that Cage was searching for mushrooms too. In conversation with him, the young conductor learned to his great surprise that Cage knew a great deal about mushrooms and had even written several reference books about them. As they walked a little ways together, Cage suddenly said, "Well, that's how it is. Our loving God lets mushrooms grow like this: one here, one there. Seemingly by chance. They don't grow in straight lines or in circles or in geometric patterns. They follow other God-given laws that depend on the humus and the moisture. This is stimulating to the imagination." Blomstedt comments on this encounter: "It was also a demonstration of his ideas. He was a very kind person, gentle, quiet, not conceited, yet tenaciously following his ideas."

Another interesting composer, who had traveled from Gällivare in the Arctic Circle, was the phenomenally gifted Bo Nilsson. Born in 1937 in Skellefteå, he had already presented at the age of eighteen two of his compositions at a radio station in Cologne during its program *Musik der Zeit*

(Music of the time) and shortly thereafter signed a contract with Universal Edition in Vienna, the most renowned publisher of New Music. They published everything Nilsson wrote; he only needed to send it—a dream for a young composer! When Nilsson started to compose, he had never heard a live orchestra. He only knew orchestral music from the radio. The single instrument at his disposal was a guitar. Using this, he tried out his self-composed sounds. His works were performed in a number of Darmstadt summer schools, including several premiere performances.

Once Blomstedt sat next to Nilsson on a train while on the way from Darmstadt to Frankfurt, Germany. The Frankfurt Radio Symphony Orchestra wanted to perform some of Nilsson's works. Bo Nilsson was very nervous and smoked like a chimney. His nicotine addiction was obvious. Suddenly he asked, "Hey, Herbert, what are the symptoms of nicotine poisoning?" He spoke about his fears of completely ruining his health. He was only nineteen!

Learning even more

In 1950, Herbert received the Jenny Lind Prize for further studies abroad. The prize consisted of seven thousand crowns and is awarded annually to a particularly promising student. Herbert asked to be allowed to use the money to attend various summer courses. At the conclusion of his time at the Royal College of Music in Stockholm, he received diplomas for the following studies: church musician, choral director, music teacher, and conductor. By this time, he had abandoned thoughts of a career as a solo violinist; instead, the possibility of directing an entire orchestra began to fascinate him more and more, especially since he loved the big symphonies. "The special attraction of conducting was the music! Beethoven, Brahms, Bruckner—music that you cannot play on the organ; it requires a full orchestra." However, the prospects were not rosy! The newly graduated and certified musician was just twenty-two years old and, with the exception of a few small orchestras, saw no prospects to find a position as a conductor. He later commented, "I have always been an all-or-nothing type of person. I would rather starve than want to earn money with anything less than good music."

Because he wanted to give his orchestras more than just the correct entrances and his ideas of musical interpretation, two years before graduating from the Royal College of Music in Stockholm, he had also enrolled at Uppsala University in Sweden and took musicology. Even today, it remains important for him to understand a composition from within its historical, cultural, and political context as well as the conceptual world of the composer and the then-current composition techniques.

During the summer, he attended a six-week conducting course in Salzburg, Austria. Every day one conducted an orchestra that was made up of students, teachers, and some hired musicians who all played together. "There was none of this unspeakably senseless practicing in front of the piano or the mirror. Only by actually conducting could one really learn something," emphasizes Blomstedt. Herbert von Karajan was announced as the speaker for some lectures, which of course attracted many people. But as it sometimes is with stars, he didn't show! Instead, Igor Markevitch took his place. His former master student is "eternally grateful for that. He was an excellent teacher, absolutely fantastic; very strict, very systematic—too systematic for some who saw music above all as inspiration and ingenuity. The most important thing for him in directing was to give the orchestra exactly what it needed. Any unnecessary gesture was better left out."

Blomstedt realized that Igor Markevitch, a Ukrainian composer and conductor who resided in French-speaking Switzerland, was just the right teacher for him. He needed this discipline, "because I was only driven by enthusiasm." Also taking the class was the Scottish conductor Alexander Gibson, whom Herbert befriended. A few years later the Scot was the musical director of the Sadler's Wells English National Opera and then the conductor of the Royal Scottish National Orchestra; in the 1960s, he founded the Scottish Opera. His special preference for Scandinavian music, especially for the composers Carl Nielsen and Jean Sibelius, certainly contributed to the fact that he got along well with his Swedish classmate. All together, Blomstedt participated four times in conducting courses given by Igor Markevitch. The second time he traveled together with Bengt Olof Engström, a former fellow student from his time at the Royal College of Music in Stockholm, who was a few years older than he was. Frank by nature and organizationally gifted, Engström had occupied a position of trust among the students at the college. Occasionally, the two young men performed music together and enjoyed fun times. It became a lifelong friendship. Later, as music director, Blomstedt recruited Engström as manager of the Norrköping Symphony Orchestra. Bengt Olof and his wife, Anne-Marie, served as the trilingual masters of ceremonies for the eightieth birthday celebration of the maestro.

In Salzburg in 1954, a very special student attended the class: the barely eleven-year-old Daniel Barenboim, a piano prodigy and, according to the judgment of various great musicians, a born conductor. In his autobiography *A Life in Music*, he writes, "I was the youngest member of the conducting class, for all the others were well over twenty years old. I remember that many of my so-called colleagues, who were conductors already, were not particularly friendly—I was, after all, a mere child. There was one exception, Herbert Blomstedt. He was very sweet to me and always took the trouble to explain things when I had language problems—I spoke very poor English and the only German I knew had been picked up in Vienna and Salzburg as a nine-year-old."[7]

Herbert had a good relationship with Maestro Markevitch, whom he greatly admired. The maestro soon realized that the young Swede was a particularly attentive student.

His trust in Herbert grew until finally he made him his personal assistant, first in Salzburg and later also in Monte Carlo and Santiago de Compostela. Markevitch's health often failed him, and so he increasingly needed support from staff on whom he could depend. He and Blomstedt had a type of father-and-son relationship. Markevitch always signed his letters to Herbert as "Papa Igor." And as with his biological father, there were some discussions about Blomstedt's religious lifestyle. However, this "father" thought it was not good that his "son" insisted on observing Saturday as a day of rest. He was convinced that in this way his student would never be able to make an international career. He expressed to Herbert only a few years before his death in 1983 that he had changed his opinion.[8]

As a student in Uppsala

At Uppsala University, Herbert was particularly thrilled by one professor: Carl-Allan Moberg, a specialist in Gregorian chant. The scholar impressed him deeply with his refined, calm nature and his extensive knowledge. During an oral exam, when Herbert saw Professor Moberg's office full of books, he spontaneously thought, *This is how I want to live!* The professor was also a great inspiration to him as a person. For his doctoral dissertation, Moberg had written about Swedish sequences, which are additional melodies to the liturgical Alleluia melismas, of which each monastery had its own tradition during the Middle Ages. Beauty and the praise of God united in music! For Herbert, this increasingly opened up a world that showed him he was on the right track. He also wanted to make music for God's glory. In his training as a church musician, he had learned a lot in this regard. The musical arrangements in the Stockholm's Protestant churches were, and remain to this day, of a high quality; many churches use only professional singers. Herbert dreamed of being the choir leader in such a church. He loves the organ and plays it remarkably well, preferably Bach: "I have wholeheartedly detested the romantic virtuoso literature: Guilmant, Widor, Vierne, Dupré, and so on. That was just meaningless chatter,[9] not church music! By contrast, Bach—every note, every note! And his predecessors naturally: Buxtehude, the northern German and Saxon tradition. For me, that was Protestant church music."

Hans Treffner, an Estonian mathematics student who had fled from the Soviets to Sweden in 1942, was a friend whom the young Herbert got along with very well on a musical level. He had a deep musical talent and was an excellent violin player; he even loved Bruckner before the future maestro had discovered him. Hans was multitalented, so he did not feel safe from the Soviet spies in Sweden and fled again to Canada, where Herbert visited him many times during his studies in the United States. In a letter, Hans requested, "Bring only good quartets. No spiritual goo! I'd rather have juicy love songs. Let your own taste determine the selection. But old folk songs are good, right? What songs did the old minstrels sing?"[10] For Blomstedt, he was

a deeply religious yet very lonely person. He returned to Sweden when he felt safer. . . . My brother and I seemed to be his only real friends. His humor was delightful, often quite spicy, and sometimes a bit crass. He was often at our home in Danderyd and was happy to be with us, but it also happened more than once that he could not come because he himself had invited other lonely people to his home! In the end, he died completely lonely in early 2007.[11]

Overall Herbert felt that with the musicology study he had filled an important gap in his education. As one of his minors, he would have liked to have taken a church history class. However, because this was not possible, he took religious history instead and is still glad that he did. There was such highly interesting literature! The four-volume collected works of Nathan Söderblom, a Swedish archbishop, about the origins of foreign religions were studied first.[12] Söderblom, who was a professor of religious history from 1912 to 1914 in Leipzig and a great lover of music, influenced Herbert "to see religion as a part of history and not just as personal piety." Herbert said, "In this way, I received an overview of other religions." There was very good religious literature in the faculty library, especially about Islam. The professor of Islamic studies at that time was the legendary Henrik Samuel Nyberg, who spoke more than ten languages fluently, including Arabic and many Arabic dialects.

For his third class, Herbert took a psychology course. This interested him primarily from the perspective of natural sciences. Professor David Katz, an immigrant German Jew who had specialized in animal psychology, left a lasting impression on Herbert in this field of study.

Learning, teaching, waiting

By now, Herbert was teaching many students who needed tutoring in preparation for entrance exams or other exams, mainly in music theory: "One learns by teaching, and excellent ear training is needed when leading an orchestra. It's one thing to hear something that is played, but another to analyze what you hear. Who is playing what? Which note is false? How is it false—too high or too low? Concerning the rhythm, does the note come too soon or too late? It is not enough to say, 'That didn't sound right.' Anybody can hear that! It's about how to get it right and find where the mistake lies."

Herbert enjoyed tutoring very much, and he was so successful that university teachers recommended him to their students. At the age of twenty, he still lived at home with his parents. He regularly visited the rehearsals of the Stockholm Philharmonic Orchestra to learn as much as he could from the conductors.

Herbert's strict observance of the Sabbath rest from sunset on Friday to sunset on Saturday led to many problematic and sometimes even peculiar situations. One day his conducting professor, Tor Mann, invited him to conduct a concert by the university orchestra, which usually took place on Friday evening. Herbert refused, as this was an event in the context of school and work. In vain, the professor tried to persuade him otherwise, using a meteorological argument: "But in October, it's always foggy here. There is no sunset!" After graduating, his insistence upon not working on the Sabbath gradually seemed to become an insurmountable obstacle to successful work applications. Once or twice a year he was able to act as a guest conductor, but a permanent position was not in sight.

Then one day Tor Mann offered to let him have the last half hour of his rehearsal with the Stockholm Philharmonic Orchestra, so he could do a trial conducting audition. The orchestra was required to remain. Herbert had prepared very thoroughly and then waited tensely in his room. But nothing happened. After about a quarter of an hour, a delegation of musicians came to him and explained: "Sorry, but we are not obliged to play under students."

In retrospect, Blomstedt says,

It was a very sobering experience, and they were correct. Yet, I had hoped for a bit of goodwill, especially since I was no longer a student. I was, however, known for being different: "This young man may be talented but has some strange ideas! He does not conduct on Friday evening and Saturday—that's just outrageous." This is certainly how they talked. I cannot say that I felt totally humiliated or was completely devastated. Life carried on. I simply continued to use the time to learn a lot, and I played a lot of organ and chamber music.

A Swede in America

At the conclusion of his musicological studies in 1952, Blomstedt filed an application for a scholarship from the Sweden-America Foundation for a year of study in the United States. The scholarship was approved, and in addition to a first-class airplane ticket, he received $150 per month as well as the payment of his school fees for international studies. In the first weeks, the scholarship recipients were introduced to the American school system and American culture. During one trip, they met Eleanor Roosevelt, the well-known human rights activist and former first lady of the United States. Once, while they were going for a walk in a forest, they heard the sound of Hector Berlioz's Requiem coming from the secluded house of a sculptor, and the Swede thought to himself, *It seems as though America actually has some culture.*

Soon Herbert was on his way to Boston to the New England Conservatory of Music, one of the best conservatories in America. Unfortunately, Herbert's teacher and mentor became ill shortly after his arrival and died soon afterward. The conservatory urgently sought a substitute teacher. "And a miracle happened: I was asked to step in! So I had the opportunity to rehearse twice a week with the conservatory orchestra as well as give concerts; that was, of course, paradise for me! The standard was even higher than in the Stockholm College of Music. But the absolutely best part was that the conservatory was very close to Symphony Hall, home to the phenomenal Boston Symphony Orchestra. I, of course, stopped by there every day and studied diligently with the scores on my lap. It was a wonderful time!"

Nevertheless, Herbert requested to go to New York to the Juilliard School of Music for the spring semester in 1953, where he saw greater learning opportunities for himself. His teacher there was mainly Jean Morel. It was an unforgettable time for Herbert. Arturo Toscanini was in his last year with the NBC Symphony Orchestra; Dimitri Mitropoulos was the musical director of the New York Philharmonic, and the principal guest conductor was Bruno Walter. "I saw these people in action on a daily basis! It doesn't get better than that. I'm eternally grateful," the maestro says today.

In Boston, Herbert got to know the music teacher and future founder of the New England Youth Ensemble, Virginia-Gene Rittenhouse, and they performed together. "Once for a worship service, I really wanted to play the third movement from Bach's Concerto for Two Violins with her," he recalls. "But she thought that the slow second movement was more sacred; the old prejudice that music in a religious context must be slow!"

Another musical friendship born during this time was with the piano and vocal student Elaine Myers. Elaine was a music teacher at Walla Walla College; in 1955, she married pianist Morris Taylor, who later as a professor at various colleges and universities such as Pacific Union College and Andrews University greatly improved the standard of music at these institutions. Together they performed with great success as a piano duo in the United States, until Elaine's tragic fatal accident in 1978. Their four highly musical children toured for a long time as the Taylor String Quartet at home and abroad. Their son Lyndon Johnston Taylor is now the principal second violin at the Los Angeles Philharmonic.

In June 1953, the scholarship ended. Herbert requested an extension in order to also have the opportunity to study at the Tanglewood Music Center where Leonard Bernstein was the teacher for the conducting class. However, Bernstein was rarely present and let his assistant Lukas Foss represent him. Bernstein himself was at the beginning of his career. Years earlier, it was rumored that Bernstein would be the successor to Serge Koussevitzky in the Boston Symphony Orchestra, but there were intrigues against him. Soon after, he became the musical director of the New York Philharmonic and "achieved great things there for many years," according to Blomstedt.

For Herbert, it was a wonderful environment. Almost every day he could listen to students rehearse. The orchestra of about one hundred musicians—the best from all over the United States—played at a highly professional level. Herbert still has a few friends from the orchestra to this day. Moreover, the musical director, Charles Munch, was to direct the center's orchestra in concert to demonstrate his solidarity with the students. In line with his personal strengths, he rehearsed a typical French program: Debussy's *Prélude à l'Aprè-midi d'un Faune*, Roussel's *Bacchus et Ariane*, but also Brahms's Variations on a Theme by Joseph

Haydn. He directed two rehearsals and then decided that he did not feel like conducting the concert. The students should do it. This was very unusual! Normally, the conductor leaves a subordinate to conduct the rehearsals and then conducts the performance himself. Herbert was allowed to fill in for the performance of Debussy and Brahms and was completely happy! However, he was overjoyed when, during these weeks at Tanglewood, a telegram arrived from the music director in Stockholm: "Offering concert with the Stockholm Philharmonic on February 3, 1954. Soliciting program proposals."

This was the same orchestra that a few years earlier had refused him a trial rehearsal! Today Blomstedt sees this experience as a good example of his philosophy of life:

> One must always be prepared! If one gets a chance, as I did with the Stockholm Philharmonic Orchestra, one must be prepared for it. If you lose ten years because you think, *there's no point*, then you will not be prepared. One should never give up and rather act as if tomorrow the chance will come. Do not lower your standards under any circumstances! Make no inferior music that drops the standards that you set for yourself. Such an attitude is always worthwhile! Of course, I also had a good dose of luck. God was with me, and it was a good point in time. That for which I had waited for so long, suddenly happened. It was like an explosion!

1. Herbert Blomstedt to Adolf and Alida Blomstedt, July 9, 1942, Herbert Blomstedt's private archives.

2. Herbert Blomstedt to UW, e-mail, March 2008.

3. All quotations, if not mentioned otherwise, are based on the author's interview with Herbert Blomstedt, March 10, 2007, Palo Alto, CA.

4. Herbert Blomstedt to UW, personal communication, December 18, 2010.

5. Herbert Blomstedt, diary entry, July 22, 2006.

6. Margarethe Undritz, interview by UW, August 4, 2006, Friedensau, Germany. All quotations by Margarethe Undritz are from this interview.

7. Daniel Barenboim, *A Life in Music* (New York: Arcade Publishing, 2003), 26.

8. Herbert Blomstedt to UW, May 4, 2012, and July 29, 2012. "Markevitch said these words to me, when I came to guest conduct his orchestra in Monte Carlo. He paid me a surprise visit in my hotel there and seemed very weak and ailing: 'Do you remember Salzburg in 1950? I was very strict with you then. But I think differently today: hold on

to your Sabbath. This is the key to your success.' In 1950, he was mad at me in Salzburg because I did not want to do the dress rehearsal for the final concert on Saturday. He then persuaded the orchestra to do the dress rehearsal on Sunday. When he told me about it, he jabbed his index finger in my chest and said, 'I think they are much more Christian than you!' That hurt me. Thirty years later, however, he had reached a different conclusion."

9. The southern German word used is *Gesprattel*, which means "a lot of talk about nothing."

10. Hans Treffner to Herbert Blomstedt, May 12, 1953, Montreal.

11. Herbert Blomstedt to UW, August 31, 2011.

12. Nathan Soderblom, *Främmande Religionsurkunder* [Foreign religion sources], 4 vols. (Stockholm: Hugo Geber, 1907–1908).

A Very Special yet Normal Family

Just as the quiet lake originates deep down in hidden springs no eye has seen, so also does a person's love originate even more deeply in God's love.—Søren Kierkegaard

A T THIS EXCITING POINT in the career of the future conductor, it might be appropriate to take a look at his private life.

The story of how Herbert Blomstedt met his future wife sounds a little bit like a fairy tale. A young "prince" hears about a poor but very beautiful and deeply religious girl from Germany. His curiosity is awakened, and he would like to get to know her, but that is not possible for the time being. It will take some years until the two can finally be wed.

Herbert's mother was a friend of a physiotherapist in Gothenburg, whom she regularly went to for treatment. They talked about this and that; one day Aunt Ester, as the young people called her, told of her sister in Hamburg. She was married to a man from southern Jutland, who was half Danish and half German. He ran a spa in Hamburg and was therefore jokingly called the "spa prince."

Their youngest daughter, Waltraud Regina Petersen, had just been accepted into a program for children and adolescents, which would send the children to Sweden to escape the post-war misery and to improve their health. Traute, as Waltraud was affectionately called, was first to be given the opportunity to improve her Swedish, and so she was sent to a boarding school in Ekebyholm. The fact that she was very musical grabbed Herbert's attention in particular.

In 1946, Traute moved to live with her aunt Ester, and one year later she passed the university entrance exams, having studied through correspondence. Then she enrolled at the University of Gothenburg in the teaching program for English and French.

"Maiden, your beautiful appearance"

That same summer Herbert and Waltraud met for the first time at a youth camp on Lake Vättern. Traute played the piano excellently, and under Herbert's leadership, a small chamber music group was quickly put together. They also sang old madrigals from the seventeenth century by Hans Leo Hassler, Orlando di Lasso, and others. The song "*Jungfrau, dein schön Gestalt erfreut mich sehr, je länger, je mehr*" (Maiden, your beautiful appearance delights me very much, the longer, the more) "fired up my imagination" as the maestro says today. He advocated vehemently for high musical culture, which matched Traute's own ideas very much. The two fell in love, and a letter exchange started between Stockholm and Gothenburg, which was to last for eight years.

As is the custom in every decent fairy tale, there are obstacles to overcome. When Traute was in Ekebyholm, she shared a room with a student named Sylvia Grundberg. Sylvia was about three years younger than Traute and came from Gothenburg; she and her family lived in the same apartment block as the Blomstedt family—in 12 Vasagatan (Vasa Street). Later, when they were both studying in Stockholm, Sylvia and Herbert had childish crushes on each other. Traute and Sylvia had also shared a regular correspondence since their time together in school. The two friends were for a time competing admirers of Herbert, a role that Traute was never keen to play.

For Traute's sixtieth birthday, Sylvia wrote a loving, detailed letter to "Traudi":

> You were then already even more sensitive and mature than I am in some ways today. I admired you for it then and still do. . . . One of your greatest strengths is certainly that you have strong convictions and remain faithful to your principles. You don't let yourself be impressed by any flattery and glittering appearances. You don't offer platitudes but come straight to the point. You never do something just because everyone else is doing it. On the contrary, you have the courage to tell people what you think and do what is worthwhile doing. There was a piano piece that I just could not listen to often enough. I still hear it occasionally on the radio, and then in my mind's eye, I see you in front of me sitting at the piano. You had short curly hair, a beautiful profile, and a correspondingly charming smile. When the piece was finished, you turned to me and nodded briefly as if you wanted to say, "There, that was for you!" Then you soon went away again. We promised to write each other. You said

that you had no desire to receive letters on a huge piece of paper with just a few words, such as, "How are you? I'm fine. Thank you for your letter. I hope to hear from you soon." I was overcome with fear and trembling. What on earth should I write that would be of importance and fill a sheet of paper? I kept all your letters that always arrived on time and were written on white airmail paper, without colorful flowers taking up half the page. In this way, and not by writing essays in school, did I learn the art of finding something in my head that was worthwhile to put down on paper. Then you showed me Hamburg! I have visited many times since then, but I get very nostalgic when I see the city from the perspective of our canoe that was decked out with pillows. We would paddle from your house past the luscious, luxurious, and beautiful gardens with weeping willows around us, past stately homes where once palace-like mansions stood, now reduced to empty ruins. It took quite a bit of skill to guide our canoe, because the oars had to propel us forward but at the same time also steer us through the narrow canals. You were so skilled at this that I could easily lie back into the pillows and relax—how lucky I was! Years later, we met on the steps of the renovated Ekebyholm. We had only a short time together for a few words and hurriedly tried to catch up on the most important things. You asked, "What was the topic of your doctorate?" And I made a feeble attempt to explain it in Swedish, but our time together was already over. I needed to come to the conclusion, and I still hadn't described my research topic properly. We smiled at one another, and you said, "Well, in the States you can get a PhD for everything, including for the topic on how to build a chair." And with that, we ended up again in our respective worlds. Since then, I have often wondered, as I once again sat on one miserably constructed chair after another at my typewriter, whether humankind would not have been better helped if I had designed a really good chair, rather than pursued my selfish interests. And now fate has let me see you again . . . and sitting next to you (in the Davies Symphony Hall) I can listen to the world of music. You strengthen my connection with Sweden, when you tell me about all the people who are dear to both of us.[1]

In 1952, when Herbert was continuing his education in the United States at the New England Conservatory, Sylvia moved to the vicinity of her own accord, "mainly because of him," she says in retrospect. In

America, however, it soon became apparent that they had very different ideals. While in the land of his birth, the budding conductor felt that he would best be able to live out his cultural ideals in Europe, but Sylvia quickly found a taste for the American way of life. She began to study medicine, changed later to mathematics and physics, became a teacher, married, and had four children. A casual friendship with the Blomstedts was maintained throughout their lives.

A decision that lasts a lifetime

Herbert says of himself that he needs a lot of time to make important decisions. To him, it was gradually becoming clearer that Waltraud Petersen was the woman whom he loved and who would be the perfect wife for him. Quickly aroused passion was not his way; instead, for him it was all about finding a partner for life, who shared his values and his faith. Many years later he described their life together by the titles of two pieces of music by Beethoven and Mendelssohn (after a poem by Johann Wolfgang von Goethe): *Meeresstille und glückliche Fahrt* ("Calm Sea and Prosperous Voyage").

Elisabet, the Blomstedts' third daughter, tells of a conversation with her father about her parents: "He told me why he had fallen in love with Mama long ago. My impression was that she had aroused his curiosity because she was German—that is, she came from the land of Bach and Beethoven. When, after having conquered her shyness, he got to know her better, he met a committed Christian, a girl who loved music and never got enough of it as my father said. Religion and classical music—these are and remain the two most important areas in his life."[2]

However, Herbert and Traute could not consider marriage yet, as Herbert still had no permanent position. Traute meanwhile had her first experiences with teaching and enjoyed the profession very much. Following the successful debut concert in Stockholm in February 1954 and soon thereafter the appointment of Herbert, the couple became engaged during *Pfingsten* (the Pentecost holidays) in 1954 and fixed a wedding date. One year later, the wedding took place in the beautiful month of May on Pentecost Sunday at Ekebyholm Castle. Herbert's father, Adolf, officiated the wedding.

Ekebyholm Castle, an estate from the seventeenth century about an hour's drive from Stockholm, would, in the ensuing period, become a central location for the growing Blomstedt family: Traute went to school there and returned after her graduation as a teacher. Later, all four of their daughters lived in the boarding school when studying at Ekebyholm.

Their third daughter Elisabet got married there in 1988. And finally, the distinguished conductor celebrated his eightieth birthday in the summer of 2007 at this castle.

It gave the quite penniless couple particular pleasure that their special day was captured on 8 mm film by Walter Boberg, a friend who worked as a documentary filmmaker. The groom got on exceptionally well with him, as he was a committed vegetarian and a "health nut."

For their honeymoon, the young couple first went to Paris, where Herbert studied for a short period with Nadia Boulanger. The legendary educator insisted that Traute be present at all private lessons. Then they went on to Solesmes Abbey, a Benedictine monastery near Le Mans. There the young conductor was to present the abbot, Dom Joseph Gajard, with a copy of a paper on the medieval Swedish sequences that his professor in Uppsala, Carl-Allan Moberg, had written and autographed for the abbot. However, the world-renowned authority on Gregorian chant had recently passed away, so the couple was unsuccessful in their endeavor and had to continue their journey.

Finally becoming parents!

On the Blomstedts' second wedding anniversary, their daughter Cecilia was born, "welcomed and longed for," as she says today. A few years ago she wrote to her father: "I feel very privileged to have received so much in life: a lot of good genes, good principles and values, good music, spiritual leadership, and more. Both you and Mama succeeded in making me feel welcomed and longed for. You have encouraged me and done everything to strengthen my self-confidence. 'Be yourself; you're good just as you are,' this was your fundamental message to me. Perhaps not formulated in these words, but I had the feeling that I was able to develop and grow, although I am neither particularly beautiful nor a superstar in any area."[3]

Farewell to Alida Blomstedt

On October 23, 1957, just a few months after Cecilia's birth, Alida Blomstedt died at the young age of fifty-eight. Her son Norman reported in "Minnen,"

> Thirty years of suffering with rheumatism had made her increasingly disabled over the years. But her suffering never broke her quiet, cheerful, and modest nature. She had a quiet humor, which smoothed out many difficulties in life. . . . Papa Adolf had returned from a pastors' meeting in Oslo, where he had contracted the Asian

flu, which was rampant that autumn. Three days after his arrival, Alida fell ill. The next day I admitted her to the ICU [intensive care unit] of my department in the hospital for infectious diseases. She got pneumonia as well, and the antibiotics had little effect. I spent the night between Sunday and Monday at her side. I tried in every possible way to ease her breathing, which was made difficult by liquid and mucus that accumulated in her lungs. She mistook the whistling and wheezing of her breathing for Karin's [Norman's six-week-old daughter] crying, [and she begged me:] "Do not let me die, Norman. I want to live and see Karin grow."

At eight o'clock the next morning, I walked home through the hospital park to get some breakfast. Twenty minutes later the nurse on duty called that Mom had just died.[4]

Herbert Blomstedt believes to this day that his brother Norman never forgave himself that he was ultimately unable to help his mother as a doctor. For all three siblings, their mother's death was a heavy blow.

Marita was only nineteen years old and emotionally still very much in need of her mother. Fortunately, her openness and love of life made it easier for her to establish new relationships. She studied at Newbold College in southern England and then trained as a nurse in Tønsberg, Norway, where she was among the top of her class. In 1964, she got married in Nyhyttan to a Swiss teacher, Bernard Pedroletti. After a few years of living in Switzerland, the couple eventually settled in Ekebyholm.

The growing family

Twenty months after the birth of Cecilia, Maria was born. The two girls shared a bedroom until Cecilia went to boarding school in Ekebyholm. In 1969, they were ten and twelve years old when Elisabet was born, followed by Kristina two years later. After her high school graduation in 1975, Cecilia helped out for half a year as a babysitter so that her mother could go back to work. Waltraud taught German, English, and French at Ekebyholm two to three days a week.

Herbert was very pleased with his flock of daughters, although he had little time for the family. Even if he could work a lot from home, at least during the first years of his conducting career, he was usually busy with his music scores. The children were not allowed to disturb him under any circumstances. If the door to the study was open, they could quietly sneak in on tiptoe to get something, but speaking to their father was not an option. Their mother insisted upon this rule being adhered to and reminded them of it once in a while. Daughter Cecilia cannot remember her father ever scolding them: "Never ever—and yet I respected him." She remembers well, however, that he was very dedicated to taking care of the children when Elisabet and Kristina were small. Whenever he was home, he insisted on being the one to take the girls to bed in the evening. In the morning, he would prepare their milk bottles and take care of them until his wife and older daughters had to get up. "By that time, he was traveling more than when Maria and I were little. I think he was trying to compensate with quality for a lack of quantity."

Moments with Dad

My father always worked very hard. When I was a child, he was often traveling. I remember how I stood with Kicki [Kristina's nickname] and Mama at Arlanda Airport: "Who will see him first this time?" A huge hug when he finally came out of customs; the scent of the big, wide world on him. . . . At home, Papa first changed into some comfortable clothes and then watched us as we unwrapped our presents. Once he took Mama, Kicki, and me with him on a long journey to the western United States. We wanted to spend two weeks in a [recreational vehicle] with family friends, the Koenigs, and in this way see a lot more of California than only La Sierra and Loma Linda, where Papa had many friends and was giving a summer course in conducting.

But Vernon Koenig suddenly fell ill, and so we had to change our plans. I'm sure that Dad would have preferred to return earlier to Sweden than originally intended. Instead, he rented a large Lincoln, and off we headed to some of our initially planned destinations: the Grand Canyon, Yosemite National Park, Lake Tahoe, and Hoover Dam. He was a fantastic tour guide. . . . My father's parenting style can perhaps best be described as leading by example. He never gave us long lectures. I remember, however, very well that he had a serious talk with me before I got married. He thought I was too young for marriage—I married on my nineteenth birthday—and made it clear to me how important it is to first complete an education. We can all say that we are fortunate to have experienced such a powerful role model in many ways. Our father shows determination, diligence, and self-discipline. Despite his great success, he has always kept his two feet on the ground and never brags about all that he has achieved.[5]

A musical house

Cecilia began playing the piano when she was six years old and had her first violin lessons at the age of eight. Her mother was able to accompany her on the piano. Waltraud had always enjoyed making music together with her husband and in the 1960s once again took piano lessons. When there was a blackout on a winter evening, she sat at the piano and played works by Brahms and Schumann from memory. She started to play the cello when she was pregnant with Elisabet, at the age of forty. The whole family now played quartet music together, although Herbert simplified the cello part for his wife. Waltraud made such good progress that after a few years she could play a cello concerto by Vivaldi. Cecilia regrets that her mother almost entirely ceased to make music when Elisabet and Kristina were small: "I think it was just too much for her because she again had two small children and one daughter suffered from diabetes." During her pregnancy with Cecilia, Waltraud sang together with her sister-in-law Lillian, under Herbert's guidance, all of George Frideric Handel's *Messiah*. She later often told how happy she felt when she sang, "For unto us a Child is born, unto us a Son is given," and she felt the kicking of her child in her belly.

Together with their father, Cecilia and Maria enthusiastically sang madrigals for three voices. The girls loved doing this. At the age of nine or ten, Cecilia remembers singing "just for fun" one of the small sacred concertos by Heinrich Schütz with her father:

> "The LORD looked down from heaven upon the children of men, to see if there were any that did understand, and seek God. They are all gone aside, they are all together become filthy: there is none that doeth good, no, not one" [Psalm 14:2, 3, KJV]. I still remember the Bible verse after forty years! What a ten-year-old could have understood by it, I do not know. Yet in this way, I learned to read music very well—something that has given me great joy later on in life.

Cecilia had a hobby of reading music scores in those days. On Sundays at ten o'clock, there was always a concert on the radio. If she could find the score for what was being played, then she was overjoyed! She sat on the sofa and read along with the music. If she got lost, she would go to her father, who showed her the right place again.

When Cecilia was fourteen, her father gave her piano and violin lessons on Sundays when he was at home and Cecilia could come home from boarding school. It was not all that easy for her to be a music student instead of a daughter. They never spoke about how he felt being her teacher. According to her father, Cecilia never practiced enough. She noted that he was disappointed, but he never scolded her. Today she realizes that the music she learned back then has brought much joy to her life and her father was always choosing the right pieces for her.

Music—choral singing and all kinds of "church music"—also played an important role during Cecilia's time in boarding school at Ekebyholm. She often accompanied the choir or the congregational singing on the piano at worship services. Sometimes the sisters played a duet, a flute solo, a piano trio, or even a string quartet together with their cousins, Norman's four daughters. Later, when they studied in Stockholm, Cecilia and Maria were involved in the music at church services.

Maria received her first cello lessons at the age of six. She was not particularly enthusiastic about the instrument; when she was a little older, she chose to play the flute and proved to be a very talented flutist.

It still gives Herbert great pleasure to listen to his daughters playing music and singing. Even though he encouraged them to develop musically, he did like to say that one professional musician in the family is enough. Cecilia and especially Maria sometimes dreamed of actually playing in an orchestra, but they knew how difficult it was to succeed in the music world. Both eventually opted for the medical field.

Sometimes the whole Blomstedt family played music together during church services and occasionally put on an entire program. However, the children were never forced to perform. Even practicing one's instrument was done on a voluntary basis. Every now and then, there were small amounts of money as rewards, but these episodes did not continue for very long. Cecilia and Elisabet report that they did not get rich in this way.

As is to be expected in every normal family with several children, the enthusiasm for playing classical music was not quite evenly distributed at the Blomstedts' house. All four daughters have adopted their parents' ideals of hard work and striving toward high goals but in different ways. Although the two older daughters were intensively involved with music, that was partly a matter of their disposition but also due to the fact that their father had more opportunities to play with them.

The two younger ones loved music and enthusiastically sang children's songs with their parents or with one of their older sisters at the piano. Elisabet studied piano and violin; but when she talks about it, it sounds more humorous than enthusiastic: "I soon stopped taking piano lessons and continued with the violin until I was about seventeen. After the birth of my first child, Oscar, I hardly played. Oscar is apparently very musical, because he woke up crying every time I resorted to playing my violin. But I did play children's songs on the piano for Oscar and Christian." Kristina, last but not least, also received cello lessons but, in her own words, felt forced to do it. "It was the worst thing in my life." As a teen-ager, she would much rather have learned to play the drums or the guitar, and she liked pop and rock music. Given the abhorrence that Herbert has for this kind of music, one can imagine that this generated tensions in the family. Now twenty-five years later, Kristina says that she enjoys listening to classical music. Several years ago she took saxophone lessons and played in a band for a short time. "But we were not very good," she notes in retrospect.

Industry and frugality

In addition to how they valued religion and music, Waltraud and Herbert shared almost all the same values in everyday life. While the pastor's son had grown up in a family where there was not a penny to spare, the daughter of the "spa prince" was strongly influenced by the hardships during the years of war. She possessed the old German virtues of frugality, discipline, a strong sense of duty, modesty, and similar virtues, which she internalized and displayed throughout her life. Sylvia, Waltraud's room-mate at Ekebyholm, saw her as being disciplined and diligent:

> She was incredibly dutiful. Everything had to be done just right or not at all. Traute taught me how to clean a room properly. It took quite a while until I could do it to her satisfaction. But she had a lot of patience with me. She was three years older than me and had acquired a tremendous amount of education in Germany, which was very different from my own, and so I found her to be somewhat domineering. She also expected that I took note of what she said. She was much stricter and more disciplined than I was. It was very good for me to have her as an example and a role model.[6]

Paradise with an outhouse

> For almost every summer of our childhood, we spent at least a few weeks at Bengtstorp, our family summer paradise. In about 1860, our maternal grandmother's grandfather built an estate near Örebro, and our grandmother grew up in this village. The farm has meadows and forests; but above all, the house is situated on one of

the most beautiful lakes in Sweden, on Lake Vikern. When we were little, it was quite primitive on the farm. There was no toilet, only an outhouse, and no running water in the house, only one water pump in the yard, no television, no phone. My father loved the silence and went into the forest every day to pick mushrooms and blueberries. My mother was not very enthused to run a household under these conditions, but she did it for our sakes. Because she didn't want to be alone with the children when my father could not be there, she often invited friends to join us. We kids loved the freedom, swimming in the lake, the nature around us, fetching milk from the farmer every morning, herding sheep, and so on. In 1984, when our parents moved to Switzerland, Maria and I, as the eldest daughters, took responsibility and ownership of the place. I was already living in Örebro, which is only twenty-seven miles from Bengtstorp. In 1992, with the help of an architect and a construction company, we thoroughly renovated the property so that it was more practical and comfortable. That was a lot of work but also a lot of fun! In the meantime, Maria also lived in Örebro and largely took care of the planning and execution of the project. Bengtstorp remained the focal point for our family. In 2001, our mother was at Bengtstorp for the last time. She lived for one more summer—the second or third without Bengtstorp since the 1950s. When Kristina and her husband were looking for a house in the country, we decided to sell them Bengtstorp. They are both very practical people and are suited to being able to keep an old house in good repair. They also love gardening. So now Bengtstorp is inhabited all year round—after two generations as a summer home. In order to still have space for family reunions, my father financed the renovation of an adjoining building. He now has his own apartment there with two rooms, a small kitchen and a bathroom. In the summer of 2006, we were able to inaugurate the apartment together.[7]

Just like his wife, Herbert was, and still is, very thrifty. When he took the night train to Copenhagen every week, he was asked why he traveled second class. His answer was, "Because there is no third class." However, since he's older now, he always travels first class so that he can conserve his energy and be ready to work as quickly as possible!

Elisabet Hafstad tells this story about Herbert:

Papa practically *always* worked, from early morning until late at night. My bedroom was directly below the living room, which also contained his study. I remember the clatter of the typewriter when my father answered the never-decreasing stack of mail on his desk, his steps on the stone floor—at home, he always wore clogs—and his piano playing and sometimes singing when again and again he would go over certain places on a score of music on the grand piano or listen to the piece of music on the stereo. I have definitely heard a good amount of Bruckner. To spend time with Papa was only possible on his terms. Kicki and I were sometimes under the grand piano or behind the couch and peered out without making the minutest sound.

The religious dimension

In later years, Waltraud used to enjoy telling her oldest daughter the following story: Cecilia was about two years old and liked it very much when her daddy played with her on the floor. One day, when he was paying particular attention to her, she asked quite impulsively, "Is it Sabbath today?"

Sabbath was the day on which Herbert took time for the family. After taking the weekly bath on Friday afternoon and welcoming the Sabbath with singing, he sometimes took out his very old, heavy, and beautifully illustrated Doré Bible, which he liked to bring out for special occasions. If the older daughters were at home, they frequently played chamber music with their parents.

On Saturday morning, the girls' father prepared "Sabbath grits," a kind of muesli with particularly delicious ingredients. Then they went to church—every week, except when they were ill.

Sometimes Herbert also took over the lunch preparations. He enjoyed it, and it made his wife happy! Quite often the family had guests for lunch, usually spontaneously invited: foreigners who had visited their church, single people with or without children, and others. When they had no guests, and their father was at home, there were mainly three different activities on Sabbath afternoon: making music, excursions or walks, and "reading" art books; that is, their father would explain the works of art to his children and tell about such artists as Rembrandt, Michelangelo, van Gogh, Monet, Picasso, and other great painters.

During the Stockholm years, Herbert served in several important positions in his local church congregation. For a time, he was the head elder and deacon; that is, he was responsible for the pastoral care of some of the church members. Of course, he also played the organ. He especially took care of a man who had made some bad choices in life and was homeless. He had long conversations with him, supported him where he could, and also invited him home to lunch.

Family worships were held every morning after breakfast in the Blomstedt home. For the younger children, there was a Bible story, and a Bible text when they were older. Their father—and in his absence, their mother—said a prayer, and then everyone joined in to recite the Lord's Prayer. In the evenings, they sang an evening prayer together. Cecilia knows that her parents continued this custom even when all of their daughters had left home, and her father, whenever he was in Lucerne and up until his wife's death, went to the nursing home every night to tell Waltraud good night and say the evening prayer with her. Even when she could no longer recognize him, she still clearly responded to the familiar folding of hands in prayer.

Waltraud Blomstedt's last years

Since the mid-1990s, Traute was more or less in ill health. There was a suspicion of Guillain-Barré syndrome, an autoimmune disease that attacks the peripheral nervous system, often causing paralysis. For her, however, it was a chronic form of pain and increasingly weaker legs. Soon mental and physical limitations became apparent. She became more and more forgetful and absentminded; she was often in pain; and her body movements became more difficult. Nevertheless, she still wanted to be there at family reunions or special concerts. For quite a while, she was still independent, could travel alone, and could go with Herbert on tour.

In September 2001, Waltraud had to be relocated to a nursing home so that she could receive the necessary medical care. Loida Doukmetzian, the wife of Herbert's close friend Karnik, remembers, "Herbert was completely devastated when he had to make the decision about the nursing home because of his travels. For a while, he talked of nothing else."[8] At the same time, he felt it was divine providence that an opening could be found in a home that was across from their apartment. They were able to wave at each other from the windows, and as long as it was possible, Herbert took his wife for walks in her wheelchair or brought her home to eat home-cooked dinners together, which he had prepared. One could feel how very burdened he was by the situation and how much his patience was stretched, but he never complained.

Beginning in November 2001, Waltraud's condition worsened dramatically. Good friends cared tenderly for her, especially during her husband's absences, particularly Dr. Ildiko Gál and Wilma Gramkow, who, in addition to working on her doctoral dissertation, rendered tireless help and assistance. In the end, she was at Waltraud's side every day; by this time, Waltraud could not recognize anyone. Herbert says about Wilma, who unfortunately died in late 2006: "Wilma Gramkow performed a labor of love that I will never forget."

Waltraud Blomstedt died on February 8, 2003, at the age of seventy-four. At the time of her passing, her husband was in Tokyo for six concerts with the Nippon Hōsō Kyōkai (NHK) Symphony Orchestra, already serving as its honorary conductor. No one could have foreseen that the end would come so quickly for his wife. Cecilia was visiting in Lucerne at the time and feels that God made it possible that she could be with her mother in her last moments. She was at her mother's bedside that Friday, and Ildiko and Wilma came for support on Saturday. As the bells of the nearby church began to ring, just before five in the afternoon, Waltraud breathed her last. "It was very peaceful," Cecilia remembers. She telephoned her father and told him the sad news. He was deeply shocked and thought he should cancel the guest performances and return home. Cecilia advised against it, so as not to let the orchestra down. He couldn't do anything for his wife at this stage; her suffering had come to an end. He was comforted by the fact that Cecilia had been there. So he honored his contract and wrote a loving, very intimate commemoration of his beloved Traute on postcards, one of which he sent home every day. At the funeral, he gave his daughters these cards so that they could read what their mother had meant to him. Over the years, the daily postcards, which he wrote to his wife during the times when they were apart, were a gesture of their unity. Herbert continued this routine for about a year after Waltraud's death, until he—like many who mourn—came to the point of accepting the reality of no longer having his wife there as his companion.

In retrospect, Cecilia says, "I think that despite deeply mourning my mother's death, my father somehow felt relieved. He no longer needed to worry. He felt extremely sorry and hurt to see how she suffered and that he could do nothing for her. And he did not have to feel guilty anymore that he was so often away from home. He had always felt that other people expected him to be at home more."

When asked whether there were musical compositions that he found particularly comforting during this time, the widower said,

> I have not explicitly searched to find comfort for Traute's death in any particular musical work. In each piece of music that I play,

I find solace, joy, and strength—a rich suite of emotions, which refreshes me. I don't need to look for comfort, because I know it can be found anywhere in music. On the other hand, certain musical works stir me to tears almost instantly. For example, the slow movement of Franz Schubert's String Quintet in C Major. Or Wilhelm Stenhammar's choral song "Sverige," which ends with the words *"våra fäder sova under kyrkohällen"* (where our fathers sleep under their gravestones). Or the final chorale of Bach's *St. John Passion*, which is about the hope of the resurrection.

The memorial service took place in Lucerne on February 28. Among the guests were friends from Germany, Scandinavia, and Japan. Pastor Paul Wright gave the eulogy. In addition to music pieces from other presenters, Maria and Cecilia played together the "Siciliano" from the Sonata in B Minor for Flute by Johann Sebastian Bach. Waltraud Blomstedt's remains were interred on August 11 in the family grave at the Vikersvik cemetery, very close to her beloved summer holiday home Bengtstorp.

Elisabet Hafstad wrote about her memories of her mother:

> My mother was somewhat reserved, and I do not know if she would have liked the idea of being mentioned in a biography. But perhaps I may tell a bit about her. She was very friendly, always interested in other people, and incredibly hospitable. Other people always came first. I think she always really wanted to have children. She was, for the greater part of her adult life, a full-time housewife, while her husband advanced his career. It must have been a demanding and sometimes thankless job to manage the entire household alone. As the mother of four daughters, she had more than enough on her plate. We were so happy that Mother lived with us for weeks at a time when Oscar and Christian [Elisabet's children] were small. Shortly after Oscar's birth in 1994, she began to deteriorate. She soon had difficulty walking, but she helped as much as she could: she cleared the table, rocked the cradle so that the baby would go to sleep, and sat down with the grandchildren to watch them while they played. Her grandchildren were her great joy. The family was simply her purpose in life. She was never happier than when we were all together.

What Herbert Blomstedt particularly appreciated about his wife was that he could talk to her about anything. She listened patiently, showed a lot of understanding, and always had a word of advice for difficult situations. In later years, she could teach again once in a while and enjoyed it very much. Lesson preparation specifically gave her great joy, and she went about it with a lot of creativity. In Stockholm and later in Lucerne, Waltraud gave seminars on developmental psychology and pedagogy, putting the materials together herself.

While cleaning out Waltraud's drawers years after her death, her husband found one of her diaries. In it, she had jotted down some of her favorite aphorisms, including "great victories are won through courage; greater victories through love; the greatest victories through patience." "Rich is he who has much; richer is he who needs little; richest is he who gives much."[9]

Today Herbert Blomstedt's daughters and seven grandchildren are "his greatest treasure." He maintains contact with them via telephone, e-mail, Skype, and letters and tries to be a part of their lives. Visits in person with his family are like celebrations to him.

---

1. Sylvia Linde, née Grundberg, to Waltraud Blomstedt, November 23, 1988.

2. Elisabet Hafstadt, née Blomstedt, to UW, personal communication, September 26, 2006. All quotations by Elisabet Hafstadt are taken from this communication.

3. Cecilia Blomstedt, interview by UW, August 15, 2006, Örebro, Sweden. All quotations by Cecilia Blomstedt are taken from this interview.

4. Notes in brackets by UW.

5. Elisabet Hafstadt to UW, personal communication, September 26, 2006.

6. Sylvia Linde, interview by UW, August 5, 2007, Ekebyholm, Sweden.

7. Cecilia Blomstedt wrote this story for the book.

8. Loida Doukmetzian, interview by UW, August 3, 2007, Ekebyholm, Sweden.

9. Waltraud Blomstedt, diary entry, April 3, 2007.

Finally a Conductor!
First Appointments in Scandinavia

E VEN AFTER THE MANY decades of Herbert's career—during
which he worked with the world's foremost orchestras—the invitation for his debut concert in February 1954 remains a very special moment for him: "That was like a ray from heaven! One cannot buy it; this
is something one has to wait for. Even if one could buy it, that would not
be a good way to start a career."

The invitation came from the CEO Johannes Norrby, a high-school
teacher and a gifted musician, who was engaged as a choral conductor
and singer. His offer was probably the result of several years of deliberations. He had heard about the young man, who was "somewhat strange"
in regard to his religion but obviously talented. Johannes Norrby was
curious but also hesitant to make contact with this slightly peculiar person. When they finally met, Herbert's four-year waiting period came to
an end. "I was well prepared because I had made good use of my time
since graduating from the College of Music, had studied repeatedly, a
perpetual student so to speak. At some point, this gives one the feeling
that this has to lead to something!"

The debutant chose a program that started with Johann Sebastian
Bach's Orchestral Suite No. 2. (Bach was still his specialty as a violinist
and organist as well as his main subject as a musicologist.) Added to this
was Ludwig van Beethoven's Piano Concerto No. 1 with the young Swed-
ish pianist Ann-Mari Fröier and Paul Hindemith's symphony *Mathis der
Maler*. This symphony was first performed in March 1934, with Wilhelm
Furtwängler conducting. In that same year, the Nazis banned the piece.
So it was still a very modern work, and Herbert had studied it in detail a

few years earlier with the Boston Symphony Orchestra under its concert-master, Richard Burgin: "I was therefore well prepared at rehearsals, and the concert was a huge success. I still cannot understand nor would ever have imagined the enormous response that followed." All seven of Stockholm's newspapers were full of pictures and the first reports! After a few days, a number of additional articles were printed.

Just two weeks later, a question came from the orchestra in Gävle: "We have heard you do not rehearse on Saturday. Is that correct?" Short and to the point! So, a quick question, a brief answer: " 'Yes, that is correct.' They politely thanked me by saying that the dress rehearsal in Gävle was always on Saturday!" Herbert was naturally disappointed but "had been consistent and was content."

Herbert's close friend Hans Treffner had lived in Gävle for some time. Knowing that the orchestra was absolutely in need of a capable con-ductor, he had repeatedly urged the local leadership to hire Blomstedt. However, during his previous summer in Canada, he had already resign-edly and sarcastically written, "It is clear that if the Gävle Symphony Orchestra prefers to keep Sunday holy, it must instead be content with a pitiful conductor."[1]

Less than a month later, a very similar request came in, this time from Norrköping. The petitioners stubbornly insisted, "Could we at least meet?" "Yes." They met in a restaurant in Stockholm. Dr. Sven-Gunnar Andrén, an epidemiologist and physician at the clinic for infectious diseases at the hospital in Norrköping and also the interim director of the Norrköping Orchestral Association, would lead the discussion and negotiations. The day after Dr. Andrén's state examination he had given his piano debut in Stockholm—a true double talent! Now he brought an invitation from the orchestra for two guest concerts in Norrköping as a means of mutual acquaintance. He had already clarified in advance that the Saturday rehearsals would instead be held on Sundays.

The two concerts were a great success. In this way, at the age of twenty-seven, Herbert Blomstedt finally got his first job. "My dream came true—I had my own orchestra! At least now I was a professional all year round; I could perhaps even marry and begin to live like a normal person."

The orchestra in Norrköping, which was founded in 1912 by the merg-ing of amateur and military musicians, was one of the smaller orchestras in the country with thirty musicians: a chamber orchestra with six first and four second violins. Nevertheless, it was an ideal choice for Bach and the early Viennese classic period! For later musical periods, especially the romantic era, more musicians for the wind instruments were contracted or the conductor adapted the parts. It was not the perfect solution, but a true challenge and an opportunity to learn a lot of new things in practice together with experienced orchestral musicians. Thanks to government grants one or more concerts could be held every week. Known as "Uncle Baton," the new conductor held concerts for young families three to four times per season—always on Sundays, he would expound on the instruments and certain selected compositions. When he was finally able to get his friend and fellow student Bengt Olof Engström to be the manager, he had all he could ever want. "We were all very happy and had a wonderful collaboration. The orchestra was fabulously good." Even today he still lauds his first appointment.

> That Engström was the right man for the job was also proven by the fact that his next appointment was for the corresponding position at the Stockholm Philharmonic Orchestra, succeeding the "grand seigneur" Johannes Norrby. When he retired, he promptly began postgraduate studies and graduated with a doctor of philosophy degree in musicology. He possessed an admirable blend of seriousness and zest for life, energy and serenity; and he was a professing Christian. And so now [at the celebration of Herbert Blomstedt's eightieth birthday], we sat at the round garden table in front of Ekebyholm Castle, both over eighty, and rejoiced over all that had been. He handed me a study of about fifty pages, containing a list of all the concerts that I had conducted with the Stockholm Philharmonic Orchestra from 1954 to 1994, over four hundred! How grateful we can be! But even more, we were happy about the present, festive day.[2]

Herbert's appointment brought great joy to the whole Blomstedt family. His father soon transferred to the fourth-largest city in Sweden and, with his wife, moved into a house right next door to the young married couple in 1 Nelinsgatan (Nelin's Street). Brother Norman, together with his wife Lillian, returned from the United States, and he started working at the municipal hospital in Norrköping. Mother Alida, now much weakened by her illness and in a wheelchair, especially enjoyed experiencing her son's concerts every week. Even today, it touches Herbert deeply when he sees concertgoers in wheelchairs; sometimes he spontaneously approaches them at the end of the concert and shares a few personal words with them. Even Father Adolf, who had since made his peace over the career choice of his son, enjoyed attending concerts when he was not traveling.

From the fire station to the music library

No sooner had the young conductor settled into his new appointment than he received another work assignment: his civil service needed to be completed! Civil service was twice as long as military service; so designed in order to deter those unwilling to do their military service (a requirement for Swedish men). Civil service also meant one and a half years of working two jobs at the same time, and one was always sent to where there was a need. So Herbert ended up in a fire brigade. After six weeks of training at the Stockholm airport, including a written final examination, civil serviceman Herbert was transferred to the airport in Norrköping. Although he found everything quite interesting, he quickly realized that this type of work was not suited to a musician's hands. He applied to be transferred and was sent to the office of the local central fire station. "I learned to type fast! I'm still reaping the benefits today!" he rejoices now. Despite agreeable colleagues and a pleasant working environment, he soon became terribly bored with typing letters and endured a real crisis concerning his sense of purpose. Finally, he was transferred to the place that he thought was just right for him: the town library. The librarians were just about to set up a music section with records, scores, and music books, and both parties were pleased with the opportunity to work together. His duties included making suggestions, submitting evaluations, and giving advice for new acquisitions. The library director Bianca Bianchini not only understood a lot about personnel management but also about music. She knew the young conductor from his concerts and gave him a free hand. He finally felt in his element and incidentally discovered an interest in library science. He could not know at the time that one day he would need the knowledge acquired here for the management of his private library, consisting of more than thirty thousand volumes.

Early music and latest insights

The young conductor deeply admired two older Swedish colleagues who had studied early music in Basel: the choral conductor Eric Ericson and the composer and violinist Sven-Erik Bäck. He was also very impressed with the viola da gamba quartet by August Wenzinger of Basel, which he heard a few times in concerts in Stockholm. When studying at the conservatory, he already realized that one could no longer perform Bach in the same way as earlier generations of teachers had. So he began to rewrite the different parts, remove slurs,[3] introduce new dynamics, and pay attention to smaller orchestra sizes. After two years in Norrköping, he decided to take a leave from concert performances for six weeks and enroll at the Schola Cantorum Basiliensis, which remains to this day an excellent school for Renaissance and baroque music.

Blomstedt remembers,

It was a glorious time. I studied scores with August Wenzinger, a wonderful, noble artist and person. With Ina Lohr, I studied Gregorian chant and *ars nova*—music of the fourteenth century. She was a fabulous lady, scholar, and practitioner, all in one person, and as a fervent pedagogue resembled Nadia Boulanger in Paris.

I stayed with Pastor Theo Schreyak, who was my father's colleague. The Seventh-day Adventist Church in Basel interested me because it was one of the first in Europe, and the first Adventist publishing house in Europe was founded there in the 1880s. Pastor Schreyak was a philosopher in the pulpit and a lover of music and art. As a preacher, he was thoughtful, reflective, and original. One did not hear any predigested, same old ideas from him. I often accompanied him to church services in smaller communities surrounding Basel and helped him with the music when there was no organist. We were a real team!

At this time, I was very active in the Stockholm Philharmonic Orchestra as a guest conductor. Every year I had four to six programs with them; I was practically the first guest conductor, albeit without the title. One day the manager, Johannes Norrby, who came from a Lutheran pastor's family, approached me. "There is something I do not understand about you. You say you want to make music for God's glory. I respect that very much and also think this is how it should be. But why don't you conduct on Saturday? Don't you want to honor God on the Sabbath?" I had no answer for him!

I began once again to systematically study the four Gospels. I knew these stories all so well but had never read them from the perspective of how Jesus kept the Sabbath! To my surprise, I found that Jesus not only healed the sick and helped the needy on Sabbath, but He sometimes deliberately did that which would anger the Pharisees. He wanted to unequivocally convince them that their observance of the Sabbath was wrong. The Bible says in many of the accounts of miracles that it was the Sabbath. This means that Jesus did it on purpose, to show the Pharisees that the Sabbath is there for man. Not so that the pious can boast about how good they are, but that people can be lifted up and draw closer to God. And one can also accomplish this through music! That was quite a long search for me. And so I eventually came to the point where I conducted my first concert on a Sabbath.

Looking back, Herbert says, "I had to follow my heart and my head. They both need to say 'Yes and Amen.' They must be in one accord. To live with a conflict between your head and your heart is simply devastating!"

I have often wished that I could meet my father again and discuss with him old and new issues from a more mature perspective than when I was a young adult. As I age, I have the growing feeling that I am becoming more like my father—both in the positive and the negative. And I would have loved to know if he ever would have been able to treat me as an equal, to go beyond the usual moralistic father-son attitude. I think he was a very good father, even though I never had the desire to be just like him in every respect. I am very grateful to him for these few fundamental attitudes and principles that have guided me through life: honesty, loyalty to God and men, the responsible use of time and money.[4]

Professor in Stockholm

In 1961, Tor Mann, Herbert's honored conducting teacher, retired, and his chair in Stockholm became open. So Herbert received a letter from his friend Bo Wallner. The musicologist urged him to apply for the professorship: "That's an order! Who but you could do it?" Blomstedt took his advice and promptly was hired. He gratefully remembers the gifted teacher who did so much for young musicians in Sweden, especially for composers: "Bo was my best musical friend in Sweden, and I have many detailed letters from him, full of enlightening observations. He was my unfailing support in everything. I was able to purchase some books from his estate. His big three-volume biography on Stenhammar is a gold mine."[5]

Never before had there been a full-time professorship of conducting at the college; this position was paid very well and had a ten-year contract. For the first time, the young professor experienced something like professional envy. In order to fulfill his obligations as a conductor, he presented his lectures in compressed sessions. He was gone for three weeks at a time, and then he was back at the conservatory. He says, "I practically worked day and night." This arrangement was not very welcome, but the conservatory administration allowed it because it was important to them that he held this position.

Each year he had three students; one student was Kjell Ingebretsen, who later became *Hofkapellmeister* (court conductor) in Stockholm, then the director of the Gothenburg Opera, and following that position, the head of the Royal Academy of Music.

Finally a full symphony orchestra

In the early 1960s, Herbert gave several very successful guest concerts with the Oslo Philharmonic. Both sides noted that there was chemistry there! His agent in Oslo, Per Gottschalk, did some further networking, and in 1962, Herbert became the conductor of the Oslo Philharmonic. For the first time, he had a full orchestra with eighty musicians. Now many musical works were possible—including those by Carl Nielsen, Gustav Mahler, and Anton Bruckner—everything new and in perfect harmony with the orchestra: "They were so enthusiastic, open, positive, and optimistic. There was simply a wonderful atmosphere! Every year when I go back there, I still get the same feeling." They played in the university auditorium, which seated about one thousand and had a huge mural by Edvard Munch behind the orchestra.

The orchestra had two tasks: radio broadcasts and philharmonic concerts. While the latter took place in the university's auditorium, which had excellent acoustics and enjoyed great popularity, the radio station only had a small hall available for the concert broadcasts. That meant fewer seats and thus a much smaller audience. The concert broadcasts took place on Sunday, with rehearsals on Saturday. Herbert's senior colleague Øivin Fjeldstad generously took over most of these Sunday concerts so that Herbert could concentrate undisturbed on the philharmonic concerts.

Kjell Skyllstad, Herbert Blomstedt's longtime good friend, recalls,

It was a great and joyful surprise that Herbert Blomstedt came to the Oslo Philharmonic. At the time, I was chairman of the International Society for New Music in Oslo. Thus, we quickly established a connection and soon became friends. We talked about what repertoire he would choose. For Herbert, it was clear that he wanted to focus on Norwegian music and include composers who had been neglected, as well as contemporary ones, into the program. I personally found this to be very significant. Many conservative critics, however, did not agree, and that was not easy for him.

For example, he performed Fartein Valen, whom we refer to as the fourth member of the Viennese School. One could also call Valen an expressionist. He developed an atonal system without a strict twelve-tone structure independently of, but at the same time as, Arnold Schoenberg. Blomstedt also performed most of the contemporary composers, such as Klaus Egge, then the chairman of the Norwegian Composers Association, and Arne Nordheim. The young maestro tried hard to acquaint Norwegian audiences with their musical heritage. It was important for him to build a bridge between Edvard Grieg and contemporary composers.

The orchestra soon changed under its new conductor. It was initially quite mediocre, but now every single musician was challenged to do his or her best. In this way, the orchestra reached a very professional level in an incredibly short time. Herbert's secret was that he had confidence in the musicians, and so their working relationship was based on mutual trust and cooperation. I had never before experienced something like this! I was at the rehearsals and came to the realization that it was something like a love affair! From the first glance, from the first note, to share such an intimate relationship is something very special. The concerts' highlights were undoubtedly the performances of standard works and premiere performances.

Today the orchestra has achieved international standards and acclaim. Successors were able to build on the foundation that Herbert laid. The special thing about him is his belief in the possibilities of musical communication at a very high level. He is simply a persona of culture. For him, music is a means of revelation of a higher power. In his interaction with the audience, one can feel his devotion, a deep penetration into the soul of the music, into its spiritual content.

Every conductor has his own idea of sound. Of course, one has to take into account the size of the orchestra when asking the question, how do I achieve my ideal sound?

Herbert also went through a lot of trouble with the scores. There were several errors in the printed music. Every performance of his represents many hours of work on the scores. For example, we sat together and worked very thoroughly on Fartein Valen's scores. This was important to Herbert Blomstedt, and the orchestra as well as the audience sensed it. For him, it is not only about technique—it's about the heart of the matter, and it shows. He never puts on any airs.

Herbert indeed came to Norway at a time when we had perhaps

not yet achieved much in terms of building up our cultural life after the war. So it was important to give some impetus: Where do we go from here? How, within a European context, can we create cultural and orchestral policies that will help us to advance? And here Blomstedt had a great impact—not only on the standard of orchestral music, but also on cultural policy in general. The orchestra was what drove the world of music during that time. Then came the conservatory and other institutions that would advance musical culture.

Today we still like to invite Herbert Blomstedt in order to "see and hear" each other again. And the audience appreciates this very much. His work is not forgotten, even if it was so long ago. His lasting merit is to have transformed the small orchestra into one that is on par with European standards. For me, he is an ambassador, who through music, creates a deeper connectedness between peoples.[6]

An invitation from the Danish National Symphony Orchestra (DNSO) in Copenhagen, which is the principal orchestra of the Danish Broadcasting Corporation, therefore came as a surprise. Mogens Andersen, the head of the broadcasting company's music department in Copenhagen, an energetic man the same age as Blomstedt, traveled to Stockholm and conducted the negotiations. He was known for his fervent commitment to New Music. The conditions that he offered Blomstedt were "like a dream" and afforded him the prospect for new experiences with an even bigger orchestra and an outstanding choir.

The manager of the Oslo Philharmonic, Eigil Beck, could not believe it when Blomstedt announced his acceptance of the offer and even burst into tears: "That cannot be true! What we are doing here is so beautiful." He did not, however, hold it against the outgoing conductor.

In "Nielsen Country"

In Copenhagen in 1968, Blomstedt became the first full chief conductor of the Danish National Symphony Orchestra, which was founded in 1925 with eleven musicians as one of the first radio orchestras in the world and gave its first performance two years later. Among Blomstedt's predecessors, there had been, as permanent guest conductors, such legendary names as Fritz Busch and Nikolai Malko and some Danish conductors.

Kjeld Neiiendam, the head of the orchestral department at the time, recalls,

The need to obtain a chief conductor became increasingly evident at the beginning of the '60s. The orchestra was in an artistic crisis; the artistic level was no longer adequate. Some saw the setback in quality as being caused by the very high average age of the musicians; others thought the problem was the changes in the repertoire to more contemporary, complicated music. The music department feverishly tried to find a chief conductor but had no success. Then, in the summer of 1965, there was a dramatic development. The head of the music department, Vagn Kappel, became seriously ill, and it soon became apparent that he would not be able to return to his post. His vice-head Mogens Andersen became the interim head, and it seemed that he was a strong candidate for the permanent position. Against this background, the DNSO began a "war" against Andersen, who brought modern music into the concert programs and, in the opinion of the orchestra, showed no understanding of the musicians. In the press, a heated debate was unleashed either for or against him. Finally, however, in December of 1966, Andersen was made head of the music department, and he immediately began every effort to find a chief conductor for the orchestra and bring it out of its artistic crisis.

After fruitless negotiations with a number of conductors, mostly from Central Europe, Andersen turned to the Nordic region. Under complete secrecy, he contacted Herbert Blomstedt, who was then just forty years old and had frequently conducted the DNSO with great success in the late 1950s. The negotiations went smoothly; Blomstedt's requirement of no rehearsals on Saturday was also readily accepted. He should take over the leadership of the orchestra as soon as possible, and so the concert plan was changed in order that Blomstedt could give a concert with the orchestra in late April of 1967.[7]

Neiiendam met Blomstedt personally for the first time a month later and was, in his own words,

impressed by his aura of integrity, honesty, and strength, and also a bit of introversion. Blomstedt clearly told the DNSO administration from the outset that he was in charge of the orchestra and not the man of the music department. He prepared them for the eventuality that there could be situations in their future working relationship, in which he would have to represent the best interests of the DNSO and not those of the music department. The DNSO wished for a boss who would limit their performance of contemporary music. After negotiations had proceeded without their knowledge, let alone their input, the orchestra feared that Andersen could have committed Blomstedt a priori to maintain the repertoire, including a considerable number of modern works. However, these fears were unfounded! Herbert Blomstedt's cooperative attitude in planning his selection of conductors, the arrangement of the repertoire, and the rehearsal schedule would soon restore peace in the DNSO again. An important factor was that Blomstedt took it upon himself to conduct a significant part of the modern repertoire and helped to make sensible choices for it. Again, it was important for him to put together practical rehearsal plans.

A period of avid record production began. Andersen and his staff wanted to record the complete works of Carl Nielsen. The crux of the matter was that, with the exception of Symphony No. 4, Blomstedt had not performed any works by Carl Nielsen! The advantage was that he was not afraid of hard work, and his new orchestra intuitively felt the compositions of their countryman, so to speak. As a result, in later orchestras he was considered, and still is, one of the greatest experts on Nielsen. In addition, works by major contemporary composers, such as Per Nørgård and Ib Nørholm, were performed and recorded.

Neiiendam says, "When Herbert Blomstedt began his appointment, the DNSO was able to perform first-class concerts with the right repertoire and the right conductor. However, significant qualitative differences in the program were noted—for example, in studio productions with young Danish conductors who did not have enough experience and in complicated modern Danish symphonic works. By dedicated and focused work and under the direction of Herbert Blomstedt, the orchestra was once again able to produce a sound compatible with international standards."

On September 15, 1975, I was appointed as Kjeld Neiiendam's assistant for orchestra administration. My work duties also included being the assistant to Herbert Blomstedt for orchestra matters, to the orchestra board, and to Mogens Andersen. In that year, the DNSO celebrated its fiftieth anniversary with a gala concert on October 28, followed by a huge banquet in the radio company's cafeteria and in different studios. On this occasion, Herbert Blomstedt received a box containing twelve bottles of a very expensive red wine, donated by the Anne-Marie and Carl Nielsen Foundation. A few days later Blomstedt brought this huge box to my office and kindly asked me to exchange the gift for grape juice, because he does not drink wine (which I am sure the representatives of the foundation did not know). So I returned the box to the wine boutique, and they agreed to exchange it for grape juice. The following day the receptionist in the entrance lobby called and asked me to please come as quickly as possible to receive a fairly large delivery, which had just been sent from the same wine boutique. I immediately went there and found five boxes with forty-seven bottles of a particularly exquisite brand of grape juice![8]

The *Carl Nielsen Letters Edition*

Carl Nielsen (1865–1931) is the foremost composer of Denmark. As a conductor, Herbert has contributed decisively to making Nielsen's works known all over the world. Blomstedt has recorded his symphonies twice, in Copenhagen (1973–1975) and San Francisco (1987–1989). A long-standing and very close friendship connects Blomstedt with John Fellow, a writer and since 2002 the editor of the *Carl Nielsen Letters Edition*, a collection of Nielsen's letters and writings, at the Royal Library in Copenhagen. In the library, Fellow came across Nielsen's huge correspondence, in which no researcher had taken an interest, studied it carefully, and spoke with Herbert about his findings. Blomstedt was immediately enthusiastic about the idea of publishing the letters and offered to give a series of Nielsen concerts whereby he would donate his remuneration to finance the project. This laid the foundation for the publication of the letters.

"Without Herbert Blomstedt's support, we would not have this edition today," John Fellow said, "but he also contributed more by allowing us to use his name, which was of course very important because he is so well known and highly respected as a Nielsen conductor. In addition, he is a professor and not just any world-renowned artist but also a musicologist. So it was that the remaining money, which was a considerable amount for thirteen years of work, was donated by foundations and eventually also by the Danish Ministry of Culture."[9]

At the time, John Fellow was the only one who knew the material, but Herbert was very interested in the content and read the individual volumes as they came out to learn more about Nielsen.

A balance of emotion and intellect

John Fellow has known Herbert Blomstedt as a conductor for forty-five years. John was thirteen years old when he discovered great music, and at the age of twenty, he met Blomstedt for the first time. Thinking back, it took some time before he could explain what attracted him to Blomstedt.

From the beginning, I heard that he had something very special that I could not find in other contemporary conductors. I had heard many classic conductors, such as Wilhelm Furtwängler, Bruno Walter, Otto Klemperer, and here, by comparison, a very young conductor came to Denmark! He did not play exactly like the old school. But in my opinion, he could hold a candle to them any day! I had a friend with whom I argued about whether Furtwängler or Walter played Schubert's Ninth correctly, then came Blomstedt—and he solved the problem for us. He played something that was between the two and was better than them! We both heard this at once.

How did Fellow arrive at this assessment? From his perspective, "Blomstedt has a sense of what happens concurrently and parallel in the music. While most conductors and musicians follow a single thread, he understands the counterpoint in the music much more clearly than others. The music is intense, less emotional in the usual way, but more emotional in a collective manner. In Herbert Blomstedt's personality, the relationship between emotion and intellect is significantly different than in most other people today. I believe that as a young man I was looking for this way to combine intellect and emotion together, both in literature— my area—and in music."

Fellow remembers that it was very fortunate for Denmark that Sergiu Celibidache often conducted in Copenhagen.

He was extremely good, albeit also extremely emotional and subjective. He built up the music in such a way that it lifted the roof; everything exploded—with a single emotional crescendo from beginning to end. Blomstedt conducted all the different voices in the music in such a way that they related to each other: fighting together, talking to each other. The highlight of the symphony was finally reached as a result of the communication between the individual parts, not as a result of the conductor's arrangement. It was fantastic! Blomstedt is able to identify with all these individual parts; in a way, he is an objective medium for many subjects.

Most Danes thought the young conductor was reserved, stiff, and very intellectual. He was considered to have great skill, more than the average conductor, but was thought of as an academic conductor. He already possessed the title of professor, and this was seen as quite negative! His longtime Danish friend has a different view:

All of these prejudices were and are not true! I believe that he simply didn't conform to the current division of emotion and intellect. He has a psyche like in days gone by, where emotion and intellect were linked together. In the ancient world, the word *ratio* referred to the whole man—that is, his intellect and emotions. Today, however, the term refers only to the intellectual realm. This shows that the emotional side of people has developed insufficiently. But not with Blomstedt, at least not when he makes music! I do not know why. Of course, his faith plays a role, probably not so much his denomination but his connection with the (belief) ratio both in music as well as in religion. And it may have something to do with the fact, as his friend Roy Branson once said, that he has wisdom, not just knowledge. But we are dealing with a topic here where there are no explanations, only different descriptions.

Does Herbert Blomstedt have a characteristic musical voice according to Fellow?

I would say that he rather lets the composer's characteristic voice be heard. He produces a special sound that probably comes from his awareness of the many voices, and one hears this immediately. In a rehearsal with Blomstedt, one can see how he illuminates every single part of the score. One understands then why he wants something a specific way and not differently. He makes all the parts sing and express themselves. Several years ago at a rehearsal of Beethoven's Ninth in Chicago, he suddenly stopped the rehearsal and asked the double basses to play alone. He explained how they should "sing" their part. Suddenly, the whole orchestra sounded like new because the deep double basses were also singing from below! In a sense, this is indeed a democratic approach in the way in which all are involved. The composer himself must have thought so, because he wrote each note out by hand. He cannot write something that he has not thought about. It is unfortunately easier to just play the notes without thinking.

Blomstedt is constantly researching. I have, for example, heard the "Jupiter Symphony" conducted by him several times in the past ten years and not one performance was exactly like the others. There was always a different interpretation of the music—and that within a relatively short period of time! That's his way of being faithful to the score: exerting a constant effort to make it even better, even more true to the original.

His very own voice is heard when selecting the music. Blomstedt does not perform everything. With the years, his programs have become even more selective than in his younger days. He puts them together so that everything makes sense from beginning to end. This is also a type of sermon—like all of his programs! Especially when it ends with a big Bruckner symphony, which occurs often. For example, in the last fifteen years, he has often performed Nielsen along with Beethoven, only the two and nothing else. I also believe that Nielsen is a special case—he is very much like Beethoven—and I do not think one can find another composer after Beethoven, who incorporates different styles throughout each symphony. Yet one only needs to hear one bar to recognize that it's Nielsen. Nielsen was aware of this and that is the reason why one can find places in his work that relate to passages from Beethoven. Not the same notes, of course, but a kind of choreographic, experiential likeness. As if to say, Beethoven was right, but civilization has evolved, and we have to think in new ways in order to still arrive at truth. At any rate, the similarity between the two composers is quite obvious! As a consequence, Blomstedt must play them together and, thus, show the evolution from Beethoven to Nielsen; thereby, they both become more meaningful!

Today there is no world-famous orchestra that Blomstedt does not conduct. That it took so long for the last of the world's top orchestras to contract him regularly, naturally, has to do with his seriousness—no showiness, no stardom! And it has to do with money. Great music has been commercialized just as much as pop and rock. The management must consider who is more lucrative. The musician who brings the old, eternal messages, or the one who follows the latest trends? In addition, Blomstedt has hardly conducted opera, and without it, one cannot be a true star. Opera speaks to the general public and brings in the most money and gets the greatest attention.

I think he finds the same values in his church as he does in the music that he plays. He already views a short movement of Beethoven's chamber music or a little early Mozart symphony as religious. And he can transmit all these values in a more general way to a larger group of people in a concert hall than in a church. I'm sure that Blomstedt is as close to God when conducting a Bruckner symphony as when he is in church—perhaps even closer. Blomstedt is a musician par excellence in a time when not only society and business, but also intellect and emotion, art and knowledge, no longer work together, but are separate entities.

---

1. Hans Treffner to Herbert Blomstedt, May 12, 1953, Montreal. Herbert Blomstedt commented on this letter: "One should not leave this somewhat exaggerated remark uncommented on. As already mentioned, my friend had a bit of an insensitive sense of humor." Herbert Blomstedt to UW, e-mail, July 29, 2012.

2. Herbert Blomstedt, diary entry, August 5, 2007. Notes in brackets by UW.

3. In musical notation, a *slur* is "a curved line connecting notes to be sung to the same syllable or performed without a break." *Merriam-Webster Online Dictionary*, s.v. "slur," accessed September 29, 2016, http://www.merriam-webster.com/dictionary/slur.

4. Herbert Blomstedt, diary entry, October 8, 2007; originally written in English.

5. Herbert Blomstedt to UW, personal communication, March 8, 2012.

6. Kjell Skyllstad, interview by UW, August 3, 2007, Ekebyholm, Sweden.

7. Kjeld Neiiendam contributed to the writing of this biography. All quotations with his name in this chapter are taken from his contribution.

8. Inge Neiiendam-Müller to UW, personal communication, January 4, 2012.

9. All quotations from John Fellow are taken from interviews by UW and his written communication to UW.

Stockholm—a "Home Game"

Come, Silence, come. With dark blue wings
cover me and rebuke
the impudent sounds
that dare to disturb the Holy Sabbath of the soul.
—Erik Johan Stagnelius[1]

I n 1960, Helmer Enwall, the grand old manager of the Konsertbolaget Agency and Herbert Blomstedt's manager at the time,
sent him far to the north of the Arctic Circle to Kiruna, the "greatest
city in the world"—purely in terms of area—to be a guest conductor
for the local amateur orchestra. Eighteen-year-old Sven Åke Landström
played the solo part in Lars-Erik Larsson's Concertino for Horn and
String Orchestra. It was a fantastic experience for the young horn player
to perform with a professional conductor. Sven was thrilled when he met
Herbert Blomstedt again after his appointment as French horn player for
the Swedish Radio Symphony Orchestra in 1967. Since that first performance together, Herbert had been a faithful and regular guest conductor
of the the Radio Symphony, with many concerts and recordings in which
he presented contemporary music.

Sven Åke Landström later became the director of artistic planning for
the Swedish Radio Symphony Orchestra and published a chronicle of
the orchestra a few years ago. He describes how Blomstedt's appointment
came about.[2]

A Swede (also) for Swedish Music

During the 1960s, the Swedish Radio Symphony Orchestra went
through some very important developments under the Romanian
conductor Sergiu Celibidache. They went on many significant

international tours. The goal for their artistic development was to give concerts in Berlin and Vienna—which happened with great success in 1969. After the Celibidache period ended in 1971, time was needed to develop new goals for both the orchestra and its leaders. At that time, Swedish broadcasting was undergoing a rigorous financial audit. The economic situation of the undertaking was to be managed as efficiently as possible. There was a lot of economic pressure and there were some hard times; but five years later the storm was over, and one could set new goals for the symphony orchestra.

The music directors decided for the first time in 1976 to appoint a principal conductor for the orchestra in an effort to create continuity and stability for the conducting position. The Swedish Radio Symphony Orchestra unanimously stood behind the proposal to extend an invitation to Herbert Blomstedt. One of their expectations was that his permanent residence be in Stockholm. He was happy to accept the offer and ended his appointment with the Danish National Symphony Orchestra.

I learned from the musical director of Denmark's National Symphony Orchestra how much they had appreciated working with Blomstedt. His reputation was already outstanding at that time.

At first, a three-year period starting with the 1977/78 season was agreed upon. Blomstedt remained the principal conductor of the Staatskapelle Dresden.[3] The head of Radio Sweden's music department, Magnus Enhörning, emphasized how meaningful it was that during upcoming tours abroad the symphony orchestra would be directed by a Swedish conductor with a feeling for Swedish repertoire.

By contrast, the music critic Åke Brandel, a few months after Blomstedt's appointment, declared in the *Aftonbladet* [Evening newspaper] that this was one of the biggest scandals and one of the worst mistakes in Swedish music history. After one year, however, he had a change of heart when he summarized the first three concerts by the principal conductor with the words "Blomstedt—a Master Conductor!" The review culminated with the words "Herbert Blomstedt conducts Swedish Radio Symphony Orchestra—a unique experience!"

Sven Åke Landström's duties included maintaining close communication with the new principal conductor concerning new appointments, rehearsals, and planning of the orchestra's schedule. It was a constructive and confidence-building cooperation for him. He remembers that Blomstedt showed great support for contemporary Swedish music during his years in Stockholm, particularly for composers of his own generation, such as Sven-Erik Bäck, Ingvar Lidholm, and Karl-Birger Blomdahl, but also for the next generation, such as Bo Nilsson, Anders Eliasson, and Sven-David Sandström.

Blomstedt also felt very connected to other Swedish composers, such as Johan Helmich Roman, Franz Berwald, Wilhelm Stenhammar, Hilding Rosenberg, Åke Hermanson, and Allan Pettersson. According to Landström, it was "characteristic of Blomstedt, to choose a great symphonic composer of Swedish music for his first concert as principal conductor in December 1977." Nils-Göran Areskoug wrote in his review in the Swedish newspaper *Svenska Dagbladet* about the performance of Hilding Rosenberg's Symphony No. 4, otherwise known as *The Revelation of John*: "Herbert Blomstedt has proved as always to be the unbeatable coordinator, with acuity and drama in the interpretation, which meant coordinating no less than three choirs."

In November 1978, there was a tour to West Germany and Switzerland. For the first time after the great success under Celibidache, the orchestra returned to the Philharmonie in West Berlin. The program included Handel's *Music for the Royal Fireworks*, Ingvar Lidholm's *Ritornell*, and Antonín Dvořák's "New World" symphony. The critique was very positive throughout.

Landström recalls,

In 1979, the music directors asked for everyone's opinion on whether Blomstedt's three-year contract as principal conductor should be extended. When the orchestra recommended a one-year extension, one could have interpreted this as a certain lack of generosity towards him. The music directors, however, decided to extend the contract for another three-year period.

A great moment came in November of that same year, as Blomstedt conducted three concerts for the inauguration of Berwald Hall with music by Franz Berwald, Sven-Erik Bäck (*Vid Havets Yttersta Gräns* [At the outermost edge of the sea]), and Hector Berlioz.

In January 1980, Allan Pettersson's Violin Concerto No. 2 was performed and a record made with Ida Haendel as the soloist. Leif Aare wrote words of praise in the *Dagens Nyheter* [Daily news]: "a tremendous work. Ida Haendel's interpretation of the solo part and the deeply dedicated, selfless work of Herbert Blomstedt on the podium was incredible." Soon after, there was a concert with Gidon Kremer as soloist in Alban Berg's Violin Concerto. "The Radio Symphony Orchestra conducted by Herbert Blomstedt played with the exact translucent clarity that Berg saw as the most important thing in his sound as it reverberated," Hans Wolf evaluated in *Dagens Nyheter*. In April, Blomstedt conducted Gustav Mahler's Symphony No. 2. Hans Wolf reported, "Herbert Blomstedt was rewarded with fanfare from the orchestra. During the whole concert, one was given the strong impression that this was a symphony that touched Blomstedt personally."

At the end of 1980, there were two special programs: a performance of Anders Eliasson's *Canto del Vagabondo* and Anton Bruckner's Symphony No. 7. After the first concert, Carl-Gunnar Åhlén spoke of "an interpretation like a monument." Concerning the Bruckner symphony, he wrote, "It is remarkable what Blomstedt does with Bruckner's music. This is not just an anonymous church organ without a living soul. . . . Rarely does one hear an orchestra so personally involved as the Radio Symphony Orchestra was on this extraordinary evening."

A highlight of 1981 was a tour to Hong Kong with the Swedish Radio Symphony Orchestra. After Herbert conducted a concert with pieces from Carl Nielsen at the beginning of February 1981, Carl-Gunnar Åhlén was again full of praise: "Herbert Blomstedt brought out the best in the orchestra, not just as expected with Berlioz and Ravel, but also in Nielsen's Symphony No. 4." Even Åke Brandel wrote a positive evaluation: "The commitment and strength of the Radio Symphony in the interpretation of Nielsen can no longer be doubted."

After a concert in March, Carl-Gunnar Åhlén raved over "Herbert Blomstedt's splendid interpretation of Mendelssohn's *Italian Symphony*." Jutta Zoff, the principal harpist of the Staatskapelle Dresden, Blomstedt's second orchestra, played the solo part in Alberto Ginastera's Harp Concerto. The evening began with Franz Berwald's overture to *Estrella de Soria*. Runar Mang wrote in *Dagens Nyheter* about a "poignant experience with dizzying splendor and a rich sound." Åke Brandel was also full of admiration: "I think of the brilliance of the Radio Symphony Orchestra under Herbert Blomstedt's outstanding performance when I call this work a gem. To my knowledge, the orchestra is not in the habit of giving any fanfare to its principal conductor, but I understand that after this performance they paid him tribute."

"However, for the next while," Sven Åke Landström said, "the newspaper articles about Herbert Blomstedt would pertain to a completely different topic."

Discord in the management

In 1982, a year before his contract expired, Blomstedt felt compelled to resign as principal conductor. He objected to some "anomalies," as he called it, in management. To his great chagrin, some discontented members of the orchestra had succeeded in ousting the powerful old troika of Magnus Enhörning, Ingvar Lidholm, and Allan Stångberg. These three men had hired him in 1977, "and they were very capable people," Blomstedt recalls.

Enhörning was the mover and shaker and a visionary; Lidholm added the musical expertise; and Stångberg was the practical organizer with insider knowledge—he had played viola in the philharmonic orchestra. But the orchestra felt that Enhörning was too autocratic and that he did not listen to them. It was during a time period when the fledgling Codetermination Act took the principle of democracy to the extreme, because everyone was given the right to make decisions. The new management team was made up of nice people, but they had little experience. I felt left alone, without the support of the old troika. Since I was also head of the Staatskapelle Dresden, I needed to be sure that my authority was upheld, even when I was out of the country. The new people were not able to accomplish this. I felt that my fundamental working conditions were challenged, and I came to the conclusion that I should go too.

Just two examples of what transpired during that time: one day I came to a first rehearsal and saw a man whom I did not know sitting in the first flutist's seat. I thought he was standing in for a sick colleague; during the break, I asked the director of Human Resources about it. I was told that this was the orchestra's new principal flutist! In my absence, the orchestra had breached our contract and held auditions for the position and selected this man—without informing me either of the audition itself nor of the outcome. I was stunned!

Then I learned that the orchestra was planning a tour of the United Kingdom with Yevgeny Svetlanov. Even this had not been discussed with me and came as a complete surprise. The new management apparently had no sense of what was proper and what constituted international practice—namely, that on important overseas tours, the musical director was in charge. I felt that I no longer received the support I needed, so I announced my resignation effective at the end of the season. The new director of the music department, Bengt Emil Johnson, responded with an angry article in *Svenska Dagbladet*, where he referred to my actions as "treason." I was very hurt because loyalty is an important value to me, and I felt as if I had been the one who had been betrayed—not by the orchestra but by the management.[4]

According to Landström, the contract resolution came as a complete surprise to the musicians. They knew what they had in their boss—not only musically but also as a person. Only two years before, he had stood up for them when it came to the issue of the musicians finally being paid appropriately and according to international standards. However, Landström recalls that "the orchestra showed appreciation for Blomstedt on the appropriate occasions. But one cannot escape the impression that both the orchestra as well as the management only fully realized the greatness of his conducting after he had left. Now he was really attractive."

Return to harmony

After Blomstedt, Esa-Pekka Salonen from Finland was hired as the principal conductor. Yet, after a break of five years, the former principal conductor came back to his old orchestra as a guest conductor, and this has remained an annual tradition.

On these occasions, he conducts mainly an international repertoire from the classical and romantic eras—with a particular preference for Bruckner's symphonies—as well as music by Paul Hindemith, Carl Nielsen, Franz Berwald, Ingvar Lidholm, and Sven-David Sandström.

In a document from the Swedish Radio Symphony Orchestra's archives, Landström discovered "that the orchestra and management had already in 1992 actively started looking for a successor to Esa-Pekka Salonen, who was under contract until 1995, but at a decreasing time commitment." During the deliberations, the name of the former principal conductor Herbert Blomstedt came up. It was known that he would leave his position in San Francisco at the end of the 1994/1995 season.[5] In a letter sent to Blomstedt in April 1993, the new music manager, Christina Mattsson, approached him on the matter, to which he responded tactfully: "One very significant question is of course whether the Radio Symphony Orchestra and I fit together, artistically and also in temperament.

Since our previous cooperation we both have changed, and our demands have increased. For this reason I look forward with interest to our concerts next April." He concluded with regret, "At this time, I cannot give you a more direct and positive response. But maybe it suffices so that you can continue in your search for a new principal conductor. With a cordial greeting also to the fine Radio Symphony Orchestra."

Mattsson was not really satisfied but asked for a more in-depth conversation, together with the executive director and the spokesperson for orchestral management. In fact, they met personally in Lucerne, Switzerland, at the end of 1993. But Blomstedt could not envision a permanent association with the orchestra. Swedish Broadcasting was under great political pressure, and only a management with the caliber of the old troika would have been able to stand up against it.[6]

In 2005, Blomstedt was appointed by the Swedish Radio Symphony Orchestra as honorary conductor. Contemporary Swedish music is still close to his heart. And so with the Stockholmers, he has in recent years performed, among others, Sven-David Sandström's *Messiah* and conducted Ingvar Lidholm's *Kontakion*, when the ninety-year-old Lidholm was presented with the Composer of Spring 2011 award in Berwald Hall.

A cordial relationship exists again—and not only with the orchestra. Bengt Emil Johnson reestablished his friendship with the former principal conductor of his symphony and gave a warm dinner speech during Blomstedt's eightieth birthday celebration at Ekebyholm. In honor of Blomstedt's birthday, he donated part of his personal book collection to the library at the school.

---

1. Erik Johan Stagnelius, "Tystnaden" [The silence], in *Samlade Skrifter af Erik Johan Stagnelius* (Stockholm: Adolf Bonniers Förlag, 1868), 368. Translation from Swedish into English by Herbert Blomstedt.

2. Sven Åke Landström contributed to the writing of this biography. All quotations with his name in this chapter are taken from his contribution.

3. See the chapter " 'It Was a Give and Take': At the Staatskapelle Dresden." Blomstedt became the music director there in 1975.

4. Herbert Blomstedt, diary entry, February 20, 2012.

5. See the chapter "Reencounter With the New World: The Time in San Francisco."

6. This is according to Sven Åke Landström's accounts.

The Summer Courses in Loma Linda

F ROM 1970 TO 1985, Herbert Blomstedt taught annual summer
courses in orchestral conducting at Loma Linda University (LLU)
in Loma Linda, California. LLU is a large Seventh-day Adventist university, with an internationally renowned cardiac surgery department at
the medical center and a campus in Riverside with liberal arts studies.
(The liberal arts college, now called La Sierra University, became its own
separate entity in 1990.) Forty-five to sixty young conductors from all
over the world participated in these summer courses; many of them
heard of the courses by word of mouth, especially since LLU did not do
much advertising. Only nine to twelve of the students were included in
Herbert's advanced class. Those who did not manage to make it on to the
short list audited Blomstedt's morning classes and participated in the afternoon sessions on chamber orchestra conducting, which were given by
Blomstedt's assistant Jon Robertson. In later years, Robertson offered a
preparatory course the week before the conducting audition for all those
interested. The summer course in the advanced class was two weeks long
and culminated with a final concert given on the last Thursday evening
on campus. In subsequent years, it was held in Pasadena's famous Ambassador Auditorium, also known as the "Carnegie Hall of the West."

Herbert Blomstedt explains how the courses came about: "Dr. Vernon
Koenig was dean of the School of Education at La Sierra University and
of German descent. He had no special musical training but intuitively
realized that the music culture on campus was not well represented. He
then took the initiative to get me involved in the conducting workshops."

An oasis of integrity

Kerry McDaniel first heard about the summer courses in 1978, when she was a music student at the University of Southern California. A fellow student and trumpet player who had taken part in the course strongly recommended that she do the same. She was actually admitted to the advanced class, and two years later she requested to take part in the chamber orchestra class and subsequently participated three more times in Blomstedt's advanced class. She especially liked

the apolitical character of the workshops. Other conducting courses in the United States were often strikingly political, with students being selected in peculiar, sometimes biased ways because they worked with famous conductors, without learning much. More often than not, it was all for show. Exactly the opposite took place in LLU, a relatively unknown oasis of integrity. Herbert Blomstedt was certainly an excellent conductor but at the time was relatively unknown in the United States. He could not have helped any of us advance in our careers, even if he had wanted to. We were just there because we loved music and wanted to learn as much as possible. Far away from the big, far more famous conducting and music centers, we were treated to a master teacher without experiencing this type of pressure or politics. I personally liked this simplicity, honesty, and integrity very much.[1]

Herbert Blomstedt always conducted the orchestra himself to begin the conducting auditions on the first evening and played a short piece of music or a passage from a composition. He called this "getting in touch with the orchestra." Kerry McDaniel's first impression was not very promising. She felt no desire to be a musician or a conductor like Blomstedt and initially felt an inner resistance to him and to what he taught in the classroom. Soon, however, she realized that this professor was, in many ways, the perfect teacher. His knowledge and expertise was so well established and widely diversified that it greatly surprised all the participants. There was no question put to him that he had not already thought about a dozen times himself. One sensed that he was particularly serious about making music. He became an invaluable mentor and a great role model for each participant who shared this responsibility and commitment in dealing with music.

The art of conducting

According to Kerry McDaniel, Blomstedt taught excellent conducting stroke techniques. One of the most important aspects of conducting is that the conductor can show the orchestra a lot with his or her hands in connection with keeping a clear tempo: phrasing, articulation, rhythm, sound, and so on, and that meaningless, superfluous movements should be omitted. This technique requires considerable discipline: one should be physically relaxed and should have done a lot of preparation beforehand and mental work. But it gives the conductor the opportunity to show how the music should sound without having to say a word. Of course, good music does not stop with the clarity of presentation, but this approach can be helpful to the musicians while performing; most orchestras appreciate this greatly. Another benefit of this technique is the time saved during rehearsals, leaving the conductor with enough time to discuss all the remaining problems that cannot be solved by hand movements.

Kerry McDaniel felt that Herbert's classes on physical relaxation were a great gift for her personally: "When I first joined the summer courses in 1978, I was extremely tense physically. My movements were one-sided and awkward. When I conducted, it looked like I was stirring something on the podium. Some of my teachers at the university had tried for years to get my motions to be more relaxed. But only by meeting Herbert Blomstedt and listening to his teaching did I really learn to relax. I have been able to implement this very successfully in other areas of my life besides music."

The morning classes were open to all participants and consisted of well-organized lectures on baton technique, behavior in front of the orchestra, how to read and prepare scores, and on general advice for conducting students. Herbert also took time to discuss specific problems regarding questions that the students had asked.

"He was a gold mine of information, detailed knowledge, and well-thought-through suggestions," says Kerry McDaniel today. "On the other hand, he always had many funny anecdotes and great stories ready to illustrate things of importance to him, whereby his talent for acting and comedy often became apparent. Some of the stories were about his own experiences; some stories he told in a hilarious and at the same time respectful way about other conductors and their exaggerated movements. He would tell us every story very engagingly and then end abruptly with a quiet and sober, 'But you should not try to imitate this.' "

In the evenings, the orchestra came together to rehearse. The conducting students would write the movements that they had prepared to conduct next to their names on a list and were then called up when their movements would be rehearsed. Blomstedt gave comments, but he waited long enough for the movement to be completed before he interrupted. "He was very careful not to make the students feel bad in front of the group," Kerry McDaniel says.

> One cannot express with words how much we all appreciated this. To our many shortcomings, he responded with patience, humor, and helpful, pertinent counsel. As one can easily imagine, his observations were very insightful, even if we could not always immediately correct our problems. Most of us shared my opinion that it was incredibly benevolent of Mr. Blomstedt to take time out of his more than busy schedule every summer to fly all the way to Loma Linda in the hot, smoggy city of Riverside, rather than enjoy his holiday or family time or study leave in Sweden. And year after year at that! He was obviously an experienced teacher and enjoyed teaching. Nonetheless, it was very generous of him.

Heart and mind

However, his former student also remembers situations that were less pleasant for her:

> Personally, I felt that my interaction with Herbert Blomstedt was not always easy. His behavior seemed at times to be extremely contradictory, depending on the mood and place where you met him. In the classroom, he was wonderful and treated us with respect. But outside the classroom, a lot of people thought of him as reserved, stiff, and cold. In the evening conducting classes, he could work with individual students with such emphatic objectivity, but always in a way that others did not notice, that some felt it as being harsh. His scrutinizing gaze made me shiver, and I almost felt like I was being dissected by him. According to him, if a problem could be taken care of quickly—for example, when it surfaced that I had an inappropriate baton—then his friendly "suggestions" were in reality orders that one could disregard only at one's own personal risk.

Herbert wrote a reflection on this perception in his diary: "Igor Markevitch was always like in an inaccessible tower, and he had a penetrating look, which was razor sharp. He was never rude to me. He had great self-control. But I never saw him as relaxed, cheerful, or collegial.

. . . Perhaps as Markevitch's assistant, I unconsciously adopted some of his mannerisms. I did admire him very much."[2]

Many who have known Herbert Blomstedt for a long time are of the opinion that he now deals with people in a more relaxed fashion than before. He himself feels he is more open-minded towards others and feels a greater need to be personally interested in people than in his younger days. Thanks to his phenomenal memory he can remember individuals and details about their occupational and family life very well and likes to ask fitting questions when they meet: "How's the family? Does your daughter still live in London?" And so on. As a highly analytical man with a radical devotion to music, he has obviously learned to connect his extraordinarily strong intellect more closely together with his pronounced emotional side and an impulsive nature.

Kerry McDaniel suspects that Herbert Blomstedt was actually very shy and adds,

Another aspect was the sheer force of his intellect. He's so smart, and this kind of powerful intellectual energy is inherently a cold energy. Interacting with him I often felt that I had to deal with the intensity of his mind and not with *him personally*. . . . In the last twenty years, he has ventured more and more outside of himself. My impression was also that he made a conscious decision to be more open towards others and more "American" in his behavior when he became the principal conductor of an American orchestra. For many reasons, I believe that his time with the San Francisco Symphony Orchestra represented a major turning point in his life.

In later years during his stays in the United States, Herbert repeatedly met former participants of the Loma Linda workshops who remembered them fondly, and some who had found very good positions as musicians. For example, his former assistant, the Jamaican-born Jon Robertson, became the conductor of the Redlands Symphony Orchestra and, according to some experts, made it the finest community orchestra in California. He was also chair of the Department of Music at the University of California, Los Angeles, where Schoenberg taught and Stravinsky had worked. He was with the Redlands Symphony Orchestra for thirty years and has enjoyed uninterrupted popularity with the musicians as well as the public. He has also guest conducted the San Francisco Symphony Orchestra. Herbert Blomstedt considers him a "brilliant teacher."[3]

A Great Song

The mathematician and physicist Peter Neumann,[4] an enthusiastic amateur musician who audited the summer courses, presented Herbert with a self-composed limerick poem in the spring of 2007 at a concert in San Francisco:

> The venerable Maestro from Sweden
> Has long ago mastered score readin'.
> Almost eighty in years,
> He always draws cheers
> From every group that he's leadin'.

---

1. Kerry McDaniel to UW, personal communication, August 10, 2007, September 25, 2007, and September, 27, 2007. All information and quotations from Kerry McDaniel in this chapter are taken from this personal communication.

2. Herbert Blomstedt, diary entry, August 14, 2007. Herbert has a friendly relationship with his student since his time with the San Francisco Symphony Orchestra. Kerry McDaniel is regularly present at rehearsals when he comes to guest conduct the symphony.

3. Herbert Blomstedt, diary entry, October 15, 2006.

4. "Peter Neumann is a computer scientist with a PhD from Harvard, but he is also a passionate musician. He visits every one of my rehearsals that are close to where he lives. On his home page, he mentions me as one of his mentors—side by side with Albert Einstein." Herbert Blomstedt to UW, personal communication, July 29, 2012.

"It Was a Give-and-Take":
At the Staatskapelle Dresden

T HE NIGHT TRAIN FROM Stockholm reached the border at about three o'clock in the morning. Shouts were heard as footsteps approached, and the doors were flung open. Suddenly, the light was switched on, and its glare fully awakened the drowsy travelers. Several People's Police officers of the German Democratic Republic (GDR), accompanied by trained dogs, began to check passports and search the sleeping compartment. They behaved courteously and were not too unfriendly. On that April night in 1969, from Scandinavia Herbert passed through the iron curtain for the first time, and the scene was scary. He had never before experienced border control measures with customs personnel in uniform such as this.

They arrived at their destination at about seven o'clock. The Berlin East train station, in the GDR part of the city, was drafty and barely illuminated. Soldiers slowly walked up and down on a ramp just below the roof, watching the few people in the station. Herbert gradually began to ask himself where on earth he had ended up. It was cold in the connecting train to Dresden, and the train attendants were rude. He had a growing sensation of not being welcome in this country. But more pressing for him were the questions of why he was there in the first place and why he didn't just go back right away.

However, immediately after arriving in Dresden, it was different. The director of the Staatskapelle Dresden, Dieter Uhrig, welcomed Blomstedt warmly, and "all at once, things suddenly became bright again and I felt welcome."[1]

At the end of March 2007, when Herbert traveled directly from San

Francisco to Dresden to once again conduct Beethoven's Ninth Symphony for the Palm Sunday concert after more than twenty years, he was taken aside for questioning at customs. "Finally arriving in Dresden, I was taken aside and interrogated by customs! Now that is very rare! And that in Dresden. It reminded me of the irritation I had when crossing the border in GDR times. The officer asked whether I got any presents abroad. The valuable Carl Nielsen autograph flashed through my head. So I said, 'Yes, I got a score.' That he thought not very interesting and let me proceed."[2]

Some thirty years after his key listening experience on his grandparents' radio when the Staatskapelle Dresden had completely mesmerized him with Max Reger's Variations and Fugue on a Theme by Mozart, Herbert Blomstedt would conduct his first Dresden symphony concert. During the previous summer, on August 21, 1968, the so-called Prague Spring had been crushed: Warsaw Pact troops had invaded and occupied Czechoslovakia, shattering the liberalization and democratization reforms made by the Czechoslovakian Communist Party under the leadership of Alexander Dubček. The Staatskapelle Dresden had thereby lost its chief conductor Martin Turnovský. He no longer wanted to work in a country where the army had played an indirect role in the invasion of his homeland, and he immigrated to Austria. In the autumn of 1968, during a tour in Sweden with a temporary conductor—Herbert Kegel from the MDR Leipzig Radio Symphony Orchestra—the Staatskapelle Dresden learned about Herbert Blomstedt.

"Kegel was a good man, but the chemistry between him and the orchestra was not right," Blomstedt observed. "It was such a delicate machinery, and if one was too heavy-handed with it, it broke down." A few months later when the orchestra needed a conductor at short notice for a concert in April 1969 in Dresden, they asked Blomstedt to help out. Although only a few weeks remained for preparation, he agreed.

Together with Ricardo Odnoposoff, the concertmaster of the Vienna Philharmonic, the orchestra had planned to perform the Violin Concerto by Johannes Brahms as well as a concerto for four woodwinds by Paul Hindemith, which Blomstedt had to learn quickly. For the major work, he suggested Carl Nielsen's Fifth Symphony—"an incredibly difficult piece for the orchestra"—which was also totally new to the musicians. Blomstedt was deeply impressed by how quickly they mastered the symphony, both technically and musically. "Actually, it was perfect after the first rehearsal." But for him, the best part was that "the same sound, incomprehensibly pliable and still always changing in expression" flowed toward him as he had remembered it, "only much more colorful. It was so beautiful, one could weep." This fascination has remained: "Since then, I consider myself fortunate every time I get to play with these wonderful artists. They awakened the sense of sound in a young boy, and with each new encounter, they show fresh possibilities of beauty."

Blomstedt was also impressed by the honesty and unbiasedness of the orchestra members in dealing with him. For example, one of them came to him and said with respect to the Nielsen symphony: "This surely is unusual music. It is probably good, but I find it hard to relate to it." He did not complain but just expressed that the whole matter would probably turn out to be quite exciting. Herbert's reaction: "I thought that these were extraordinary, mature people, not only wonderful musicians. They can stand back and view all this from a distance, even when an unfamiliar task demands all of their attention."

Some orchestra members offered to do things for him and were prepared to drive him to attractions, such as the Silbermann organ in the Freiberg Cathedral and to Saxon Switzerland (a national park). All this meant that the maestro from Scandinavia "fell totally in love with the Staatskapelle from the first day on." This feeling was quite mutual. The invitation for another concert came promptly.

In the following years, the working relationship became stronger. Since the guest conductor from Scandinavia also took over representative tasks, such as the anniversary concert of 1973, celebrating the 425th anniversary of the Staatskapelle, as well as foreign tours—including a first trip to Japan—he was soon considered their secret boss. When the official invitation came, he nonetheless hesitated a long time to accept it. There was the fame of the orchestra with the skill and sensitivity of its members, which had impressed him almost too much, leaving him to consider whether he could actually be adequate to the task. He had also never conducted opera, and this was expected in Dresden, especially since the Staatskapelle was primarily responsible for the opera. The performances took place in the Schauspielhaus (play house), since the Semperoper (Semper opera house), which was destroyed during the war, had not yet been rebuilt. There were several reasons for Herbert's lack of experience in this area, the primary reason being that opera does not have the same emphasis in Scandinavia that it does in Central and Southern Europe.

There were only a few opera houses, and the audiences as well as the conductors were more focused on purely instrumental music, choral works, and songs. Herbert was himself an instrumentalist and focused more on pure music. In an opera, language and acting are added to the music, and that was in the first instance "too much art" for him. As an avowed orchestral trainer, he was also aware of the fact that frequently playing opera music could slightly jeopardize the high level of the Staatskapelle's playing. Finally, he was rather opposed to the opera because of its content: adultery, murder, and homicide. Those were not for him! Moreover, he can't see blood; "I already get dizzy when the doctor has to take a blood sample."

But the bigger problem for him was the atheist and communist ideology of the GDR government, and as a confessing Christian, he found it to be a hostile ideology:

> I was aware of the attitude of communism towards religion and how ruthlessly it can take action against people. Therefore, I was deeply burdened by the fact that the government had agreed to the negotiated terms of my contract, allowing me the freedom to work as I saw fit, and so on, but who also harassed many of my fellow believers by not allowing them to study or to work in certain positions. . . . Should I become an advertisement for this, just so that one could say, "Look here, we live in a socialist state, but we're very tolerant"?
>
> This is what caused me a lot of consideration. I think the Staatskapelle knew this and very skillfully moved the discussions along.

Eberhard Steindorf, concert dramaturge of the Staatskapelle from 1969 to 2004, writes,

> Of course, Herbert Blomstedt's decision for Dresden was not an easy one despite all the clearly positive artistic aspects. . . . From the outset, he felt directly confronted in this position by the communist ideology, its practical implications, and all the officials from the municipal to the national level, who—usually less jovial than dogmatic—represented it. As it turned out, his Christianity became an annoyance to one or the other of these people (unfortunately, it also sometimes gave occasion for cheap ridicule). Many however—since it was well known throughout the city that he attended the Seventh-day Adventist Church—took this as an encouraging sign and as an example because his testimony was lived out quite practically in his person and in his thinking and actions. One must openly admit that it was at times a challenge when planning the or-

chestra's performances, especially when on tour, to make sure that we didn't schedule rehearsals on "his" Saturday, but fortunately, "in house" among the musicians, there was understanding and openness regarding this issue: one should show respect for an artist of this stature and for his clear conviction, even if one did not agree with him. Besides it was just impossible to deny him anything.[3]

In GDR times, it was difficult to hire a conductor—and a devout Christian on top of that—from the capitalist West for an orchestra in the socialist East. Today Herbert Blomstedt can only guess at the obstacles that had to be overcome, the many phone calls and discussions, the applications and paperwork that were necessary until everything was arranged and watertight. In Blomstedt's own words, he will never forget the fact that the Staatskapelle considered him worth all this effort. One day after Blomstedt had guest conducted a performance, Peter Sondermann, the solo timpanist, whispered in his ear, "Professor, you *have* to come to us; we pray for this every day." And the musicians dispelled his concern about his lack of opera experience with these words: "We will make every effort to help you. You can do it! We will carry you through this."

Being thus pursued, Herbert finally agreed; starting with the 1975/1976 season, he officially became the chief conductor of the Staatskapelle Dresden.[4] At this point in time, he had already directed the traditional Palm Sunday concert for many years as well as the annual requiem, which commemorated the destruction of Dresden in February 1945. He had also gained some experience with opera performances: since 1972, he had performed Beethoven's *Fidelio* several times with the Staatskapelle. They had already made a recording of its first version, the "old" *Leonore*, with Edda Moser in the leading role.[5] To date, it is Blomstedt's favorite opera because its contents reflect high ethics—namely, loyalty, freedom, and humaneness. Moreover, the music is more symphonic than typical opera music and thus corresponded very well to Blomstedt's preference. Soon *The Magic Flute* by Wolfgang Amadeus Mozart would be added to the repertoire. Additionally, Blomstedt discovered *Pelléas et Mélisande* by Debussy to be "quite fantastic music."

The conductor from Scandinavia also felt warmly welcomed by the audience. In a performance with the Staatskapelle as a guest conductor in the spring of 2007, he noted, "The public was typically 'Dresden.' Long silence after the final chord. Then applause that did not want to stop."[6] He is convinced that many citizens of Dresden in the mid-1970s felt gratitude not only that they could hear beautiful concerts but also that an outsider came to them and created a quasi connection to the world behind the tightly sealed border.

He also did not behave like a rich Swede but lived modestly. There was still a great housing shortage at that time in the GDR, and so for the first year of his commitment, he lived in a guest room in the building that housed the Seventh-day Adventist church in Haydn Street. In 1976, the opera offered him two rooms—a so-called shared rental—in an apartment on 4 Zeppelin Street. It was located in White Deer, a preferred residential area high above the Elbe River. The singers Theo Adam and Peter Schreier lived very close by. Professor Manfred von Ardenne also had settled there with his research institute. The view of the Blue Wonder—a cantilever truss bridge built in the late nineteenth century between the districts of Blasewitz and Loschwitz[7]—was legendary.

Mrs. Dressler, a retired teacher, lived in the other two rooms of the apartment and was not only a lover of art but also enjoyed cooking for her co-tenants. It was not always easy for vegetarians in the GDR to find a variety of foods for their diet; but the chief conductor received preferential treatment, and on the side here and there was a package of fruit or homegrown vegetables from admirers of his art. When he was invited somewhere, he expected no special diet but ate what the family ate.

Pastor Jochen Graupner recalls,

When Herbert Blomstedt was our guest, he always knew how to give small pleasures to the children; however, they were actually big pleasures for them. He gave them small foreign coins that he had in his wallet. He explained what country they came from, what could be seen on the coin, how one spoke in that country, and what is unique about it—everything that interests children. He communicated on their level, explained things that were new to them, and also played with the children. In another family, where the children all played an instrument, he made music with them. We were particularly impressed by his knowledge of languages. Those who work in other countries must also be able to communicate there. This motivated our children to devote themselves to learn the languages taught in their school.[8]

Herbert summarizes his working relationship during this special time with the Staatskapelle as a "give and take" over the years. Musically, a whole new world opened up for him. Due to the unique musical traditions of the orchestra, he discovered, for example, works by Richard Strauss in addition to the world of opera. He had not performed works by Strauss before because they seemed rather superficial and all about external splendor.[9]

The Staatskapelle, however, was and is still regarded as a Strauss orchestra because the composer was connected by friendship to the orchestra for more than sixty years as both composer and conductor. Nine of his operas were premiered in Dresden, and he dedicated his *Alpine Symphony* to the Staatskapelle.

In fact, it was not long before the practical challenge concerning the works of Richard Strauss became a reality for Herbert. He was hardly sworn into office when he was commissioned by the city to perform the waltz from the *Rosenkavalier* (*Knight of the Rose*) with the orchestra for a promotional film about Dresden. With short notice, the date was set. What to do?

In addition to the Staatskapelle, there is another outstanding orchestra in Dresden—the Dresden Philharmonic. Their chief conductor until 1964 was Heinz Bongartz, who also lived in the White Deer residential area and was by this time regarded as the éminence grise among conductors. Blomstedt asked for his help. With great courtesy, Heinz Bongartz introduced his much younger colleague to the Straussian world of music and especially to this famous opera, a musical comedy with lush instrumentation of about one hundred musicians. Blomstedt confesses that he began to discover "the musical magic that is possible with Richard Strauss," and has over the years become an "ardent Strauss admirer."

According to Eberhard Steindorf, Herbert Blomstedt knew "how to become a Dresdner to the Dresdners. This identification made him an eloquent advocate of the city and, of course, especially of the orchestra around the globe. Those who witnessed a press conference or an interview with him in New York, Tokyo, or in any other European city got a sense of this. His whole focus was to preserve and promote not only the high technical skills of the ensemble but also the distinctive orchestral sound, which had impressed him so deeply as a young boy."

The Austrian newspaper *Wiener Zeitung* once aptly reported, "The best proof of Herbert Blomstedt's artistic abilities is that he is able to demand such a culture of perfect performance from the orchestra. Anyone who is just a little informed can appreciate how difficult it is to maintain such a standard."[10]

The former concert dramaturge sees it as part of Blomstedt's personality that the conductor, "with intelligence and heart," "could always rely on the sensitivity, discipline, and spontaneity of the Staatskapelle" and that he "gave the decisive impetus, but in reality almost entirely stepped back behind the work and the orchestra. He wanted, together with them, to just be there for the music and the listener. During the final applause, he preferred to stand among his musicians, and when they left the stage, he was waiting backstage to shake each hand and thank them personally. He always gave his best and expected the same from the Staatskapelle—regardless of whether the hall was sold out or not." Steindorf remembers, for example, a concert at a cultural center in a Saxon industrial area, to which no more than 250 people had come, but Blomstedt "conducted with an intensity as if he were in Carnegie Hall."

Herbert's meticulous knowledge of the musical score, which is considered as phenomenal as his memory, makes Eberhard Steindorf think of a certain premiere when, to a famous composer's amazement, Blomstedt presented the composer with a comprehensive list of errors that he had found while studying the score. Steindorf adds, "It is quite evident that he conducts the Vienna classics—like those of the twentieth century or the romantic standard repertoire—from memory; but everyone was astonished when he did not want a conductor's music stand even for rarely performed works, such as Hector Berlioz's *Grande Messe des morts*, which he had never previously conducted."

Eberhard Steindorf writes,

> Over the years, Blomstedt performed a remarkably varied repertoire with the Staatskapelle. Besides the classics, romantics, and the great masters of the baroque, they performed works from the "orchestral archives," such as Jan Dismas Zelenka, Johann Gottlieb Naumann (whom he then also introduced in Sweden), Johann Friedrich Fasch, Francesco Morlacchi, Carl Gottlieb Reissiger, and of course Richard Strauss. In Dresden, he conducted his first Mahler and—based on his childhood experience—also Reger. And he closely acquainted the audience with the major composers of the twentieth century from Germany, Austria, Russia, France, Hungary, Switzerland, England, and of course Scandinavia. With Blomstedt at the helm, the Staatskapelle gave twenty world premieres and almost as many Dresdner premieres. Finally, he conducted about 250 guest concerts in Europe, North America, and the Far East with the Staatskapelle. During his era, the touring activities of the orchestra reached a hitherto unknown extent. In the studio, they recorded more than one hundred titles.[11]

These recordings include all of Beethoven's symphonies and the original version of *Fidelio*; also Anton Bruckner's Symphonies Nos. 4 and 7; Antonín Dvořák's Symphony No. 8; Edvard Grieg's complete incidental music to *Peer Gynt*; Wolfgang Amadeus Mozart's last symphonies, Nos. 38 through 41, and his divertimenti as well as the Oboe Concerto; all of Franz Schubert's symphonies; Max Reger's Violin Concerto; most of Richard Strauss's tone poems; and Carl Maria von Weber's clarinet concertos with Sabine Meyer, and his Piano Concertos Nos. 1 and 2 with Peter Rösel.

Steindorf summarizes,

> Only those who experienced it for themselves would probably be able to fully understand it: the listeners in those years revered the conductor Blomstedt not only because of the many thrilling musical experiences, but because they saw him as a person who was infinitely devoted to them. In the midst of their political and cultural seclusion—"behind walls and barbed wire"—they saw in him something like a small window to the world; one who kept a connection for them to the outside, who repeatedly and with unchanged affection came back to them and who by his whole being symbolized a piece of freedom for them. I only know Herbert Blomstedt as a friendly person who always treats people around him warmly, openly, and without reservations. I have seen him strict and uncompromising—but never unfriendly or even rude. I personally witnessed him like this once, when by means of an article written by an author from Berlin, I thought I needed to ideologically "justify" a controversial Schoenberg performance, which did not fit the official cultural policies during the GDR times. He did not like that at all. One can tell that he shares the joys as well as the burdens of the people who are close to him. As far as possible, he wants to be there for them.

An excursion to the New World

In 1979, there was a very special premiere for both the Staatskapelle Dresden and Herbert Blomstedt: they went on tour for the first time to the United States. In addition to concerts in New York's Avery Fisher Hall, the Kennedy Center in Washington, DC, and other cities including Philadelphia, it was a very moving experience to play for the United Nations anniversary in the United Nations General Assembly Hall. The program included the overture from *Die Meistersinger von Nürnberg* by Richard Wagner, *Responso* (a concerto for orchestra) by Siegfried Matthus,

Vier letzte Lieder (*Four Last Songs*) by Richard Strauss with the soprano Leontyne Price, and Ludwig van Beethoven's Symphony No. 8. Before a performance in the packed five-thousand-seat Eisenhower Hall Theatre, the musicians from the other side of the iron curtain were invited to West Point, the most famous military academy in the United States; they were given a tour of the grounds by cadets and were served a festive meal.

Throughout the four-week tour, the response was fantastic. Audiences heard the very distinctive sound of the orchestra—a well-balanced and expressive sound—and were thrilled. For Americans, who Blomstedt says have a good sense for music, "it was like a revelation to hear something like this." Columbia Artists Management, Inc. (CAMI), the almost monopolistic management agency for the best artists, signed Blomstedt while still on tour. This made Herbert Blomstedt, in his own words, almost instantly famous in the United States.

Also on this tour were GDR cultural functionaries, who traveled with the orchestra, apparently as ideological safeguards. Nevertheless, the whole journey was marked by solidarity: when one musician's foreign currency was stolen, all his colleagues chipped in so that he did not have to go home without souvenirs.

Herbert Blomstedt drove in the orchestra buses every day, invited the musicians out to eat, chatted with them as they were literally experiencing a "new world," and accompanied a critically ill orchestra member to the hospital in the middle of the night and interpreted for that person.

With long-term consequences

In the United States, there are many symphony orchestras that have a very high standard, equal with, and in some respects even superior to, the best European orchestras, because they are better organized and better paid. The best American orchestras are called the "Big Five." They are in New York, Boston, Chicago, Philadelphia, and Cleveland. Later on in his career, Blomstedt received invitations from these orchestras and is now a regular guest conductor in the United States. But in the late 1970s and early 1980s, immediately after his tour with the Staatskapelle, he received inquiries from some other top-quality orchestras. CAMI knew that the Detroit, Minnesota, Pittsburgh, and San Francisco orchestras were looking for a chief conductor. By and by, Blomstedt auditioned with each one of them and found them all to be very good. But he hesitated at first to make a decision. Detroit launched a particularly intense campaign to sign him. He did like the orchestra, but he did not like the city. Because the musicians were so disappointed that he declined their offer, he committed himself to go to Detroit once every year as a guest conductor. In Pittsburgh, he found the administrative management to be not serious enough, and Minnesota did not really convince him either. Eventually, he became convinced that out of the four orchestras, the San Francisco Symphony was qualitatively the best fit for him.

Now he had to prepare for the farewell in Dresden. At this time, the GDR was in decline. The economic situation was steadily becoming more and more hopeless and hampered the work with the orchestra. More and more often the Ministry of Culture and the artist agencies divided up individual musicians of the Staatskapelle into smaller ensembles and sent them to perform in Western countries in order to obtain foreign currency for the state. Thus, important musicians were missing during concerts in Dresden and during guest performances with increasing frequency. In addition, for political reasons, a number of musicians were banned from participation in international guest performances. The Ministry of Culture brazenly suggested that in such cases one could simply hire good musicians from other orchestras. Serious confrontations arose when Herbert Blomstedt repeatedly pointed out that in this way the special character of the Staatskapelle could no longer be guaranteed; finally, the bureaucrats in East Berlin ended the friendly collaboration.

The Semperoper, which had been destroyed during the war, had undergone a comprehensive reconstruction since 1977 and was now nearing completion. Blomstedt's contract expired in July 1985—five months after the opening of the rebuilt High Renaissance–style opera house. "I performed opera in Dresden, even enjoyed it, but that could never be my main concern. I have always considered myself primarily a concert conductor. Now I would, of course, have had to conduct much more opera. This made the decision to leave a little easier!"

Herbert Blomstedt felt that his official farewell as music director in the summer of 1985 was "rather lukewarm": "Of course, the *Generalintendant* [artistic director] in Dresden then was Gerd Schönfelder, one of the most awful Stasi men, and he was not interested in honoring a Westerner who had dared to say some hurtful truths about the cultural policies of the ailing GDR."[12] Many musicians from the Staatskapelle would have liked to see their outgoing chief conductor receive the conductor laureate title, but he was not granted this honor. (HB received the title finally in May 2016 in Dresden!).

Farewell to the East—and to the North

However, the departure had a positive side effect, because Herbert Blomstedt had never moved his wife and children to Dresden. He explains, "I, of course, did not want my family to live voluntarily under the Marxist banner." During all the years with the Staatskapelle, he commuted between Dresden and Stockholm.

Artistically speaking, the Dresden years were a milestone in his biography; financially, they would have to be rated as less profitable. Most of his salary was paid to him in East German marks—a currency that he could not take out of the country and were worthless in the West. He received only a small portion of his salary in West German deutsche marks. So he and his family lived mainly on the income received from performances in other countries. With the East German money, he financed donations to churches in the GDR, which he would otherwise have donated in other countries where he earned money. He also took the opportunity to buy many books because the quality of publishing in the GDR was very high. In addition, he bought a number of newly crafted stringed instruments and pianos, which he gave to his daughters, friends, and churches in Scandinavia.

However, a big problem also arose for Herbert in that the Swedish government wanted him to pay tax on his income from the GDR. Because the GDR currency was not convertible, he simply could not pay his taxes with it. This developed into a ten-year legal dispute, and the unpayable tax liability hung over Blomstedt like a permanent sword hanging above him. He did not want to disappoint his friends in Sweden by simply leaving the country for economic reasons: "I felt I had a great duty there. So I stayed, hoping and trusting that this would all be resolved somehow. I am an incurable optimist. And so it eventually happened." At the last minute, so to speak, his lawyer found a clause in the double taxation law that exempted him from the tax liability in Sweden. Unfortunately, shortly after this, the government changed this clause in the law, so Blomstedt would have faced the same problem in the future. When he inquired about it, the tax authorities gave Blomstedt two options: either stop working in Dresden immediately or leave Sweden! Thus, the Blomstedts transferred their residence from Danderyd, near Stockholm, to Switzerland, and a year later they moved to picturesque Lucerne. Herbert's departure from Dresden and the new position at the San Francisco Symphony then solved the tax problem conclusively.

Herbert still feels today that it was a "happy transition": "Altogether I am very grateful that these transitions always took place painlessly and naturally for me. It often happens that one parts in anger and with resentment so that disappointment and maybe even bitterness remain.

That was never the case with me. When I made the decision that I needed to move on and left an orchestra, the musicians often shed a tear. . . . For me, in any case, the change was definitely good and very interesting."

"Even after he moved to the San Francisco Symphony in 1985," Eberhard Steindorf said, "Herbert Blomstedt regularly returned to his former Dresden workplace, and he still remains much more than just a welcome guest but a friend of the musicians and of the music lovers in the city. It is almost a miracle that, even after more than twenty-five years, the people of Dresden still see him as being one of them—and love and celebrate him accordingly."

Overall, Herbert Blomstedt worked longer in Dresden than in any other city: five years in the "secret service" as he and his musicians jokingly called it, and then ten years in his official capacity as chief conductor. After the Berlin Wall had come down and the Stasi informants had been exposed, the former music director received, in his own words, "heartbreaking letters" and even personal visits from some of his old Dresdner musicians. The regulations stipulated that exposed former Stasi employees had to leave the orchestra immediately and irrevocably. Blomstedt tried to assist those who had turned to him for help, "but the orchestras were merciless. I do understand them, and they do have their rules. Unfortunately, my hands were tied. However, what surprises me is the fact that even today, after more than twenty years, no pardon is in sight."[13] The former music director knows exactly what became of the affected musicians. Even if, in terms of his beliefs, Blomstedt saw himself as an enemy of communism ("the ideology—not the people"), he was never indifferent to the people's fate, even if they may have deserved it. Blomstedt has never requested his own Stasi files (that would have identified other Stasi informants).

For his eightieth birthday on July 11, 2007, the former principal conductor received a very special gift: "I was 'decorated' by Jan Nast with the Staatskapelle's Golden Badge of Honor. It is pure gold with a diamond—a noble gem with the tiny decorative S of the Staatskapelle on it. But much more than all of this is the fact that only three people have previously received this award: Giuseppe Sinopoli, Colin Davis, and Bernard Haitink. It is an outward sign of a musical love affair, and as such I am deeply moved."[14]

Three months earlier he had once again conducted a special traditional concert in the Saxon capital:

In April 2007, I was back in Dresden, and on Palm Sunday, I

performed the Ninth with my beloved orchestra. The Frauenkirche [Church of Our Lady] was rebuilt—the city and I myself were in rapture. In the cathedral, where Heinrich Schütz had played with his choir and musicians in the seventeenth century, even I, a later successor, now stood and interacted with my audience. I realized that I had filled musical leadership positions in Saxony for twenty-two years—more than in any other country. And I was grateful. Even a little proud (but not more than is allowed).[15]

During a conversation with Jan Nast and Tobias Niederschlag in the Dresden Schlosskapelle (castle chapel) on Palm Sunday in 2007, Herbert saw the former principal harpist of the Staatskapelle in the audience. In the following lines about her, he expressed his appreciation of all his former orchestra members:

Fortunately, I spotted Jutta Zoff right in front of me in the second row. She was solo harpist of the orchestra during my tenure and one of the greatest musicians I have ever known. Now I could make her *pars pro toto* in showing my respect and love for the Kapelle. I remember a passage in Strauss's *Ein Heldenleben* where after the passionate central love scene the music calms down to a soft G-flat major chord in *pppp* (*pianississississimo* [played very, very, very softly]). The strings come to rest in this sweet harmony, and then the harp confirms it with a simple chord, *dolcissimo* [played with sweet, soft, tender emotion]. I used to look at her a bar or two before this. It is the simplest chord in the world to play, still she prepared herself for it far in advance. I could see how her imagination was working and how she adjusted her seat on the chair ever so slightly before actually striking the chord. And when I heard it, it was more tender than any kiss. I don't know how she made it. But I have never heard something like it.[16]

Memories of a longtime concert visitor

For many Dresdner music lovers, if the Palm Sunday concert in 2007 was something special, it was because Herbert Blomstedt performed with the Staatskapelle and continued this tradition. Music critic Hartmut Schütz said in his review of the concert that the Dresdners have remained appreciative of this conductor for generations. Looking at my family and my circle of friends I can only agree with him!

"It Was a Give-and-Take": At the Staatskapelle Dresden

Herbert Blomstedt's many years of working with the Staats-kapelle does not alone explain this sympathy. I think of Erich Käst-ner who wrote in his autobiographical children's book *Als ich ein kleiner Junge war* [*When I Was a Little Boy*]: "If it is correct to say that I can not only judge of what is horrible and ugly, but also of what is beautiful, I attribute this gift to my good fortune in having grown up in Dresden. . . . I could breathe in beauty as foresters' children breathe in woodland air."[17] Kästner was referring primarily to the architectural beauty of historic Dresden and its scenic sur-roundings. I would like to broaden this statement to include the musical life in and around Dresden. Which other city of the size of Dresden has two internationally acclaimed orchestras, two boys' choirs, and many other musical ensembles with a long tradition and excellent quality? And I could be a part of the concert life—fore-most through the subscription for the philharmonic. Since about 1978, we had the good fortune of being able to attend three or four concerts of the Staatskapelle each year, in addition to opera, cham-ber concerts, recitals, concerts of the *Dresdner Kreuzchor* [the boys' choir of the Dresden Kreuzkirche (Church of the Holy Cross)], church music. As a young teacher at the Kreuzschule [School of the Cross] where members of the boys' choir go to school, each performance was a great pleasure for me. Although I had little knowledge of music theory, my music choices developed in this way.

My encounters with Herbert Blomstedt as conductor of the Staatskapelle Dresden occurred during a time in my life when I attended concerts most frequently. He always strode to the podium with quick steps—as if he could not wait for the concert to start. At the end of the performance, he stood beside the orchestra members; the applause should go to everyone, not to him alone. His modesty towards the musicians as well as towards the respective musical work appealed to me. In the two or three school concerts I experi-enced with him, Blomstedt not only conducted but also introduced the pupils to the music. And here his charisma, his knowledge, his humor, and his modesty became even more apparent: twenty-four hundred young people in the Kulturpalast [a concert hall], who moments before were talking enthusiastically and not always be-having appropriately, suddenly fell silent and attentive when Blom-stedt turned to them after welcoming the musicians. It was im-pressive and admirable how he briefly, pointedly, and humorously introduced them to the musical work or the composer. I especially remember the performances of Bedřich Smetana's "My Fatherland" and Richard Strauss's *Ein Heldenleben* [*A Hero's Life*]. Concerning Smetana, Herbert Blomstedt remarked that the Bohemians were the musicians of Europe, and Dresden was indeed close to Bohemia—a lovely compliment to Dresden!

After the inauguration of the Semperoper on February 13, 1985, and the concerts of the Staatskapelle rang out from this wonderful venue, it was clear even to the layperson how difficult the acoustic conditions in the Kulturpalast had been and still are. Herbert Blomstedt became the principal conductor of the Staatskapelle despite these conditions, the shortage of foreign currency, and the iron curtain. This showed me that our Staatskapelle still sounded like the "magic harp" that Richard Strauss had spoken of. But I realize now, even more than at that time, that Blomstedt gave us internationality, which is what art needs.[18]

Transparent, yet exciting—a note from two members of the Staatskapelle

Eckart Haupt, solo flutist of the Dresden Staatskapelle, remembers the time under Herbert Blomstedt:

In the fall of 1981, when the Staatskapelle was being enlarged and they were looking for a principal flautist, I moved from the Dresden Philharmonic to the Staatskapelle. The transition went smoothly without an audition because Blomstedt was behind it. In my inaugural concert, I played the most virtuosic of all Carl Philipp Emanuel Bach concertos, the Flute Concerto in D Minor. These concertos are all extremely difficult and challenging to play, not only because the technique is demanding, but also due to the composer conceptualizing everything from the perspective of the piano, without being interested in how the individual instruments would implement it. I had a practical edition of the score where one could read the original score and, at the same time, the editor's additions, and I had originally planned to play this excellent edition. But no, Blomstedt insisted that we play the original score; after I had reconstructed the score so that it also met musicological requirements, we could premiere the work under his leadership. Afterward, I was very happy that I did this because a few years later I was able to record a CD of all five of these concerts with the Staatskapelle Berlin.

There was no mercy with Blomstedt; the interpretation had to meet musicological requirements and at the same time be emotionally acceptable and convincing. I found it wonderful that Blomstedt pushed for this. Back then; I probably would have taken the laxer, easier road. He forced me to go the more difficult route! I still thank him today!

Herbert Blomstedt was considered the undisputed authority, not only because he had clear ideas about the works, which he was also able to implement in a musically credible way by his conducting technique, but also because he acted like a deeply spiritual man, which he is. It was very apparent that he not only lived with us on a musical level, but one felt that he had an anchor. I always had the feeling that somehow he—this must have something to do with his faith—felt supported, which led him to have an inner confidence that flowed over into his artistic production and consequently also into the artistic outcomes he achieved with us. This security that emanated from him meant that he was credible. I've rarely met individuals in which the person and the vocation are so well correlated with each other as with him. He was, of course, different from the other conductors whom I had witnessed before: Kurt Masur, Günther Herbig, Herbert Kegel. . . . But what particularly fascinated me was his holistic credibility. I could see that every kind of music was worship for him, even if it was a piece of Stravinsky. He not only made music from his gut instincts, but it was, at the same time, a service to the musical work or service to God. To me, he was always an excellent example of what is good and beautiful, whose tool is musical interpretation. For me, as a young man, this also explained many of his behaviors. On tours, he helped those who had fallen ill, and if anyone had problems, he would inquire about family details. He had wonderful integrative and communicative skills. This was not something to be taken for granted. It hadn't been too long before that conductors were seen as tamers and taught along these lines by their own conducting teachers. He subscribed to none of this but was rather a credible father figure and a role model. Because he not only had an emotional but also a spiritual grasp of the works, it naturally sometimes happened that his ideas were different from mine. I had not come to the Staatskapelle without experience but in earlier years had found my own interpretational solutions for some pieces that we also played with him. While I also agree that there is no *one* specific way, one does have to readapt to the conductor's intentions every time. Herbert Blomstedt implemented his artistic ideas unconditionally and precisely; not with brute force but so that sometimes with a joyful heart—or clenched teeth—one carried out his intentions. That he managed this is, of course, a sign of a good conductor. That meant sometimes, when it came to using *pianissimo* (and I can play quietly!) that we had to go to the limits of technical feasibility. Nevertheless, one can only find good art when one explores the boundaries and pushes them further. In this respect, it is always an existential matter to be able to make good music. You have to give of yourself fully and at the same time withdraw at least somewhat in such a way that making music does not always have to do with a gush of feeling and venting one's emotions but with incredible composure, amazing self-control, and mental tension. Blomstedt required this from us and lived it himself! He tested the entire dynamics palette. In this way, tremendous artistic results are achieved! Today it is common—and I regret this very much—that in some orchestras the volume begins at *mezzo forte* [moderately loud] and increases to *fortissimo* [very loud]. With the Staatskapelle Dresden, it starts with *ppp* (*pianississimo* [very, very softly]); this is, of course, a much stronger musical impression. Although as an opera orchestra we were used to holding back on the dynamics when playing with vocal soloists, Blomstedt further refined these orchestral virtues and brought many instinctive behaviors in the orchestra to a conscious level. In this way, he has definitely influenced the younger generation who came to the orchestra at that time.

In addition to the dynamics, Herbert Blomstedt trained us to listen unreservedly to each other. He demanded structural clarity, and that meant he fine-tuned the articulation and increased the musicians' sense for what they have to do with the articulation to elicit a certain impression. Much of what I had learned from my teacher Friedrich Rucker during my five years at the Music Academy Dresden met Herbert Blomstedt's expectations. So I did not have to relearn anything.

Blomstedt also has a sense for what seems to be impossible but is actually doable. We once recorded Mozart symphonies—G Minor and C Major—and he actually drove the *pianissimo* usage to the extreme. That was such an important lesson because one was forced to push the apparent limits even further. One noticed that there is still another way of doing this! In this respect, he has hereby generated new sound spaces, new possibilities, and new instrumental techniques. In 1998, we premiered Siegfried Matthus's Concerto for Flute, Harp, and Orchestra in Dresden. I was very glad that Herbert Blomstedt could direct this performance. From the outset, he had a clear idea of the work and basically didn't show any consideration for the musicians. That sounds critical, and it was indeed hard; but in hindsight, it was absolutely correct because he achieved the correct tempos and the tonal transparency was guaranteed. Playing it generated an exhilaration in us that was very inspiring.

I guess that one of the reasons for Herbert Blomstedt's enjoyment and outstanding interpretation of Anton Bruckner is because he takes pleasure in Bach's music. He plays the great romantic works systematically and judiciously and in general sees music as architecture in musical form. I believe I can say from an orchestral and a soloist perspective that all good conductors see music in this way. There is also a very specific intellectual component with Blomstedt. I see the fact that he can conduct the works all from memory as a sign of this great spiritual overview. This is not something external but testifies to a tremendous intimacy with the musical idea.

One of Blomstedt's particular merits was that his great reputation opened up the American market for us in a difficult time when being cut off from the world in the GDR meant more disadvantages than advantages. He helped us to be cosmopolitan again, and we were more internationally recognized because of the tours to the United States that he initiated. The Staatskapelle Dresden was definitely an orchestra that always traveled in GDR times, even to the West. I traveled from the beginning of my career, without ever having been a member of the Stasi. Being a large orchestra, we were used by the East German government as a cultural showcase. This meant that we acquired a broader and larger understanding than our compatriots, and we did not view the other social systems as solely positive. One did not have to be a communist to perceive the errors in the Western system. The East Germans, who knew of the West only through contraband magazines or from West German television, were in danger of developing unrealistic ideas about the other German state. This was not the case with us!

The Blomstedt era was an important time for us as an orchestra and possibly for him as a person as well. An orchestra was made available to him with centuries of tradition and with established playing styles, which he was able to develop further. For me, as one of the younger musicians, it was significant at the time to see how he dealt with such established machinery, which also maintained, educated, and organized itself and, furthermore, created something unique based on its collective notion of music. From an artistic perspective, it must have really meant something to Blomstedt when he came to us in Dresden. The fact that we had an outsider as conductor did not make us untouchable to those in power; but he was the point of contact for us rather than the authorities, and he always stood up for us. It was a comfortable situation.

Under Herbert Blomstedt, I learned that music has a very strong spiritual component, and I was enabled to express my feelings. He was very skilled with the orchestra; he did not preach but simply did his job and implemented his ideas. He was pragmatic and used the spiritual component to understand the work and to persuade the musicians of his idea. Psychologically, he was very competent and never offended anybody—at least, I have never experienced it. He was strict, sometimes aloof but never used the wrong tone. Over all the years, this is quite something!

I was always impressed by how he directed the musical works; he did not spare himself or us. He could be uncomfortable, but he never escalated disputes. If there was an unpleasant remark from the orchestra, he either ignored it or dismissed it with a gracious response. That was the only right thing to do!

Occasionally, he gave one the feeling that if one just spent enough time on something, that if one was diligent enough, then anything could be accomplished. Years later, when Blomstedt once again did an outstanding work at the Leipzig Gewandhaus Orchestra, I realized that he had moved away from the notion of the unconditional interpretation of music. Later he allowed more individual freedom to soloists to add their own interpretation. I have the impression that he matured in this respect; for example, when a wind soloist suggests something to him, he accepts this and continues to build on it. After his time in Dresden and during the subsequent years, he increasingly allowed the individual design of a solo line, a melody line, by the respective leading solo performers. In the mid-2000s, I heard him perform Beethoven's Ninth, where this balance of intellectual assertion and allowing things to happen was present, which was something new for him. With time, he has probably noticed that if he gives and at the same time lets go, or to put it roughly, if he not only slows down, but also steps on the gas, then it will be wonderful. Music and flying have so much in common! At times, one simply has to entrust oneself to the wind or to the tracks of the musical path. This is what distinguishes the mature Herbert Blomstedt of today. He now has more confidence in the musicians. That's wonderful! The five elements that have made him the man he is are musicality, intellect, concentration, discipline, and experience. His strictness never resulted in an oppressive atmosphere. There was always a cheerful air about him. This empowered him to request anything. He gave us everything he had and required everything from us. Herbert Blomstedt has left many traces in the hearts and minds of his musicians and his audience.[19]

Peter Mirring, the former concertmaster of the Staatskapelle Dresden, came as a novice to the orchestra in 1969 and got to know Herbert Blomstedt at this time:

> Mr. Blomstedt was chief conductor of the Staatskapelle Dresden from 1975 to 1985. But even before and, of course, after that, he was a regular guest with us. In this long, fruitful, and wonderful collaboration, I got to know him as an extremely amiable, extremely competent, and a completely unassuming person. I have known him to be an incredibly hardworking and a comprehensively educated person.
>
> He introduced us to the music of his homeland, such as Sibelius and Nielsen. His repertoire spans from Bach to modern music. In all our concerts, he was always so well prepared that he never needed a score—an incredible accomplishment—and I cannot remember that he ever made a mistake.
>
> I was able to make many recordings and perform many concerts with Herbert Blomstedt and the Staatskapelle as well as with the NHK Symphony Orchestra. We performed, among other things, Richard Strauss's *A Hero's Life* more than forty times together at home in Dresden or while on tour. I was very much molded by this experience.

Peter Mirring concurs with his colleague Eckart Haupt that Herbert Blomstedt has matured: "We played Beethoven's Ninth relatively often with him. A few years ago he was here and conducted the Ninth once again. I felt that his perspective of this music had deepened."[20]

Most honored, dear Professor Blomstedt!
    . . . More than four decades connect you to us, the Staatskapelle,

with almost all of our members. It's wondrous how the relationship between us started and developed. And under circumstances that I do not wish to describe here in detail, but perhaps it was these very issues that led us to become so close! We can only be grateful that you took it upon yourself to share our fate with us, to join us, and to encourage us for so many years. We traveled the world together, played music from all periods, had an open podium also for our composers, and were able to keep a wonderful audience. The school concerts remain an unforgettable experience for me where you single-handedly managed to address the young people and to reach out to them and strengthened our hope that even in a changing society music would have an important place!

One had to be there! It is difficult to convey these feelings and experiences to the next generation by telling them the stories. I'm sure that most of my former colleagues share these feelings with profound thanks!

Dear Mr. Blomstedt, I would like to say, "*ad multos annos*" [to many years] or, as Goethe liked to conclude his letters, "And so henceforth!" It is in God's hands alone, we may simply ask him![21]

---

1. Herbert Blomstedt, interview by Eberhard Steindorf, in *450 Jahre Sächsische Staatskapelle Dresden: Eine Festschrift, 1548–1998* (Dresden: Sächsische Staatsoper Dresden, 1998).

2. Herbert Blomstedt, diary entry, March 26, 2007; originally written in English.

3. Eberhard Steindorf contributed to this book. All quotations with his name in this chapter are taken from his contribution.

4. "*Staatskapellmeister* [state music director]—a government official—that I never was. My colleague in the opera, Siegfried Kurz, carried that title." Herbert Blomstedt to UW, personal communication, July 29, 2012.

5. The first version of the opera premiered in 1805. A second version shortened the opera to two acts. The libretto was revised again in the third and final version. "By convention both of the first two versions are referred to as *Leonore.*" *Wikipedia*, s.v. "*Fidelio,*" accessed October 3, 2016, https://en.wikipedia.org/wiki/Fidelio.

6. Herbert Blomstedt, diary entry, April 2, 2007; originally written in English.

7. See *Wikipedia*, s.v. "Blue Wonder," accessed October 3, 2016, https://en.wikipedia.org/wiki/Blue_Wonder.

8. Jochen Graupner was a pastor in Dresden, serving in an administrative capacity from 1974 to 1985. He wrote a contribution for this book.

9. Herbert Blomstedt had jokingly called this music "Coca-Cola"—bubbly but without any nutritional value!

10. Quoted in Eberhard Steindorf's contribution.

11. Eberhard Steindorf.

12. Herbert Blomstedt, diary entry, April 1, 2007; originally written in English.

13. Herbert Blomstedt, diary entry, February 22, 2007.

14. Herbert Blomstedt, diary entry, July 11, 2007.

15. Herbert Blomstedt, diary entry, July 16, 2007.

16. See Blomstedt, diary entry, April 1, 2007.

17. Erich Kästner, *When I Was a Little Boy* (Danbury, CT: F. Watts, 1961), 47.

18. Dr. Fridrun Hantke taught German and history until her retirement. She penned her memories for this book.

19. Dr. Eckart Haupt, interviewed by UW, October 1, 2009, Dresden.

20. Peter Mirring to UW, private conversation, October 1, 2009, Dresden.

21. Joachim Ulbricht to Herbert Blomstedt, July 11, 2012. Joachim Ulbricht, a former solo violist, wrote this letter to congratulate Herbert Blomstedt on his eighty-fifth birthday. Herbert writes, "This letter moved me deeply. He found just the right words. These are the words of an exceptionally well-educated, very sensitive, and warm person." Herbert Blomstedt to UW, July 29. 2012.

Reencounter With the New World:
The Time in San Francisco

I still enjoy fine meals in fancy restaurants, but I would rather eat gruel with Herbert Blomstedt than caviar with any other conductor I know.—Peter Pastreich[1]

D URING HIS TIME AS the musical director in Dresden, Herbert Blomstedt was also the head of the Danish National Symphony Orchestra for two years until 1977 and then head of the Swedish Radio Symphony Orchestra until 1982.

Meanwhile, far away from northern and Central Europe—namely, on the American West Coast—the San Francisco Symphony (SFS) was looking for a new music director. Peter Pastreich, the managing director of the SFS at the time, first heard about Herbert Blomstedt from Kurt Masur, who was then the music director of the Leipzig Gewandhaus Orchestra. At that point in time, Blomstedt was not really known in the United States. However, as Pastreich did a bit of research, he found out that many musicians knew the Swede, even dating back to his time at the Juilliard School of Music. All the other graduates from his generation had established their careers in the United States, whereas Blomstedt had mainly conducted orchestras in Scandinavia. In the United States, however, one hardly ever heard news about the musical culture from Scandinavia or the then Soviet countries.

In 1982, Pastreich attended several of Blomstedt's concerts in Dresden and Los Angeles and introduced himself. Pastreich later related his first impression: "I immediately noticed that Blomstedt was absolutely straightforward. He was likable from the start. He didn't gossip, play games, or try any tactical maneuvering. I did not immediately feel the warmth that he emanates; however, it wasn't difficult to talk with him."[2]

There was a long list of proposed candidates for the advertised

127

position, and Blomstedt's name was near the bottom of this list. Pastreich recommended him to the election committee, and so he was bumped up to tenth place. Blomstedt was among the first three candidates for a conducting audition after the election committee did some intensive research.

Michael Steinberg, the director for publications and an artistic advisor to the SFS at the time, also traveled secretly to see Blomstedt in Detroit, where they were also interested in signing the Swede. Steinberg was impressed by the sincere and efficient rehearsal as well as the serious yet lively concert. He remembered the dinner with Blomstedt afterward as a wonderfully long evening filled with a wide range of conversational topics. It seemed to him that the musical director from Dresden was a well-kept secret: respected in his field, known in certain circles because of several recordings, but the general public didn't know his name. His personal opinion was that "it was a risk for both sides: on the one hand, bringing a person to San Francisco whose most striking trait was his studied avoidance of show and glamour; and on Herbert Blomstedt's side, to enter a world that was completely different from the one he knew so well."[3]

Technical performance machine meets European musical tradition

There were also other considerations for Blomstedt. He was a relatively young conductor when he became head of an orchestra with a tradition spanning many hundreds of years, and he had been able to learn a lot. Now he received the offer to direct a highly accomplished orchestra, which lacked the connection to a rich history. Blomstedt felt called to acquaint this technical performance machine with European musical tradition. Even though he had other offers in the United States, he finally favored San Francisco.

For an orchestra, there is no decision of greater importance than that of choosing the conductor. On February 8, 1984, Blomstedt made his debut with the San Francisco Symphony. The program included the "Unfinished Symphony" by Franz Schubert, Alban Berg's Violin Concerto with Gidon Kremer, and Beethoven's Fifth Symphony. He was already impressed at the very first rehearsal: the orchestra played perfectly, even though Beethoven's very popular Fifth Symphony is extremely difficult to play and does not perform itself automatically! Everything seemed possible with the San Francisco Symphony, both musically and technically.

Blomstedt conducted subscription concerts for two weeks. The audience was thrilled, and the orchestra was enthusiastic about his expertise, his courtesy during the rehearsals, and his determination to bring out the best in them. He was offered the position of music director. He asked for time to think it over.

On March 27, the SFS announced that Herbert Blomstedt would become the tenth music director in the fall of 1985, succeeding Edo de Waart. De Waart had left the legacy of an orchestra with predominantly young, top musicians who still needed a lot of intense musical training and discipline. Blomstedt would give this orchestra a character and collective vigor.

In June, before his official start, he conducted the SFS Beethoven Festival. He approached Beethoven's best-known works, the nine symphonies, with an intensity and enthusiasm that would become characteristic; this resulted in a dramatic introduction for the new music director and a sensationally exciting reencounter with Beethoven.[4]

In early October, the newly minted music director made his official debut with Richard Wagner's Overture to *Die Meistersinger von Nürnberg*, Roger Sessions's Symphony No. 2, and Richard Strauss's *A Hero's Life*. Over the next decade, he would perform works by Strauss nineteen times.

The initial enthusiasm of several musicians in the orchestra gave way to increasing disenchantment. Those aspects that they initially appreciated in their new director, in fact, meant a lot of work! He was very thorough with every single note, so some felt he controlled too much of their playing. He told them in detail how they had to play—that took the fun out of it! However, Blomstedt is known for his incredible patience; he never yells, and he never is verbally abusive. He simply rehearses the same passages again and again until he is satisfied. For him, this meant that composer so-and-so was played this way and no other way! The orchestra was not used to this, but the musicians gradually came to appreciate his thoroughness.

John Kieser, the director of operations at the SFS at the time, recalls, "Herbert Blomstedt simply brought discipline into the orchestra. Music, like any art, needs the right tools. It is also a language, and one must study and practice in order to express oneself properly. The maestro brought all of this home to the orchestra."[5]

Looking back, Pastreich realizes that Blomstedt showed an incredibly intense seriousness with regard to classical music and that he was able to impart this to the orchestra. For many conductors, their egos are paramount, but this is not the case with Herbert Blomstedt. It is not important to him to be admired for his elegance. Of greatest significance to him is what the composer wished to express and how to convey this.

Word spread quickly in the SFS about Blomstedt's steadfast religious principles. Hitherto, Saturday had been a normal working day for the orchestra; now, of course, a new schedule had to be devised. Saturday rehearsals were rescheduled to Friday mornings and the choir practices to Monday nights because many choir members were otherwise employed. In addition, negotiations with the labor union had to be conducted. The head of administration took care of this and also informed the orchestra of the changes. In the beginning, the change was difficult for the musicians, but in actual practice the rescheduling proved to be uncomplicated.

Soon it became apparent that Blomstedt, with his unwavering belief in his own principles, was tolerant of others' convictions and lifestyles. John Kieser comments about the now honorary conductor: "He is known here for his piety but also for his broad-mindedness. So it was and is easier to accept his stance."

However, the most important thing for the SFS was that Herbert welded the orchestra together and made it a strong ensemble.

In March 1986, their first tour with Herbert as conductor led them to Chicago, Illinois; Ann Arbor, Michigan; Saratosa, Florida; and Orlando, Florida. The program included Carl Nielsen's Symphony No. 4 ("The Inextinguishable"), Jean Sibelius's *Tapiola*, and Ludwig van Beethoven's Seventh Symphony. The *Chicago Tribune* reported on the concert: "The orchestra's two-week American tour gave every indication that conductor and players . . . already have settled into a productive rapport that exalts music over manner, substance over surface, restraint over rhetoric. It augurs well."[6] The results of the orchestra's work spoke for themselves and were overwhelming.

The reluctant star

The new music director also showed substance in his lifestyle. San Francisco had never before known such a conductor! Instead of frequenting cocktail parties and expensive restaurants and instead of buying a costly car and a dream house, the maestro lived like a monk! He only ate vegetarian foods and preferred spelt porridge for breakfast; he neither smoked nor drank alcohol. He even sublet a place far outside town, even though he could afford something better than that!

But music was obviously his whole purpose in life. He did not need luxury. He wrote a postcard every day to his wife, Waltraud, in faraway Switzerland and never dreamed of flirting with his many young female admirers. In later years, when Waltraud often visited from Europe, the couple rented a simple apartment in San Mateo, then a relatively unassuming suburb. They found most of their friends in the Seventh-day Adventist churches of the Bay Area, where there were many intellectuals who had season tickets to the symphony and quite naturally came backstage after concerts to greet the conductor and talk about the music. This was a delightful experience for Blomstedt because he felt understood in two spheres: his music and his faith.

Blomstedt concluded his first season with Beethoven's *Missa solemnis*—a work that he would also perform nine years later at his farewell concerts.

In February and March 1987, the orchestra toured Europe for the first time since 1973, performing in seventeen cities, including Paris, Berlin, Munich, and Vienna. Some critics predicted a long-term partnership between Blomstedt and the SFS. In Vienna, everyone was full of praise for the outstanding rendition of Anton Bruckner's Symphony No. 6. A Munich critic described the orchestra's playing as "the stuff that dreams are made of."

Intermezzo in Germany

In Munich, Blomstedt also met Lothar Schacke for the first time. Schacke later became his manager and still works with him today. Herbert's general agent, Hanna Zubrzycka, had recommended Blomstedt contact Schacke after her agency in Amsterdam, Interartists, was bought by a company in Hanover, and Blomstedt no longer felt competently represented when his advisor there, Michael Hocks, left the company. The maestro remembers Hanna Zubrzycka, a Polish Jew, as

a grande dame and very good manager, extremely competent professionally, as loving as a mother to me, and firmly demanding towards our orchestra partners. We mostly communicated by phone, rarely by letter, except of course when contracts were involved. I created an ideal image of her in my mind. When I met her personally in her office for the first time after many years, I was shocked: She was overweight, with ugly makeup on and always had a cigarette in her mouth. Her office was on the third floor of her house, and she rarely ventured out of it, especially since her bedroom was right behind her office and the stairs in this canal house were steep and dangerous. Her employees did her shopping for her as she sat enthroned in her domain like a queen, knowing that she would soon die of lung cancer—she even named the month. That is why she recommended Lothar Schacke to me as her successor. Until the very last, she acted wisely towards her artists, but very unwisely towards herself.[7]

At the time, Schacke was working for, among other people, Eugen Jochum and accompanied him on all his concert tours. Because Blomstedt was a great admirer of Jochum and communicated with him in writing, not much persuasion was needed for the change to the *Künstlersekretariat am Gasteig* (Munich Artists' Agency at the Gasteig).

Sadly, Eugen Jochum died on March 26, 1987, and was buried in Munich. In July, a memorial concert with Blomstedt conducting the Bamberg Symphony took place in Jochum's hometown of Babenhausen. It was a program exclusively featuring Mozart, with the Symphonies Nos. 34 and 38, and the Flute Concerto with soloist Rudolf Pohl. Two days later Herbert performed Bruckner's Seventh Symphony with the same orchestra in the Ottobeuren Basilica; it was a long-planned concert, which Jochum was originally going to conduct. As it was, it became a memorial concert for him at the very place that had meant so much to him. Beforehand, Blomstedt made use of the opportunity to meet Jochum's daughter (who is also a gifted musician) to get a glimpse of Jochum's scores with his notations and comments.

Lothar Schacke comments on this, "Mr. Blomstedt has in the meantime taken Jochum's place in Ottobeuren to a small degree. He is well loved there because he is such a religious person. Every time he visits he resides in the guest apartment of the monastery where he feels very much at home."[8]

Lothar Schacke remembers how he met Herbert Blomstedt:

This is a very interesting story! In compliance with my father's wishes, I studied architecture in Wuppertal, Germany, in spite of the fact that I would much rather have attended a music college. In the course of time, it became more and more clear to me that I just had to do something with music. I played the organ, passed an exam, began learning the piano, and was a church organist in a small Romanesque church near Gummersbach for twelve years. The minister there, an organist himself, had initiated a small series of concerts. When he was transferred, I took over the organization of the concerts. That was far more interesting than my studies. I made program booklets all day long! And that is when I discovered that I was interested in this whole business of music management. I sometimes even conducted the small concerts in my church.

I got to know the daughter of an acquaintance from a choir in Wuppertal, Elisabeth Ehlers, who is now my office partner and was then undergoing training in a concert agency. She promised to take me to a concert in Wuppertal one day, and when it worked out, it was on May 3, 1977, with the Staatskapelle Dresden under Herbert Blomstedt! The program included *Till Eulenspiegel's Merry Pranks* by Richard Strauss, Dmitri Shostakovich's Piano Concerto No. 2 with Rolf-Dieter Arens as the soloist (later he became a professor of piano and the director of the University of Music "Franz Liszt," Weimar), and Antonín Dvořák's Ninth Symphony. As I recall, I didn't go backstage, but I arranged with Mrs. Ehlers so that she would introduce me to her boss in order to possibly get a job at his agency in the near future. After I graduated as an architect, I would have no need of further studies; but as a gifted autodidact, I could perhaps get a job there. And, in fact, they really did want me! Isn't this meaningful: the decision for my current job was triggered by a concert with Herbert Blomstedt! When he asked me twenty years later whether I would like to become his agent, I was, of course, extremely enthusiastic and said yes. And so things came full circle for me.[9]

Spotlight on contemporary American composers

Back again on the Pacific coast, Blomstedt conducted Symphony No. 2 by John Harbison in May. This work by the American composer, whom Blomstedt particularly appreciated, was commissioned by the SFS. In the coming years, this piece as well as Roger Sessions's Symphony No. 2 would often be part of the program and also on international tours. Later, a CD recording was made of it. At the end of his tenure, Blomstedt had conducted thirty-eight American works, including twelve world premieres of works commissioned by the SFS.

At the end of 1987, the time had come: Blomstedt and the SFS made their first recordings for London Records/Decca, with whom they signed an exclusive contract. Carl Nielsen's Symphony No. 4 and Symphony No. 5 and works by Hindemith, including *Mathis Der Maler*, were recorded. Shortly afterward, in February 1988, the SFS went on a tour to Asia, giving concerts in Hong Kong, Japan, and Taiwan. The *Hong Kong Standard* wrote that Blomstedt was able to make his musicians play in such a way that the performance culminated in a combination of interpretation and spiritual experience. One couldn't do any better than this.

A Great Song

A few months later Blomstedt performed Grieg's complete incidental music to *Peer Gynt*, comprising twenty-six parts, with the SFS orchestra and choir. The recording won the Japanese Record Academy Award.

Gradually, word spread about the evolving quality of the SFS. While on tour on the East Coast, they performed the national premiere of Elliott Carter's Oboe Concerto with Heinz Holliger as the soloist. In Washington, DC, and Boston, choruses of praise erupted from the critics. "Some critics have recently suggested . . . that it may be time to add the name of San Francisco to the legendary list of America's 'Big Five' orchestras," the *Washington Post* wrote.[10]

The following spring the recordings from London Records/Decca, including Carl Nielsen's Symphony No. 4 and Symphony No. 5, won one of the most prestigious record awards in the world, the French Grand Prix du Disque, as well as the Belgian Caecilia Prize.

A few months later the SFS were back on tour to the East Coast. In order to show solidarity with the entire state of California, the SFS toured northern California—followed by southern California a few months later. A performance in the remote town of Weed, at the foot of Mount Shasta, attracted music lovers from near and far. A happy concert visitor said, "This was the greatest thing that has ever happened in Weed. And it will probably also remain the greatest."[11]

Special highlights of the 1989/1990 season were the American premiere of the recently discovered Violin Concerto by Leoš Janáček with the concertmaster Raymond Kobler, and the world premiere of the Violin Concerto by Elliott Carter, which was commissioned by the SFS, with Ole Böhn as the soloist. The world premiere of the oratorio *Genesis*—a work commissioned to resident composer Charles Wuorinen—happened at the same time. This extremely complex work on the theme of creation gave Blomstedt, the SFS Choir, and the SFS an opportunity to play on *Morning Edition*, a news program on National Public Radio.

On October 17, 1989, an earthquake with a magnitude of 6.9 on the Richter scale shook the Bay Area of San Francisco for fifteen seconds. The epicenter was located near the Loma Prieta peak in the Santa Cruz Mountains. It was the strongest earthquake in the region since the big quake of 1906 and caused significant damage in a radius of about sixty-two miles, especially in San Francisco and Oakland. Sixty-three people were killed, and about four thousand people were injured. Herbert Blomstedt had originally planned to spend a couple of weeks with his family in Lucerne, Switzerland, but he immediately changed his plans. The shocked population now needed encouragement and solidarity. So, on the following Sunday, he conducted Beethoven's Ninth with the famous "Ode to Joy" in the Golden Gate Park. With free admission, the concert had an audience of more than twenty thousand and remains an unforgettable experience for many.

"HB" and "PP"

In the meantime, Herbert also got to know more and more of the big city of San Francisco. At first, the city appeared to be full of vice, and his only interest was in the concert halls, but he began to discover the beauty of the area on his working walks with Peter Pastreich, his administrative director. They especially loved the path around a reservoir, which was actually closed to the public. They greatly amused themselves with the thought of the possible media reaction if the conductor and the manager of the SFS were caught on the forbidden paths. Later on, they went to Golden Gate Park and other places in the center of the metropolis so that Blomstedt gradually got to know the beauty of the city.

One day Peter Pastreich took his chief conductor sailing. Blomstedt loved it but had "virtually no free time, because he was constantly studying music scores. Even at his Swedish summer residence in Bengtstorp, he sat at seven in the morning in front of the house with a Bruckner symphony score in hand, even though this symphony was not going to be played in the next season! HB's response was, 'I only studied it once again,' " Pastreich recalls. A friendship developed between the two men that continues to this day. In his speech commemorating the end of Blomstedt's time as musical director of the Leipzig Gewandhaus Orchestra, Pastreich remarked, "I called him HB and he called me PP. I was particularly pleased about this because *pianissimo* is his favorite dynamic."

Orchestras in the United States do not receive public funding; instead, they rely on donations and grants. Thus, the maestro once showed his athletic side for this good cause. Herbert insisted on throwing the ceremonial first pitch at San Francisco Giants' season opener as publicity for the SFS—and he gave it all he had.

Right across Europe, and alterations at home

In August 1990, the SFS went on a very special tour with Blomstedt: sixteen cities with eighteen concerts in major European music festivals were scheduled, including first performances at the Salzburg Festival, the Edinburgh International Festival, and the Lucerne Festival. It was one of the most successful tours of the SFS. In an acclaimed performance in Salzburg, they played only one piece—Bruckner's Fifth Symphony, which one critic determined was the most excellent that he had heard at that festival. The following morning London Records/Decca announced the renewal of the contract with Blomstedt and the SFS for another four years. The *London Times* wrote about the concerts in Edinburgh: "Blomstedt's two San Francisco concerts were revelations, the undisputed critical hit of the music programme."[12]

On September 6, 1990, the SFS also performed a highly acclaimed concert in the Gewandhaus in Leipzig, featuring Mozart's Symphony No. 32, *Death and Transfiguration* by Richard Strauss, and Nielsen's Symphony No. 4. They even played an encore: the overture to Nielsen's opera *Masquerade*. After the concert, Blomstedt had a momentous encounter with Hartmut Brauer, a solo cellist and board member of the Leipzig Gewandhaus Orchestra. Brauer said, "I 'ambushed' him backstage in the artists' lounge. One usually received many rejections on occasions such as this. I thought to myself, *What will the outcome be this time?* And I just spoke to him! We immediately got along well, and I asked him, 'Could you image yourself conducting the Gewandhaus Orchestra?' And he replied, 'Yes, of course.' I asked for the name of his agent, we spoke three or four more sentences, and everything had been decided. It was the beginning of a wonderful artistic collaboration!"[13]

" 'Great orchestras deserve great halls,' Herbert Blomstedt told a press conference in 1990, shortly after the European festival tour, when he revealed plans for an acoustic renovation of Davies Symphony Hall"—a project that he had advocated for some time.[14] A year later the first part of the renovation was complete: a new canopy made of plastic panels hung above the stage, and risers were installed on stage for the orchestra. The musicians noted a significant improvement because they could now hear each other much better, and the audience gained a completely different sound experience.

Meanwhile, Blomstedt gave concerts with the SFS in New York's famous concert halls Carnegie Hall and Lincoln Center, performing works by George Perle and Peter Lieberson. It is part of the orchestra's tradition to perform as much contemporary—especially American—music as possible. Herbert chose successively Charles Wuorinen and George Perle as composers in residence. Like Elliot Carter, another of Blomstedt's favorites, they are perceived as technically complex academics and are difficult to grasp for some audiences. The maestro also conducted other works that were not so much to his personal liking, but he always ensured that he could make them his own. He discussed every piece with the respective composers and had countless questions. A thorough study of the musical scores was also imperative to him.

One of Blomstedt's greatest wishes was to introduce the orchestra and the audience to Scandinavian music, especially Carl Nielsen and Jean Sibelius. Until then, the former was completely unknown in San Francisco. *Peer Gynt* by Edvard Grieg had been performed once previously, but "with Blomstedt, it was an entirely different world," Peter Pastreich recalls.

Many years later, in November 2008, when Herbert Blomstedt once again stood as honorary conductor on the SFS podium, he stated, "No orchestra plays Nielsen's symphonies better than the SFS. They have the virtuosity, the strength, and the sensitivity that is needed for it. We have not played the 'Sinfonia Espansiva' since the CD recording more than twenty years ago. But the music sits like a rock in their inner selves. And the new orchestra members absorb it from the fingers and lips of their older counterparts. This is quite remarkable. The audience responds with the same enthusiasm as after a Beethoven or Mahler symphony."[15]

Winning awards

In 1991, for the two-hundredth anniversary of Mozart's death, the SFS opened the Mozart and His Time Festival by performing the Requiem by the late genius. Arts organizations throughout San Francisco participated in the festival.

On the occasion of World AIDS Day on December 1, Blomstedt conducted the first West Coast performance of John Corigliano's Symphony No. 1, a work to commemorate all those who have died of AIDS. Shortly afterward, the recording of Nielsen's Symphony No. 2 and Symphony No. 3 was presented with the *Gramophone* Award for the best orchestral recording of the year. It completed Blomstedt's cycle of Nielsen's symphonies with the SFS; for him, it was the second recording of the six works.

One day Peter Pastreich suggested that they incorporate *Carmina Burana* by Carl Orff into the program. The piece had not been performed in a long time; some subscribers, musicians, and members of the board solicited a new production. "Not exactly a work which one would connect with HB," the former SFS manager smiled, "but he wanted to think it over." The maestro promised to thoroughly view the work during the upcoming Asian tour and then to decide whether he could do something with it. Finally, he decided that he liked *Carmina Burana*, and so the work was performed. It was a huge success. Once again they made a recording, for which the SFS with its choir and conductor were awarded their first Grammy Award for the Best Performance of a Choral Work in March 1993. But Blomstedt's typical way of working out every detail of the score and making every voice perceptible, displeased a critic, who saw this as limiting the passion and wrote: "Here, there is an excess of hygiene."[16] This in turn led to loud laughter from the one being critiqued.

Before that, the Asia tour had, in the course of nineteen days, led them to Tokyo, Osaka, Taipei, and to Okinawa Island, where the concerts were part of the festivities for the twentieth anniversary of the return of the island to Japanese administration.

Finally, the second and larger phase of the renovation work at the Davies Symphony Hall was completed. The orchestra's new permanent home was inaugurated with a gala performance of Beethoven's Ninth, followed by two weeks of subscriber concerts featuring Mahler's *Resurrection Symphony*. The recording of *Resurrection Symphony* received the German Record Critics' Award in 1995 and was nominated for a Grammy Award.

At the end of 1992, Herbert announced that he would cede his position as the SFS music director effective in the fall of 1995. The orchestra thanked him for his ten-year appointment by naming him their conductor laureate—a distinction that did not exist before. Shortly thereafter, he received the Ditson Conductor's Award from Columbia University for distinguished service to American music.

The year ended with the world premiere of John Harbison's Oboe Concerto, a work commissioned for the principal oboist William Bennett. The work was also included in the repertoire for the European tour in the spring of 1993. The *Frankfurter Neue Presse*, a newspaper in Frankfurt, wrote the following about the performance of Bruckner's Symphony No. 4: "A full, cultivated sound of broad dynamic extremes and primary strength, which became orgiastic in the finale."[17]

When Herbert Blomstedt conducted Mahler's Symphony No. 8 with the SFS in the fall of 1994, it had not been played in San Francisco for ten years. Striking differences were now apparent with regard to the orchestra, the choir, and the acoustics.

Then the news arrived that Herbert had received an Oscar! He is real, can move, and makes sounds—and is Waltraud and Herbert Blomstedt's first grandchild. But this was not the only reason that it was high time to return to Europe.

"Ten years is a long time," Blomstedt says in retrospect. "The risk of falling into a routine increases. That would be fatal, that must not happen!" In a conversation with Peter Pastreich, it was agreed upon that the music director would take his leave at the end of the season. "I gave my best," he concluded. "In Europe, new responsibilities were waiting."

Reencounter With the New World: The Time in San Francisco

In dealing with orchestra members, Herbert Blomstedt has always adhered to a principle:

> I have always avoided close friendships with musicians in order to give no reason for envy. I was friendly with everyone and appreciated everyone, even those who were a bit odd. Artists are often a little strange, but they are kind! And when they play, one can forgive them everything! I found my friends mostly outside of the orchestra.
>
> Over the years, a very trusting relationship developed with Peter Pastreich. I knew him as an extremely gifted person who loved music with his whole heart. It is important that one is willing to make sacrifices for music and not only adhere to sober calculations. With him, I immediately felt he had a musician's heart! Originally, he studied medicine at Yale and played the trumpet. He organized concert tours for the university orchestra and thereby discovered his calling to concert management. After studying in France, he proved to be absolutely brilliant in this field and still enjoys an excellent reputation worldwide as a problem solver. Incidentally, early on I noticed certain resemblances to my father—especially his inclination towards perfectionism. Our shared vacations in Bengtstorp where we roamed the woods like two little boys are unforgettable to me—simply wonderful!

Herbert Blomstedt performed one more time with the orchestra on a European tour. This time there were acclaimed performances in Vienna, Budapest, Warsaw, London, Madrid, and Lisbon. In June 1995, he ended his tenure, as mentioned before, with four performances of Beethoven's *Missa solemnis*.

At the end of his ten-year commitment, there were twenty-eight CDs documenting a "fantastic musical partnership," as it reads on a thank-you plaque from Decca; there were memories of "incredible musical highlights," says Peter Pastreich; and there was "an orchestra and an audience at their best," according to Michael Steinberg. As the only honorary conductor of the San Francisco Symphony, Blomstedt would in the future give several concerts each year with the orchestra.

The 1996 Grammy Award for Best Choral Performance in Classical Music awarded to the SFS under Herbert Blomstedt for their recording of *German Requiem* by Johannes Brahms was like an encore so to speak.

Did I request the two works that were awarded with Grammys? They were part of the subscription series. A program committee prepared the season; I, as the chief conductor, was head of the committee and made the decisions after extensive consultations. Nothing was played without my sanction. The ideas came from all sides, not only from me. No one had to propose Brahms's requiem to me—but perhaps it was a special request from the choir—I do not remember. *Carmina Burana* is indeed a very popular work and guaranteed sold-out halls. I'm just spontaneously skeptical towards too popular works—perhaps sometimes unjustly so. But then I studied the work in detail and considered it worthwhile. On closer examination, one can always find something of value in every seriously intentioned work.[18]

Elijah in San Francisco:
A choir rehearsal with Herbert Blomstedt

It is March 14, 2007, and the music director's assistant is punctual as always as she picks up the honorary conductor in her car for the first choir rehearsal. Because her boss, Michael Tilson Thomas, is currently guest conducting on tour in Germany, Marcia Kimes can devote herself entirely to her guest, Herbert Blomstedt. It is about an hour-long drive up to San Francisco's Davies Symphony Hall from Palo Alto, where, for the duration of his visit, Blomstedt is staying with his good friends Bill and Bonnie Blythe. In the parking lot behind the hall, we meet several members of the orchestra, who are on their way to a performance. They happily greet their former chief conductor. One of them says, "It's so good to see you again, Maestro. We're glad to have you here." And the musician assures Blomstedt of how much he is looking forward to working together. Herbert greets the employees in the technical service department and at the gate personally and has a kind word for everyone. In each encounter, one can sense how much he is appreciated.

The rehearsal takes place in Zellerbach Rehearsal Hall on the ground floor.[19] Herbert collaborates with the choir for the first time in almost twelve years. During his tenure as music director here, they had many fine performances together, culminating in the first two Grammys that the SFS ever received. For the performance of Felix Mendelssohn's *Elijah*, there are 162 singers; thirty of these are professional singers. The others are amateurs who have received considerable music training. The choir has studied with Ragnar Bohlin, a Swedish choral conductor who came to San Francisco recently.

Reencounter With the New World: The Time in San Francisco

Herbert and Ragnar greet each other warmly at the door and immediately begin conversing in their mother tongue. There is enthusiastic applause when the maestro steps in front of the choir. He thanks them with a bow. Then he greets the singers and asks, "Are you fit for the fight?" Loud consent. Now they can begin.

At the choir's request, the oratorio is sung in English. In fact, the premiere of the work, originally composed in German, was performed in English on August 26, 1846, in Birmingham, England, under the direction of the composer. Mendelssohn himself had supervised the translation and placed great emphasis that the texts remain as true to the original as possible. The libretto is composed exclusively of biblical texts, and the message was very important to him.

As always, Blomstedt has studied this work very thoroughly. He had the score in front of him most of the time while traveling—even on the train from Lucerne to the Zurich airport and then later on during the transatlantic flight. Now the maestro asks the choir to sing the first piece: "Help, Lord!"

He interrupts the singing. He explains that the pronunciation needs to be clearer as this is a loud cry for help and there should be no vibrato, for there wasn't any water left in Israel. The people would have no feelings left to spare!

The pronunciation is now practiced only by speaking: "Will then the Lord be no more God in Zion?" The murmuring of the people should increase to a scared, urging, fearful, and protesting questioning.

One section of the music is marked with the *sforzato* dynamics notation, indicating a sudden emphasis. Blomstedt comments on this, "Leopold Mozart once said that *sforzato* should sound as if one strikes a bell. And the quieter you sing, the more clearly you must sing."

The work begins with Elijah's curse that there will be no dew or rain for many years "but according to my word." For this section, the composer used descending diminished fifths, which sound eerie; these are repeated by the brass players almost like a confirmation. The same sequence of notes now appears in the chorus and is to be sung as a curse without vibrato.

Suddenly, an elderly lady with a frozen smile raises her hand and gives the signal for the first break. The maestro knows the American labor unions very well and has arranged so that rehearsals with the choir are not stopped in the middle of a piece. However, the power of the union officials in the United States in this regard is merciless: there has to be a break after exactly forty-five minutes, regardless of what is being rehearsed at the time. Blomstedt knows this well enough from his time as chief conductor in San Francisco. By his own admission, he feels like someone who is caressed with one hand and slapped in the face with the other. One has to see the comedy in the situation; otherwise, it can be hard to accept.

While the members of the choir stretch their legs and get something to drink, their conductor doesn't get to take a break. Ragnar Bohlin pounces on his superordinate colleague with the score and asks him many questions. Blomstedt answers them as seriously and friendly as ever. Ragnar Bohlin studied under Eric Ericson and has a Nordic vocal ideal—predominantly a mild head voice with little vibrato—whereas his predecessor tolerated more vibrato and favored a chest voice. The choir has to relearn this.

Two members of the choir, a woman and a man, one after the other, come over to me during the break and ask, "Did you come with the maestro? Then please tell him how much we have been looking forward to having him here. He enriches us so much, especially spiritually." "Yes, tell him, please, that he is always very welcome here. It benefits the choir so much when he practices with us thoroughly again." They both assure me that they dare not speak to the maestro personally. He is a person of great respect. Orchestral and choir members usually address other conductors in the United States by their first names, but he has always remained "Mr. Blomstedt." Only his closest colleagues, after a few years of working together and with his permission, call him "HB."

The break is over, and they continue the rehearsal with the piece "Blessed are the men who fear Him." Blomstedt again lets them sing the beginning of the piece and then explains, "This piece is full of character. First and foremost, its character is very quiet—*pianissimo*." Once again, the strong vibrato bothers him: "Are you afraid or freezing?" General laughter.

As for the text, Blomstedt now explains that the composer placed great emphasis on the accuracy of the translation into English. Whereas the blessing in German applies to the individual—"Blessed is *the man* who fears the Lord"—the English text is translated as "Blessed are the men who fear Him." Mendelssohn therefore made a point of asking the translator why he had not used the singular as in the German text. He wrote back that the King James Version, which for an Englishman had about the same importance as the Luther Bible for Germans, uses the plural. Mendelssohn's answer to him was, "I'll leave it up to you." But Blomstedt uses this example to make it clear that the composer would have preferred the singular here because personal religion was important to him, and by his own admission, he wanted to rouse each person in the audience with his work. Then Blomstedt tells of the Mendelssohn statue on his grand piano in his home in Lucerne that looks across at him when he plays: "I often have profound conversations with him." Some choir members laugh, but he is actually not joking.

Now the choir sings the appeal of Baal's priests, "Baal, we cry to thee, hear and answer us!" The maestro explains that this music, which is linked to the early pentatonic scale, is supposed to sound heathenish and primitive. In the final cadenza, the traditional harmony resounds again. Herbert says, "Even the devil knows something about beauty; we have to give him that." Again the singers are amused.

After Baal's priests and the people have not managed to persuade the idol to burn up the sacrifice, Elijah demonstrates the power of crying out to the living God: fire falls down from heaven and consumes the burnt offering! The people are deeply moved and acknowledge in amazement, "The Lord is God!" The choir expresses this by means of a gradual *crescendo* ending in *fortissimo* (singing very loud). Blomstedt says, "The conviction grows slowly, towards a powerful confession."

Because the soloists are not present at this rehearsal, the maestro sings the passages in between to facilitate the choir's entries. He has to pass over Elijah's instructions: "Take all the prophets of Baal." He says, "That's too fast for me. I hope you can do it!"

He comments on the implied execution of Baal's priests, "This is history. Today we would probably not do that. Two thousand years of Christianity have effected a change in thinking." Doubtful murmurs and undertones of contradiction come from the choir.

After several short choral passages, the first part of the oratorio ends with the people thanking God who sent the rain again. "A victory has been won," says Blomstedt. "But only for a certain time period, as with all the victories in this world." With this, the rehearsal is over.

Just two days later the orchestra will also be at the rehearsal. Initially, it takes the honorary conductor quite some time to arouse real enthusiasm for the work among the musicians. However, in his opinion the soloists are an "almost perfect quartet" from the outset: Juliane Banse, with her wonderful soprano, sung effortlessly and equally lyrically but, at the same time, with the ability to dramatize; Annette Markert with her warm, expressive mezzo-soprano; the youthful tenor Christoph Genz, a former member of the *Thomanerchor* (St. Thomas Boys' Choir) and a full-blooded musician, who sings so naturally and has an incredible voice; and finally, Alan Opie of the English Royal Opera, with an expressive baritone and much vibrato, which does not suit the maestro at first. After futile discussions, he states, "It is probably better for the work and the baritone that he sing a good Opie instead of a bad Blomstedt."

His conclusions at the end of the two weeks: "The three performances were outstanding. The orchestra quickly grasped the character of Mendelssohn's last significant work and lived up to its reputation. The associate principal cellist, Peter Wyrick, played a moving solo in 'It Is Enough'; in some of the arias, the clarinets and bassoons played *pianissimo* in a way that one is not likely to forget. . . . It was a great success for the choir, and Ragnar Bohlin made an excellent start as the choir director."[20] And then he quietly adds, "For a while, we were in God's presence through this work."

After the matinee performance on Sunday—the third performance in total—there is a pre-birthday celebration for the honorary conductor. Besides witty speeches that show the lasting bond between the SFS and Herbert Blomstedt, he is presented with a score of Carl Nielsen's second opera, *Saul and David*, which was autographed by the composer with a dedication to his teacher Orla Rosenhoff, dated July 15, 1904. Later, Poul Sørensen, a Danish songwriter who owned the score, eventually gave it to his friend Kjell Roikjer, a bassoonist and composer. It is an original piano score, a quarto-sized book from 1903 in black linen, with a libretto from 1896. The recipient of the gift gives a small acceptance speech in which he extemporaneously and briefly touches on the biographies of these artists. It's exactly the right gift for Herbert Blomstedt, the bibliomaniac with the encyclopedic memory. Perhaps he will perform the work one day? He declines by saying, "I would need several months to study and practice it; I just don't have the time."

Time—this is exactly the right cue for a hurried departure to the airport. The former music director has a rehearsal with the Staatskapelle Dresden the following morning. Herbert's response to my surprise at his schedule for the next day was, "Jetlag—what's that?" What will be performed? The plane hasn't taken off yet, and he is already studying the score from Beethoven's Ninth Symphony. Of course, he knows it by heart. But being prepared is everything!

Reencounter With the New World: The Time in San Francisco

1. Peter Pastreich, speech for Herbert Blomstedt's retirement, July 1, 2005, Leipzig, Leipzig Gewandhaus Orchestra archives.

2. Peter Pastreich, telephone interview by UW, October 2006. The description of Herbert Blomstedt's public image during these years is largely based on this interview.

3. Michael Steinberg, quoted in the prologue to *A Salute to the Blomstedt Decade: Herbert Blomstedt and the San Francisco Symphony, 1985–1995* (n.p.: n.p., n.d.). Unless otherwise indicated, all newspaper articles, concert critiques, and part of the concert chronicles are taken from *A Salute to the Blomstedt Decade* in the SFS archives.

4. "A Blomstedt Album," in *A Salute to the Blomstedt Decade*.

5. John Kieser, conversation with UW, March 25, 2007, San Francisco, CA.

6. John von Rhein, "San Francisco Symphony Showcases Its Potential," review of San Francisco Symphony concert, with Herbert Blomsted conducting, Orchestra Hall, Chicago, *Chicago Tribune*, March 13, 1986, http://articles.chicagotribune.com/1986-03-13 /news/8601190169_1_young-orchestra-herbert-blomstedt-san-francisco-symphony.

7. Herbert Blomstedt to UW, personal communication, October 17, 2010.

8. Lothar Schacke, interview by UW, July 23, 2009, Munich.

9. Ibid.

10. Joseph McLellan, "San Francisco's Stellar Symphony, More," *Washington Post*, December 4, 1988, https://www.washingtonpost.com/archive/lifestyle/style/1988/12/04 /san-franciscos-stellar-symphony-more/7cd902b2-2f8b-4915-abda-e5f181e9d60e/.

11. "A Blomstedt Album," in *A Salute to the Blomstedt Decade*.

12. Quoted in Larry Rothe, *Music for a City, Music for the World: 100 Years With the San Francisco Symphony* (San Francisco: Chronicle Books, 2011), 213.

13. Hartmut Brauer, interview by UW, September 30, 2010, Leipzig.

14. Rothe, *Music for a City*, 214.

15. Herbert Blomstedt, diary entry, November 8, 2008.

16. Herbert Blomstedt, discussion with UW.

17. Quoted in "A Blomstedt Album," in *A Salute to the Blomstedt Decade*.

18. Herbert Blomstedt to UW, personal communication, October 29, 2010.

19. The author attended the rehearsals and performances of the SFS during March 14–25, 2007, in San Francisco.

20. Herbert Blomstedt, diary entry, March 17, 2007.

Interlude in Hamburg

I just think music.
—Johannes Brahms

IN 1995, HERBERT BLOMSTEDT returned from America to Europe to stand at the podium of a very young orchestra. He had been a guest conductor of the Hamburg-based Norddeutscher Rundfunk (NDR; North German Radio) Symphony Orchestra as early as 1969 and had been invited again a year later. In 1981, he guest conducted in Düsseldorf and Antwerp, performing Franz Schubert's Symphony No. 9—the "Great C Major"—and Beethoven's Piano Concerto No. 3. Two years later they performed *A German Requiem* and the Violin Concerto by Johannes Brahms. At the end of 1994, in his last season with the SFS, Blomstedt once again conducted the Hamburg orchestra, performing Paul Hindemith's symphony *Mathis der Maler*, Johannes Brahms's Concerto for Violin, Cello, and Orchestra, and the Symphony No. 4 in E-flat Major by the Swede Franz Adolf Berwald. At the opening concert of the Schleswig-Holstein Music Festival in 1995, they performed *Glagolitic Mass* by Leoš Janáček, *The Wound-Dresser* by the American contemporary composer John Adams, and Arnold Schoenberg's arrangement of Johann Sebastian Bach's Prelude and Fugue in E-flat Major. Shortly thereafter, Herbert signed a second contract with a German orchestra on the Elbe River; in the fall, he directed a special concert—50 Years of the NDR Symphony Orchestra—performing Richard Strauss's tone poem *Also sprach Zarathustra* and Johannes Brahms's Symphony No. 4.

The British, Brahms, and Buxtehude

Immediately after the Second World War ended, Hans Schmidt-Isserstedt established the Hamburg ensemble known as the Hamburg

147

Radio Symphony Orchestra by order of the British military. He had approached musicians from disbanded orchestras who were in prisoner-of-war camps in Schleswig-Holstein and invited them to audition upon their release. In this way, the first concert took place in November 1945 in the undestroyed Hamburg music hall, with none other than Yehudi Menuhin playing the solo part of Mendelssohn's Violin Concerto. Schmidt-Isserstedt was the chief conductor in Hamburg until 1971, and concurrent with this appointment also served as chief conductor in Stockholm from 1955 to 1964. The two music directors knew each other from this latter time period. Schmidt-Isserstedt was born in 1900 and, according to Blomstedt, "had his eye on him," saying that Schmidt-Isserstedt potentially would have liked to welcome the young Swede as his successor in the Hanseatic city. However, Blomstedt was still engaged in Scandinavia when "Schmisse" died in 1973. By that time, Moshe Atzmon had already been at the head of the Hamburg orchestra for two years; Klaus Tennstedt and Günter Wand were later musical directors. And now, in the mid-1990s, Blomstedt recalls, "There was something in the air. The orchestra needed a successor to Sir John Eliot Gardiner, and they came back to me. One was hoping for a longer, more stable, and—from both a personal and musical perspective—happier period."

Blomstedt was persuaded and took on the task. The collaboration with this first-rate orchestra proved to be excellent; Herbert was a friend of the manager Rolf Beck, whom he had gotten to know during the time when Beck had managed the Bamberg Symphony. Back then, Beck had wanted him to be the Bamberg orchestra's leader, but the picturesque town on the Regnitz appeared too small to Blomstedt—with all due respect to the Bamberg musicians—especially since the alternative was San Francisco.

But now Hamburg! Many things delighted the Blomstedts about Hamburg: the cosmopolitanism of the city; the culture of the whole region, with its many old churches and wonderful organs from the baroque period; and the proximity to Lübeck, with all its traces of Bach and Buxtehude. In a short time, they found not only good friends but also a few of Waltraud's relatives and Schmidt-Isserstedt's widowed second wife, the ballet mistress Helga Swedlund, also a native of Sweden. Hence, they enjoyed plenty of opportunities to socialize.

Short, content rich, and not all sweet
Yet, from the outset, a shadow of transition hung over this idyll: the Leipzig Gewandhaus Orchestra had "proposed" to Herbert Blomstedt, and this was a request he simply could not refuse! "An all too important

orchestra! I could have delayed it a bit in order to honor the three-year contract I signed in Hamburg," he says today. "We didn't even consider a dual appointment of Hamburg and Leipzig because both orchestras are in Germany and that would have meant unhealthy competition. But Mr. Beck was, of course, very disappointed. I could understand that. He was of the opinion that since I had no intentions of staying, I should rather dissolve the contract. There was certainly a prickly tone."

Finally, they agreed on two seasons in Hamburg: from August 1, 1996, to July 31, 1998. This was by far Blomstedt's shortest time as chief conductor of an orchestra.

From the start, like any radio orchestra, the NDR Symphony Orchestra was commissioned to perform a lot of New Music. However, they noted that no orchestra could develop at the highest level without a central repertoire. Thus, Blomstedt introduced his musicians and the audience not only to Scandinavian music but also to the Vienna classics, including Haydn and Mozart, which, in his own words, "are essential for orchestral culture."

Blomstedt's tenure immediately began with a finale: the final concert at the Schleswig-Holstein Music Festival in August 1996. This was directly followed by an appearance at the Rheingau Music Festival, with Richard Strauss's *A Hero's Life*, György Ligeti's *Atmosphères*, and Joseph Haydn's Cello Concerto No. 1 in C Major, featuring Yo-Yo Ma as the soloist. In November, the soloists whom Blomstedt particularly esteemed, the soprano Juliane Banse and the baritone Matthias Goerne, sang Johannes Brahms's *A German Requiem* together with the NDR Choir and the Budapest Radio Choir. The pianist Gerhard Oppitz and the violinist David Garrett performed with the orchestra on the tour of Japan in February and March of 1997. The children's choir of the Hamburg State Opera, the *Hamburger Alsterspatzen*, participated in Arthur Honegger's *A Christmas Cantata* during the week of Christmas in Hamburg and Kiel.

At the beginning of the second season, in the late summer of 1997, the orchestra did a three-week tour through South America. In São Paulo, Buenos Aires, and Montevideo, they performed works by Béla Bartók, Antonín Dvořák, Franz Schubert, and Johannes Brahms, with Frank Peter Zimmermann as the soloist for Brahms's Violin Concerto. A month later, on a small tour of northern Germany, Thomas Zehetmair performed the violin solo of Karl Amadeus Hartmann's *Funeral Concerto*. In addition to works by Sibelius, Strauss, György Kurtág, and Beethoven, they performed the Viola Concerto by Alfred Schnittke, featuring Kim Kashkashian as the soloist. A rarely performed sacred work by Felix Mendelssohn, the oratorio *St. Paul,* was presented with the NDR Choir and the Budapest Radio Choir in late October and early November of 1997, not only in Hamburg but also in Leipzig, Blomstedt's future workplace. Right at the beginning of 1998, following performances in Hamburg and Lübeck, they went to Spain. Immediately thereafter, the orchestra toured through Germany and Switzerland, featuring the illustrious soloists Helen Huang in Mozart's Piano Concerto No. 21 and Sabine Meyer in Nielsen's Concerto for Clarinet. In May 1998, for Herbert Blomstedt's final concert as chief conductor of the NDR Symphony, they performed Gustav Mahler's Symphony No. 3. The Hanover Boys' Choir and singers from the NDR Choir sang together with the mezzo-soprano Iris Vermillion as the soloist.

But with that, the collaboration by no means came to an end. In early 2000, Blomstedt was once again conducting the NDR Symphony, performing Beethoven's Symphony No. 6 and Nielsen's Symphony No. 4. They had not parted in discord and resentment but with propriety and respect. A worthy successor was promptly found in Christoph Eschenbach. Six years later Christoph von Dohnányi took over the position, and since 2011 Thomas Hengelbrock has held the chief conductor's baton. For Herbert Blomstedt, this is proof "that Rolf Beck has a good eye and a sixth sense."

Every year Blomstedt serves as guest conductor for the NDR Symphony Orchestra—still under Rolf Beck's management—"to make up for something. The musicians have become even better, and to me they play like masters. I enjoy being there, and we're the best of friends. The orchestra is very spirited; and if one respects and motivates the excellent musicians, they play excellently."

Memories of Hamburg

My first concert as chief conductor of the NDR Symphony Orchestra was a wonderful performance in the Marienkirche [St. Mary's Church] in Lübeck: Bruckner's Mass in F Minor. The huge Gothic brick church, where Dietrich Buxtehude had worked as an organist and cantor until his death in 1707, was during his lifetime a place of the most wonderful musical performances. Buxtehude, born in Helsingborg, Sweden, was the greatest Protestant church musician in the generation preceding Bach, and his *"Abendmusiken"* [evening music]—five concerts on Sunday afternoon during the Advent season—were known far and wide. Even twenty-year-old Bach made the pilgrimage of four hundred kilometers [249 miles] on foot from Arnstadt in Thuringia to Lübeck just to hear Buxtehude. He had four weeks of vacation—but stayed four times as long! The old master must have impressed him tremendously.

And now almost three hundred years later, I was able to make music with some of the best musicians and singers of our time in this sacred place. An Adventist in a Lutheran church interpreting Catholic music! In the light of the great eternal God, our doctrinal differences disappear, and we can only marvel at everything that is human and sublime in music. One can only be grateful.

Almost exactly three months later, on November 22, 1996, we were guests in Greifswald. Northern German Radio has the largest coverage area in Germany, and we wanted to show the furthermost eastern region in Germany that they also belong to us. After the Peace of Westphalia in 1648, Greifswald came under Swedish rule for more than 150 years, so I came home as it were! In the Cathedral of St. Nicholas, we performed *A German Requiem* by Johannes Brahms, a native of Hamburg. It was a memorable performance, recorded live by NDR television. The Bible texts, which Brahms had selected with great care and set to music, took on a special meaning in this context. Christian Friedrich, brother to the great painter Caspar David Friedrich, designed the sanctuary, which served as a backdrop to the orchestra and choir. We sang and made music together magnificently—unforgettable.

During the two seasons of my work in Hamburg, we did two big tours abroad, to Japan and South America. In Japan, we received a rousing reception. The last concert in Suntory Hall in Tokyo was again devoted entirely Brahms—Hamburg's greatest composer. The orchestra has a special affinity for his music. Incidentally, Johannes Brahms's father's double bass was still played in the orchestra. Hence Brahms's original sound! A year later we read that this performance was chosen by the audience in this city of eleven million inhabitants as the best concert of the year.[1]

---

1. Herbert Blomstedt to UW, personal communication, February 23, 2011.

The Leipzig Gewandhaus Orchestra: "I Couldn't Say No"

Res severa verum gaudium.[1]
—Seneca

I N THE SUMMER OF 1995, Hartmut Brauer, the principal cellist of the Leipzig Gewandhaus Orchestra (LGO), was vacationing with his wife in Austria when he received a call from Leipzig: "You have to go see Herbert Blomstedt!" Brauer, who was the chairperson of the orchestra board at the time, immediately contacted Blomstedt's manager, Lothar Schacke. With such short notice, they agreed upon an initial interview in Anif, Austria, which is near Salzburg and halfway between the agency office in Munich and the Brauers' holiday location.

Brauer remembers that in the ensuing weeks they "telephoned wildly back and forth."[2] While the orchestra board had a lot to discuss before making direct contact with Blomstedt, Herbert also had to think twice about how to proceed because he was in the process of signing a three-year initial contract, which contained a release clause after two years, with Hamburg. Therefore, the Leipzig orchestra's board members were not without reason in feeling that they had to hurry. Herbert Blomstedt had gained all sorts of experience in changing from one orchestra to the next over the decades. Never before, however, were the circumstances as dramatic as now.

Tradition in transition

Since 1970, Kurt Masur had stood at the head of the LGO, the largest professional orchestra in Germany with about 185 musicians. The orchestra's roots date back to 1743—"the oldest continuously existing civic orchestra."[3] Masur, who was exactly one week younger than Blomstedt, had to discontinue his musical studies during the post-WWII hunger winter in Germany. Nonetheless, being highly gifted, he took on the leadership of his first orchestra at a very young age, after short stints at the Komische Opera company in Berlin and at the Dresden Philharmonic. In Leipzig, he made a significant contribution not only musically but also through his remarkable participation in the Leipzig Monday demonstrations of 1989. He rendered invaluable additions to the musical culture of Leipzig through his commitment to the construction of the Gewandhaus, which opened in 1981, and the restoration of the Mendelssohn House.

Masur's contract was expiring in 1996. He was also the chief conductor of the New York Philharmonic since 1991 and had already alluded to his possible resignation in March 1994 in an interview with the *London Times*. He stated clearly that he had a successor in mind, a personal favorite, a so-called shooting star. This person was, however, bound by contract, so that idea was never pursued further.[4]

It was clear to the orchestra's board members, who were responsible for finding a new music director, that only the world's best would be considered during their selection of Masur's successor. Hartmut Brauer, who had a close and trusting relationship with Masur for many years, said in retrospect,

> After such a long time, an abrupt departure is actually a disaster for any orchestra. Now it was our turn to find a new boss! Of course, our colleagues said, "We have to aim high"—but that was far from easy! What person would take it upon him- or herself to accept an orchestra that had been strongly influenced by the same musical hand for a quarter of a century? For me at least, there was only Mr. Blomstedt! I had already watched him once as I was a substitute player in the orchestra, and I was enraptured on the one hand by his warmhearted way of making music, how he spreads happiness, and on the other hand by his—I wouldn't call it strictness—but relentlessness in music. I thought, *He really brings out the good in the orchestra, and that, which one sometimes has to cultivate—that is, performance practice and a classical repertoire all the way to the Haydn symphony—he will impart to us.*

Other members of the orchestra were also in agreement: Blomstedt should come back because they "were hooked," as Peter Michael Borck, violist and at that time a member of the orchestra board, recalls. "It was clear where we would have to go now first of all. This ultimately spared us a lengthy and possibly complicated search for a music director."

The Leipzig Gewandhaus Orchestra: "I Couldn't Say No"

In Brauer's opinion, Blomstedt was

the only one who had the caliber, the strength, and the perseverance, and above all, a very clear musical concept. I knew of only a few people who, for our core repertoire—especially the *B*s: Brahms, Beethoven, Bruckner, but also Johann Sebastian Bach—would have as much to contribute. [I liked him for] just this alone; for example, he approaches Bruckner with a Bachlike performance practice: unrelenting insistence on short and long, stressed and unstressed; nothing escapes him! This has greatly influenced the sound of the orchestra, improved it, and purified it somewhat, and made it more agile. It was not as dramatic as before, but the sound itself was there, of course.

Peter Michael Borck remembers a guest performance with Günter Wand a few years before the Blomstedt era, when Bruckner's Symphony No. 5 was performed:

Wand suddenly did only that which was written in the score! That was very difficult for us as an orchestra. No *ritardando* [a gradual decrease in tempo] was done if it wasn't in the music. And an incredible sound was created, in that it was simply together. The Gewandhaus Orchestra has, of course, always sounded great, but there was always some vagueness. Blomstedt has brought precision and thus, according to me, a much-better sound effect, clearly focused, and therefore much more powerful in tone. This has ultimately brought warmth again; I think this is one of his very great merits.

"Hand in hand with this went the lowering of the underlying orchestra dynamics," Brauer adds. "He just simply required it: 'It has to be *piano*! *Pianissimo*, it has to really go down in volume! And not just softly but also melodiously.' This is extremely important."

"Because this is the only way to expand the range," Borck explains. "At some point, one can't get any louder; of course, there is a limit to softness, too, and yet somehow not really. I have been sitting in concerts here, where we played so quietly that one could hear an ambulance passing by outside, which is not normally possible. Blomstedt once told an oboist that he should start the sound in such a way that one could not hear him at first. I had never witnessed that this is possible! But he did it."

The Gewandhaus in Lucerne

The board of directors was in agreement, and in the summer of 1995, Hartmut Brauer, Peter Michael Borck, and Clemens Röger, the principal horn player, drove to Lucerne. Brauer recalls,

> It was a rather dramatic experience for us, and we, of course, thought, *What on earth are we going to talk about?* At six in the evening, we rang the doorbell at Rosenberghalde [Herbert's residence] and spoke into the intercom, "The Gewandhaus Orchestra is here." We took the elevator to the fourth floor and were soon seated on the sofa, making small talk. Finally, as the chairman, I plucked up my courage and asked the question, "Mr. Blomstedt, can you envision becoming the music director of the Gewandhaus?" That was a pretty direct question, and after a moment of reflection, he gave a direct answer. He simply said, "Yes."

Later Blomstedt commented on his consent, "I thought to myself, *If it's the Gewandhaus Orchestra that is requesting, one cannot possibly say no.*"

During the evening, the maestro led the three representatives to his office and showed them, among other things, his bust of Arthur Nikisch (the Gewandhaus Orchestra's music director from 1895 to 1922), who had always been a great role model for Blomstedt and whom Bruckner had known personally. Now things were coming full circle, so to speak.

Hartmut Brauer recalls,

> Elsewhere—in the media, record industry, and so on—it was rumored that Masur's successor could be Blomstedt. This was somehow in the air. As an orchestra looking for a boss, one could go to the city's senior-most employee, which in Leipzig is the mayor, and ask what should be done, or one starts with the orchestra. In the case at hand, following a meeting with the orchestra, the board was instructed to contact Mr. Blomstedt. The matter was precarious, as we initially had to agree not to disclose anything because Blomstedt first wanted to start in Hamburg and was also under contract there. So for about three-quarters of a year we had to keep our orchestra colleagues waiting.
>
> Meanwhile Mr. Schacke negotiated with the city. These are always complex and lengthy discussions. Finally, the lord mayor, Dr. Hinrich Lehmann-Grube, came to the Gewandhaus and informed us of the official decision. He met me at the stage door, and we

walked up the stairs together. He was aware of the fact that the orchestra knew nothing official yet. Halfway up the stairs, he turned around and asked, "What will you do if the colleagues disagree?" We had already asked ourselves this question. I just said, "They will agree." We went into the hall; the lord mayor announced the name; and there was long-lasting applause. I saw Dr. Girardet [deputy mayor of cultural affairs in Leipzig from 1991 to 2009] sitting three chairs away from me. He looked at me briefly, and it was as if both of us felt a weight being lifted from our shoulders now that the problem was solved.

The timing of handing over the baton in Leipzig should have gone seamlessly. In June 1994, shortly after the previously mentioned *London Times* interview, Kurt Masur had agreed to an extension of his contract until 1998. In actuality, he left the Gewandhaus with short notice because of further frustrations in late 1996.[5] The audience, many members of the orchestra, and prominent cultural representatives were shocked. His designated successor, whose appointment was officially announced in July 1996, stood under contract as the head of the NDR Symphony Orchestra and could only begin in Leipzig in the 1998/1999 season.

Hartmut Brauer remembers,

> Before Kurt Masur, even in the '70s, there were endeavors to bring Herbert Blomstedt to Leipzig. But the city leaders were very red [particular regarding national politics at this time] and apparently had a problem in giving a non-GDR citizen a leading cultural position. In this regard, the Staatskapelle and the Semperoper were cleverer, or they had more leeway. Since the postwar period, however, the LGO constantly had guest conductors from the West and made recordings with them, including many with Herbert von Karajan. What we didn't really know at the time was that the relationship between the artistic agencies in the GDR and the major international agencies, even CAMI, played a role.

One day during Herbert's time as music director in Leipzig, an elderly lady in a park approached him while he was on his way to a rehearsal. She told him, to his surprise, that during GDR times she was a secretary in the Ministry of Culture and knew therefore that he had already been strongly favored in the late sixties as the preferred candidate for the LGO. However, socialism prevented this from going any further.

A Great Song

The beginning of a wonderful collaboration

All four Blomstedt daughters traveled from Scandinavia for the inauguration of the eighteenth Gewandhaus music director on September 1, 1998. Blomstedt also invited his seriously ill former classmate Gunno Södersten. Södersten was wheeled in on a stretcher and was able to listen to the opening concert. He had only a few more weeks to live, but he wanted to be there. Blomstedt knew he would have little time for him because hundreds of people certainly would want to speak to him. In the afternoon before the concert, he went to visit his old friend in the hotel where he was staying, so as to have more time to see each other. It was a moving last encounter for the both of them.

On the program for the "enthronement concert"—as Rolf Beck humorously called it—was Anton Bruckner's Symphony No. 3 from 1873. The concert was preluded by organ music. Michael Schönheit played Johann Sebastian Bach's Fantasia and Fugue in G Minor and Felix Mendelssohn's Organ Sonata No. 6. Afterward Yehudi Menuhin gave a speech and stated that the position of music director of the Gewandhaus was made for the American Swede.

"One heart—one mind. There is nothing that they could not achieve together," the newspaper *Frankfurter Allgemeine Zeitung* said in its report on the inauguration with regard to the collaboration between the music director and his new orchestra. The *Welt* newspaper summarized, "Blomstedt conducted a wonderfully balanced orchestra. At the end of the second movement, Bruckner's glory was complete."[6]

> My first suggestion was that Queen Silvia of Sweden should give the speech. Her uncle, Ernst Sommerlath, was a theology professor in Leipzig, and I knew her cousin, Margaret Ledig, from the Seventh-day Adventist Church in Dresden.
>
> But the queen was not available. Then I suggested Yehudi Menuhin, as we had performed together several times, and he said yes. His speech was quite fantastic. He died six months later in Berlin.[7]

Two days later the Bruckner symphony was played again; this time they performed Arthur Honegger's "Liturgique" before the intermission. They went on tour with this program, performing at the Chorin Monastery and in Dresden, Lucerne (debut at the festival), Besançon, Montreux (with another program), and Linz in the Brucknerhaus (Bruckner House) as the opening concert of the Bruckner Festival. The Viennese newspapers

Der Standard and *Kurier* were deeply impressed.

In Leipzig, the Blomstedt couple moved into a very special second home: it was high up under the roof of the historic Mendelssohn House on Goldschmidtstraße (Goldsmith Street), just a stone's throw away from the Gewandhaus. However, their first residence remained Lucerne. Three years later when Waltraud had to move into a nursing home in Lucerne, they moved out of the three-bedroom apartment.

"A very authentic personality"

Herbert Blomstedt always placed great importance on a very good personal and artistic collaboration with his respective orchestra managers. Even before his inauguration, he hired Andreas Schulz to be the Gewandhaus director. He was a young and very capable music manager, who had already established considerable credentials elsewhere. In retrospect, Andreas Schulz referred to working with Blomstedt as "the most valuable time" of his career thus far and answered some questions in an interview with the author.[8]

> URSULA WEIGERT (UW): *Professor Schulz, how did you get to know Herbert Blomstedt?*
>
> ANDREAS SCHULZ (AS): I had worked at the Schleswig-Holstein Music Festival since 1996. At first, I was responsible for the master classes at the Lübeck Academy of Music and then since 1994 for the Schleswig-Holstein Music Festival's orchestra at Salzau Castle. In that year, I met with Herbert Blomstedt and his agent, Lothar Schacke, several times to contract Mr. Blomstedt for a work assignment with the festival's orchestra. I recall each meeting, because all our conversations were memorable. We talked less about the organizational content of the work assignment than about topics relating to music, about our families, and about our faith. I was fascinated by his personality, his vast knowledge, and his gentle and modest nature.
>
> UW: *What are your experiences of the chief conductor?*
>
> AS: His tenure as Gewandhaus music director from 1998 to 2005 was a great and very sustainable win-win situation. Even today we benefit from Blomstedt's fundamental work with the orchestra. Rehearsals, for example, were marked by great mutual respect and high esteem. Mr. Blomstedt always sought out the best in each musician and tried to cultivate it

with great patience. Yet, he was also a strict orchestral trainer in the best sense of the word and rehearsed the work very intensely until the last second.

He initiated significant changes, such as introducing the German orchestral seating arrangement. The repertoire has been expanded significantly, and because of invitations to conductors in the field of historical performance practice,[9] we have received many new ideas. He also strongly supported the performance of works from the baroque period. In particular, works by Johann Sebastian Bach were often included in his program.

Herbert Blomstedt also worked intensively on the Gewandhaus Orchestra's sound, focusing on the shaping of the string sound and a clear delivery of the music. The first years were not always easy for the orchestra or the audience, but everyone witnessed the impressive fruits of his labor in the last season of 2004/2005. What he achieved continues on to this day, with Riccardo Chailly adding to it through his own emphases.

The extensive changes were difficult to implement and resulted in many, sometimes intense, discussions. Herbert Blomstedt listened, explained, persuaded, and worked continuously and unwaveringly. At his departure in 2005, he left an almost perfect orchestra behind.

UW: *How were your private meetings?*

AS: Herbert Blomstedt is a very authentic personality. He deals with people in his professional life in the same way that he does in his private life. I have visited him several times in Lucerne, where we spoke about professional and private issues while going on long walks. Every so often we would stand still and admire the fantastic views or the beauty of nature.

In 2007, my family and I were invited to Sweden for his eightieth birthday celebration. We traveled with our camper to visit Mr. Blomstedt at his summer residence in Bengtstorp a few days prior to the celebration and spent a wonderful time with him. I especially remember searching together for blueberries in the forest, which we then ate in the evening with pancakes. A few days later we went with him to the birthday festivities. Our five daughters, my wife, Mr. Blomstedt, and I all piled into our van and spent the long drive telling stories and singing. Mr. Blomstedt started us off on canons, and we sang four-part choruses. At the birthday party, there were many guests from around the world; most of them did not know each other personally; and yet there was a very warm and friendly atmosphere that emanated from the host. Herbert Blomstedt was the connection between us all. For my family and me, these days in Sweden will always remain in our memories.

UW: *Some speak of the "aloof Swede." How do you see that?*

AS: If one only observes him from a distance, then one could come to this conclusion. However, as soon as one speaks to him and gets to know him better, then one can feel his warmth and become attracted by his fascinating personality. He really is not an "aloof Swede." If anyone thinks so, then I would recommend the person attend one of his concerts and listen to how he interprets the music. Then you will experience all of his depth, and I guarantee that you will be thrilled.

I am also grateful and happy that I could work with Mr. Blomstedt for seven years. This has enriched my life; it was a precious time for me.

UW: *Mr. Blomstedt is known for his very religious attitude.*

AS: I myself come from a pastoral home, and it was a nice experience for me when he and I had our first lunch together and he said grace. And so it was every time that we ate together; whether we were in the office or on tour, he always took the initiative and thanked God for the food and our time together. We often talked about my church, the Holy Trinity Church in Leipzig, which is a member of the Independent Evangelical Lutheran Church. My family and I have benefited from getting to know wonderful friends in the Adventist church in Leipzig through Mr. Blomstedt.

UW: *Another typical characteristic known by insiders is his sense of humor.*

AS: Yes, his sense of humor is special. At first, one does not suspect he has such a profound and witty humor because he acts rather serious and focused. But when you discover, for example, how he collects cartoons from the *New Yorker* or how wonderfully he can tell anecdotes about other artists and how pleased he is when he gets to the punch line, then his laugh is so contagious that you just have to laugh! Although I heard some of these stories two or three times in the seven years of our collaboration, each time I had to laugh with him again but more so because of how Mr. Blomstedt told the stories in words and gestures.

UW: *How would you describe his dealings with people in positions of responsibility?*

AS: Mr. Blomstedt had a very good relationship with the lord mayor of Leipzig and with the relevant committees. If there were serious cultural or political problems, he wanted to get involved himself. At the beginning of his tenure, for example, a local political party commissioned a study to examine the size of the Gewandhaus Orchestra. Together with Mr. Blomstedt, I invited the relevant board, the Cultural Executive Committee, to the Gewandhaus. In an interesting lecture, Mr. Blomstedt outlined the various necessary appointments based on the scores of selected concert pieces and operas and the church music repertoire. He could explain a complex matter in a simple and understandable way. He answered the many queries of the politicians with patience using numerous examples. In the end, the study was shelved.

Herbert Blomstedt was highly respected by all political leaders, and he still is today.

UW: *In your opinion, do you think he has certain qualities that made him particularly suitable for the Gewandhaus Orchestra?*

AS: He already knew the Gewandhaus Orchestra very well. He came to Leipzig several times during his tenure as chief conductor of the Staatskapelle Dresden. It was a very wise decision by the Gewandhaus Orchestra and in particular by the orchestra board chairman at the time, Hartmut Brauer, to seek out Mr. Blomstedt as Kurt Masur's successor.

In my opinion, Mr. Blomstedt is a music director in the best sense of the word. Many of his musical and personal skills were necessary for the new task in Leipzig. But he convinced me not only by his musical work, but also in all aspects of management. Blomstedt, Volker Stiehler, who was the managing director of the Gewandhaus at the time, and I were responsible for restructuring the Gewandhaus and developing long-term strategies. We discussed all ideas intensely and found diverse solutions, which I was able to implement in my daily work. This included, for example, many very small but important details, such as the spatial reorganization of offices. In many cases, we took down walls between offices in order to improve communication.

Mr. Blomstedt also had decisive ideas with regard to concert planning. Here in particular one needs to mention the launching of family concerts. He narrated these concerts in an impressive manner. From the beginning, the family concerts were sold out. Blomstedt has also shown his talent for storytelling in many other concerts. Even though he was always very thoroughly prepared, he could use simple, clearly stated words to inspire the listener, whether young or old.

We also initiated some unusual projects with him. In 1998, two of my friends from Munich, Peter Gartiser and Nicolas Steenken, had the idea of setting up a manager's orchestra. We first developed the project together, and then I introduced it to Mr. Blomstedt. He was excited about it straightaway, and we began implementing the Management Symphony. From the beginning, this orchestra, made up of leaders in the German industry, was a huge success. This is largely due to Mr. Blomstedt, who has succeeded, together with colleagues from the Gewandhaus Orchestra who were responsible for the auditions, in making a real orchestra out of the manager's orchestra. Since then, we do this project every year.

UW: *The office of Gewandhaus music director is of great importance in Leipzig. What role did Mr. Blomstedt play in Leipzig society?*

AS: A significant role because the Gewandhaus music director is, generally speaking, the most important music representative in the city of Leipzig. Mr. Blomstedt's advice was just as sought after, as were his comments and statements on particular cultural policy issues. At the same time, his extensive international experience played a prominent role in this.

At important receptions, for example, Mr. Blomstedt was always present with welcoming words for sponsors of the Gewandhaus. I will never forget one reception for our long-term car sponsor BMW, where he spontaneously manufactured a comparison between a 12-cylinder BMW and a complex music score. The guests were amused, and it left a lasting impression.

One hardly ever met Mr. Blomstedt at other receptions

in town. He always did what was necessary for the Gewandhaus and the Gewandhaus Orchestra. Other receptions were rather boring for him or even a waste of time. He would rather study a score or read a good book. So he was not a person who could be found at all social occasions.

However, his presence in the city was still very large. He went shopping and was well known in bookstores, antique shops, and various restaurants. He attended the performances of the motets in the St. Thomas Church and went to concerts at the Bach Festival. He visited museums and exhibitions and showed great interest in the cultural life of the city. Often people in the city would stop and speak to him. He was treated with great respect but was greeted in a very friendly and openhearted manner. The people in Leipzig appreciated Mr. Blomstedt very much, and he takes the stage as a guest conductor today to warm applause.

Musical highlights

One cannot enumerate all of the concerts that were performed during Blomstedt's seven-year tenure in Leipzig. However, an overview of particularly notable performances at home and on tour can give one an idea of the wealth of musical experiences that the Gewandhaus Orchestra gave their listeners under its Swedish conductor.

At the beginning of 1999, the *Financial Times* in London rejoiced that the LGO was expanding its horizons by including Arthur Honegger, Carl Nielsen, and Pierre Boulez as well as Felix Mendelssohn, Bruckner, and other well-known composers in the repertoire. In fact, during Herbert Blomstedt's first season, the Gewandhaus Orchestra performed seventeen premieres and two world premieres.

In May 1999, the orchestra performed in Japan for the first time, giving ten concerts with Blomstedt. Further tours in Japan followed in 2002 and 2005. After the first season in 1999, the headlines of the newspaper *Leipziger Volkszeitung* emphasized that a trip to the Leipzig Gewandhaus Orchestra is like visiting the pinnacle of symphony culture.

In Leipzig, there were many annually recurring highlights for Herbert Blomstedt, such as the New Year's Eve concert with Beethoven's Ninth or the UNICEF concerts during the Advent season with popular pieces of classical music, which were narrated ingeniously by the music director. Other unforgettable occasions included the regular performances at the Bach Festival, such as conducting Johann Sebastian Bach's *St. John*

Passion at the end of July 2000 in St. Nicholas Church; or the festive *Zehn Jahre Wende—Wir sind das Volk* (Ten years of reunification—we are the people) commemorative concert of October 9, 1999, in St. Nicholas Church, which featured Beethoven's Fifth Symphony as well as excerpts from Mendelssohn's *Elijah* and Bach's Mass in B Minor, in which Viktoria Mullova, Nancy Argenta, and the St. Thomas Boys' Choir participated. (The latter concert is now available on DVD.)[10]

Following a performance of Mendelssohn's Symphony No. 3 and Bruckner's Symphony No. 6 in Hamburg's Laeiszhalle concert hall, two of Hamburg's newspapers, *Harburger Anzeigen und Nachrichten* and the *Hamburger Abendblatt*, reported on February 14, 2000, about the "enthusiastic cheering" and "fervent excitement" without any of the customary Hanseatic reserve. The *Leipziger Volkszeitung* reported on the same performance and concluded, "Blomstedt, Gewandhaus Orchestra, and Bruckner; this is a combination of the very best."[11]

Go away, mournful spirits!

It was Friday, May 14, 1999, towards the end of my first season as Gewandhaus music director. We had returned home the day before, happy but also tired after a long tour in Japan. In Leipzig, the Bach Festival was in full swing, and after a day's rest, we were also going to take part in it.

Friday would renew our strength, and we were sincerely looking forward to finally being at home a whole day without any obligations. But then I saw that the Eric Ericson Chamber Choir from Stockholm would be singing in the evening at the St. Nicholas Church. I could not miss it! Not only is it one of the best choirs in the world, the wonderful singers are also my compatriots, and their director is a lifelong, good friend of mine. So I asked Mrs. Pless, my faithful assistant, to organize two tickets for me. The concert was sold out, but Mrs. Pless made the impossible possible. Yet, she could not organize someone to accompany me. Everyone from the Gewandhaus was tired, or they had other obligations.

In the evening, I went to the St. Nicholas Church to pick up the two tickets at the counter. Somehow I was convinced that someone would want to be "a victim of my generosity." In front of the church, there was a long line of people who had the same goal as I—a longing for music, for a rare spiritual feast. I was painfully aware of the fact that though people noticed me, I saw no familiar faces.

Then, when I finally reached the counter, I realized why I had not found a companion. Because he was standing there! I didn't know him, but there was a man with a sad face and a sign on his chest that said "homeless." I asked him whether he would like to go to the concert with me; he wouldn't have to pay anything but would be my guest. The man pointed to his lack of appropriate clothing, made a few awkward objections, but finally did come with me, and we walked down the aisle together to our seats. They were numbers one and two in the first row.

What may devout visitors have thought as they saw this unusual pair walk toward the front? He was unshaven and smelled of alcohol, and I must confess I was afraid he might be a disturbance. When we had found our seats, he elbowed me and whispered again and again, "Why are you doing this?" I could give only one answer, "Because you're my friend."

As the choir took the stage, he fell silent. The first work on the program was the Bach motet *Jesu, meine Freude* (Jesus, my joy). He followed the text closely in the program, and as the fourth verse was sung, he sighed deeply. "Go away, mournful spirits, for my joyful master, Jesus, now enters in." A beam of light illuminated the soul.

One can never know what is going on inside another person, but I had the impression that he listened with his whole soul and that he was doing some thinking. Three months later I received a letter from him: he had decided to stop drinking and start a new life. Unfortunately, he only partially succeeded, but we are still friends today. He also, like me, always needs new encounters with the "Master of joy" to stay mentally and physically fit.

Especially at Christmastime, we have ample opportunity to open the doors wide for joy and love. May it last for the whole year. It is inexpensive and enduring. Go away, mournful spirits.[12]

Peter Korfmacher, the editor and music critic, commented on the article as follows: "With no one else, am I so sure that it's not just all pious words, but [you are] someone [who] carries the essence of the good news in his heart and doesn't speak because of the prospect of beautiful gifts. I have learned a lot from you in this regard and also try to teach this to my children. I am pleased that you will soon be back in Leipzig."[13]

Gewandhaus meets university

In May 2001, the new Great Hall in the University of Music and The-

166

ater "Felix Mendelssohn Bartholdy," Leipzig, was opened after bombing in 1944 destroyed the previous magnificent concert hall. The new hall, built through the commendable efforts of the composer and former rector Siegfried Thiele, was from its inception an outstanding example of contemporary architecture. An opening concert worthy of this great hall was devised, with the Gewandhaus Orchestra's music director on the podium, and some contemporary works along with Schumann's Symphony No. 1 and Haydn's Sinfonia Concertante in B-flat Major on the program. Herbert thought it would be fitting to select one of the student's compositions. Rector Christoph Krummacher suggested a Chilean student, Andrés Maupoint. He was in Paris for a semester as an exchange student and could hardly believe his good fortune when he received the news. During the 2000/2001 Christmas holidays, he met the maestro in his Leipzig apartment on the top floor of the Mendelssohn House to explain his compositions and to propose a piece for the performance. Blomstedt could remember that he had once met Maupoint at church and was happy to see him again. They talked about music for more than an hour, and finally Maupoint recommended his composition *Fünf Bilder* (Five images) as particularly suitable for a conservatory orchestra. "The images are very different. I explained the examples for each and my thoughts, the symbolism, playing instructions, and so on. Herbert Blomstedt took the score and a CD recording of the composition and subsequently let me know that he wanted to include this piece in the program. His comment was that it was a wonderful piece with clearly recognizable architecture and coherence. He added, 'The composer knows exactly what he wants. That makes the conductor's work easy.' "[14]

Professor Kluttig, the chair of conducting, directed the first rehearsals and then Blomstedt conducted the last three *tutti* rehearsals. The orchestra was very well prepared, which of course is not to be taken for granted with a contemporary piece. Maupoint knows this from experience. "Many young musicians are skeptical, are not motivated to play it, and usually have little experience with New Music. In the beginning, there is often a certain detachment there, but when people see how the form slowly emerges and how they should react, then they enjoy it. In one of the *Bilder* [images], the musicians have to make sounds with their mouths—for example, *tsk, tsk, tsk, tsk, tsk,* or *a!* That was new to them; some were initially embarrassed or simply reluctant. But after a while, everyone joined in."

When rehearsals began, Maupoint was quite anxious, although it was not a premiere, and he knew how the piece sounded. But when

Blomstedt began to talk about tonal colors (timbre) and to draw the orchestra's attention to them, Maupoint felt this was a real godsend because he works with blocks of sounds and timbres when composing. He had provided comments for each of the parts of his composition. During the rehearsals, he could express his wishes that something be played in a very particular way. The young composer felt the maestro was completely open to his piece, kept strictly to the score, and did not want to change or replace anything:

> Sometimes I, and also some of my colleagues, have encountered orchestras that did not like to do something extraordinary—for example, making sounds with their mouths or using other objects in addition to their instruments to produce tonal color. A more conservative conductor once said, "I know my musicians. They don't need to do it like this." I was very pleased with Mr. Blomstedt's attitude, because he respected me one hundred percent as a composer and held to the score. I thought he would perhaps think some things were funny. When talking with other musicians about Blomstedt, they instantly make the association "Blomstedt equals classics." He is not very well known for performing contemporary music, except for, of course, such well-known composers as Krzysztof Penderecki, György Ligeti, and the like. I think he probably does not often have the opportunity to perform contemporary music. In Leipzig and elsewhere, the public generally wants to hear something familiar, so one has to perform this as well. It is a vicious circle.

When asked about this, Herbert corrected this assessment somewhat: "In fact, in my early years, I performed quite a lot of contemporary music, including many premieres and pieces by composers who were not so well known. At the same time, enough other colleagues take this on. Now I see my task rather as introducing a still underrated and little-known composer such as Anton Bruckner to the concert audience and not leaving the classical and baroque eras entirely up to the experts of original sound."

Maupoint felt that the three rehearsals in the university were

> very pleasant because Blomstedt is a pleasant conductor. The students really loved him because he has a wonderful personality. The musicians from the Gewandhaus say the same thing. At the same time, he is very strict and knows exactly what he wants. He knows a

vast amount and sees things clearly. It is rare for a conductor in his position to get along well with others. He is very professional, but he also takes time for people in all possible positions, regardless of their background. His relationship with God, with the Bible, with Jesus, has, of course, shaped him—consciously or unconsciously—so that his Christianity is deeply rooted within him in a very natural and self-evident way. One can feel that music is not work for him but service to God and humankind. As a result, he can be strict and very caring concurrently with the orchestra. Perhaps not all the musicians know that he is a Christian and an Adventist, but they appreciate his approach. And so, he also gets treated with a lot of respect.

The young composer was also impressed by the fact that Blomstedt found a printing error in his piece: at one point, there was a low B in the score for the viola, which does not exist for this instrument! Now, in this composition, the individual instruments were noted *divisi*; that is, each had a different part. "There are thousands of notes in the score, and the maestro finds an incorrectly printed one. That is like finding the proverbial needle in a haystack!"

Dr. Christoph Sramek, an honorary professor at the University of Music and Theater in Leipzig and a member of the Saxony Music Association (an association for the promotion of contemporary music in Saxony), feels like a "partner of contemporary composers." When Maupoint was Dimitri Terzakis's student, Dr. Sramek had taken note of him because of the world premiere of one of his chamber music works and ever since had thought him to be an interesting composer. When he heard *Fünf Bilder,* conducted by Blomstedt, at the Great Hall's opening ceremony,

I was so moved by this music that tears ran down my face in the middle of the piece. And I felt that Herbert Blomstedt is a conductor with a special sensibility for musical timbres. Already in the past I have sometimes thought when listening to recordings of his interpretations of traditional music, "Where did that instrument come from? I have to look it up in the score; I've never heard that before." And indeed, there it was! Blomstedt makes timbres blossom and has a flair for the ratio of orchestral timbres, one to another, like no other conductor.

Once, during the 1980s, I taught an interpretation seminar, and we looked at a Bruckner symphony—I believe the third. I simply compared different recordings with each other, including one with

Blomstedt—whom I did not yet know personally—and the Staats-kapelle Dresden. Back then I experienced the same thing. I thought, *Now I have heard several recordings of this symphony with other con-ductors. Where is this instrument suddenly coming from?* I had never noticed it in the score before. I think this is basically one of his special strengths.

Maupoint, who deals so remarkably with musical timbres and is influenced somewhat by Olivier Messiaen, had found a master conductor who turned his composition into such music that I was moved to tears. The person seated next to me asked whether I was not feeling well, but I could only say, "No, but I've been waiting for a moment such as this for twenty years." After having accompanied and paved some of the way for the composers of my generation, who are now fifty to sixty years old—like Bernd Franke, Reinhard Pfundt, and, to a certain degree, Steffen Schleiermacher—I had been looking for a composer from the younger generation who could develop a similar energy, but I just did not find anyone. By this, I do not want to say anything against different Leipziger com-posers, some of whom are my friends. But I suddenly felt that here is a composer who, illuminated by Herbert Blomstedt, could unfold his full energy. Since that time, I have been working with Maupoint.

Sramek was aware of the fact that this was his subjective impression. Anxiously, he waited to see how the audience would respond at the end. It gave him "great joy" that his colleagues and the students also shared his impression that something big had started here. There was never-ending applause when the last note died away, and the general consensus was that the new hall of this university, so rich in tradition, was inaugurated with a worthy piece.

Nordic tradition in Leipzig

Scandinavia and Leipzig have a lot of history in common. In addition to trade relations that span many centuries, people such as King Gustav Adolf, the theologian Nathan Söderblom, and the composer Edvard Grieg, left their mark in the Saxon metropolis.

Christoph Sramek says,

Nordic music is linked to some extent to Leipzig's University of Music, because the most significant student was Edvard Grieg. I found it very interesting that Mr. Blomstedt brought Nordic music, which is at home here, a little closer—even going beyond Grieg. His appointment was in this respect a fortunate coincidence for the city of Leipzig.

Renowned musicologists, especially Theodor Adorno, have questioned the Finnish composer Jean Sibelius concerning inner dynamics, which are often contained in the progression of a symphony, suggesting that he did not respect these. But if one understands something of the mentality of northerners, one can sense that this was not at all important for Sibelius. Applying German standards to his music would therefore prove to be completely inadequate. Some conductors have been trying to cheat and have endeavored to generate what was not there naturally. But Sibelius—a man who was influenced by his relationship with nature—took a very different approach. One becomes aware that issues such as the foreground and background, the main theme and transitions in the sense of the Viennese classics are not applicable here.

Herbert Blomstedt, in his interpretations of Sibelius, never tried to make him into a German composer but simply knew how to perform his music. In my opinion, he played Sibelius as he should be played: with colorful nuances throughout but not with added-on dynamics.

Herbert Blomstedt is aware of the social dimension in music. In the 1950s, there was a tendency to focus only on the structural development in the music. However, Blomstedt is conscious of the fact that there are always spiritual backgrounds to compositions. It is very evident that he incorporates this aspect in his interpretations. He always tried to find the spirit of the music, whatever that may look like. This is more difficult because the spirit speaks without words; thus, it's about music stirring something spiritual and not just superficially performing or playing techniques.

In memory of someone great—to Edvard Grieg

The Norwegian Edvard Grieg was one of the most significant among the many foreign students of importance at the conservatory founded by Mendelssohn in Leipzig. The Leipzig publisher C. F. Peters published his works, and the publishing director, Dr. Max Abraham, was his personal friend. Grieg often remained for months with his friend in Leipzig, who provided him with two rooms in his publishing house in Talstraße 10 [Valley Street]. The now beautifully restored home houses the Grieg Begegnungsstätte [meeting place]. On September 19, 2009, a bust of the composer, designed and sculpted by Felix Ludwig, was placed in the garden in front of the house. Before his retirement, the artist was a bassist in the Gewandhaus Orchestra and has a great sense of musical qualities also as a sculptor. I donated the impressive artwork of my compatriot with joy.[15]

Tours on four continents

Following summer performances in Edinburgh, Manchester, and at the London Promenade Concerts, the twentieth anniversary of the new Gewandhaus was celebrated in October 2001 with a program purely of Brahms—the Violin Concerto, with Nikolaj Znaider, and Symphony No. 4.

Straight afterwards they went on a tour in the United States, and a month later Blomstedt was a guest at the Santa Cecilia Orchestra in Rome with two performances of Brahms's *A German Requiem*.

The spring of 2002 brought another tour to Japan; this time with stopovers in Hong Kong and Taiwan. They played works by Beethoven, Bruckner, Mozart, and Sibelius. Flooding in central Germany gave rise to a benefit concert in August, in which Mahler's Symphony No. 5 and Mozart's "Haffner" Symphony were performed. The day before the concert the orchestra had performed the same program at the *Festspiele Mecklenburg-Vorpommern* (a music festival in Mecklenburg-Vorpommern, Germany).

Two months later the LGO did a tour of Germany with concerts in eight cities across the country, ending with a trip to the Barbican Centre in London for Leipzig Day.

The actor Ulrich Mühe was a guest at the UNICEF concert on December 1, 2002; in between Jean Sibelius's *Swan of Tuonela* and Paul Dukas's *The Sorcerer's Apprentice*, he read Johann Wolfgang von Goethe's ballad of *The Sorcerer's Apprentice*.

The LGO's year had a festive ending with Nancy Argenta, Michael Chance, Christoph Genz, and Johannes Mannov as soloists in Handel's *Messiah*.

A Beethoven cycle was presented in the 2002/2003 season, which was warmly welcomed by the public as well as by the media and followed with great interest.

Besides complete symphonies, works for soloists and the orchestra were performed; the *Missa solemnis* was played on March 6, 2003, and featured Juliane Banse, Iris Vermillion, Christian Elsner, and Thomas

Quasthoff. The *Missa* was Blomstedt's first concert with the Gewandhaus Orchestra after the death of his wife, Waltraud, on February 8. At the time of Waltraud's passing, he was guest conducting the NHK Symphony Orchestra in Tokyo. He never failed to appear for a single concert in the following weeks despite a very tight schedule, and by mid-March, he had conducted three concerts with the NDR Symphony Orchestra. In early April, he performed seven concerts with the SFS in San Francisco.

In June, there was a premiere of a special kind when the Gewandhaus Orchestra performed with Blomstedt in Australia. In Melbourne and Sydney, they presented Beethoven's "Pastoral" Symphony, Schumann's Cello Concerto, and the overture to Mendelssohn's *A Midsummer Night's Dream*. On the second program performed in Sydney, Brisbane, Kuala Lumpur, and Singapore were Richard Strauss's *A Hero's Life* and Wolfgang Amadeus Mozart's "Jupiter Symphony."

Curiosity, impressive knowledge of the score, and a guiding hand

Sebastian Breuninger, the first concertmaster of the Gewandhaus Orchestra, wrote the following about Herbert Blomstedt:

> It is by no means an easy task to do justice to a personality like Herbert Blomstedt with words. One can learn an immense amount about music and how to perform it from him. It's exemplary how he explores all things. There is no bar in the score on which he could not give exhaustive information. He knows a lot about the composers and their works. His curiosity to learn more and advance further has not diminished with age. Each of his interpretations is an exciting, new production, in which faithfulness to the text and impressive knowledge of the score are fundamental requirements. Perhaps restraining one's own personality creates a poignant authenticity of expression. Although there is deservedly much talk about his Beethoven, Bruckner, and Brahms interpretations, his respect for music in general makes him one of the foremost advocates of many other composers, including those who sometimes are brushed over or treated inadequately. He has done great things for Sibelius, and other less well-known Scandinavian composers have also played a major role in his programs. With very few exceptions, personally, I have performed only real milestones of music history with Herbert Blomstedt, even when he has often, with great dedication, performed lesser-known music, especially from Scandinavia, with

us and also with other orchestras. His ability to grasp things thoroughly and without bias, as well as wanting to and being able to ennoble and refine everything, is important for an understanding of his consistently respectful attitude.

I also remember a particularly emotional *Pathétique* by Pyotr Tchaikovsky, where this work sounded unusually pure, clear, and definitive through his guiding hand. He uses every available opportunity to make the music comprehensible to the listener but, above all, to make it admirable and to transmit his love for this particular art form to anyone who has the smallest openness for it. Children in particular have a strong sense of truthfulness. I'll never forget the farewell that Leipziger children and teenagers gave Herbert Blomstedt after his last school concert. One had the impression that there must be a great pop star in the place, and there stood an almost eighty-year-old man on stage, who made no fuss about appearances. No performer is better suited than Herbert Blomstedt to illustrate how one can go beyond the limits of one's own personality in making music by subscribing to an entirely universal idea.[16]

Early in the 2003/2004 season, the Gewandhaus Orchestra played at an open-air concert in Rosental, a park in Leipzig. Despite rainy weather, their performance of Maurice Ravel's *Boléro* and Camille Saint-Saëns's *Carnival of the Animals* provided a cheerful atmosphere, with "epic and witty" narration between movements by Herbert Blomstedt.[17]

In September, the Gewandhaus music director went to Amsterdam, performing Beethoven's and Tchaikovsky's fourth symphonies with the Concertgebouw Orchestra. In January and February of the following year, they did a four-week tour through the Netherlands and across the United States.

At the beginning of October 2003, the Violin Concerto by Antonín Dvořák was performed with Julia Fischer, a young violinist from Munich, and repeated on October 16 in Munich. The "new star in the violin sky," together with a "brilliantly performing orchestra," received "cheers from the audience, a hug from the Gewandhaus music director, and played Paganini's Caprice No. 2 as an encore," reported Katrin Seidel from the *Leipziger Volkszeitung* on October 4, 2003.[18]

On Reformation Day, *Elijah*—"a brilliant commencement" to the Mendelssohn Festival—was performed by the LGO, together with the Gewandhaus Choir and Gewandhaus Chamber Choir. *Elijah* also featured the soloists Sibylla Rubens (soprano), Nathalie Stutzmann (contralto), James Taylor (tenor), Christian Gerhaher (baritone), and Michael

Schönheit (organist). A live recording of the performance was released by RCA Red Seal in 2005.[19] The critic Tobias Wolf voiced the opinion of many listeners with his enthusiastic review: "Surreal . . . more surreal . . . breathtaking . . . magical moments."[20]

Incident in Turin

For the first two months of 2004, Blomstedt was guest conducting various international orchestras before he went on a smaller tour with the LGO, which led them from London via Dortmund and Bregenz to Italy. As usual, Herbert's assistant, Marie Theres Pless, accompanied them on this trip. She remembers the dramatic hours when her boss had to cancel a concert for the first time due to health reasons:

> On May 4, Mr. Blomstedt conducted a concert with the LGO, performing Richard Strauss's *Don Juan* and *Till Eulenspiegel's Merry Pranks* and Antonín Dvořák's Symphony No. 9 in the Kurhaus of Meran. As usual, we arrived in the morning. Mr. Blomstedt rested after lunch, then there was an acoustic rehearsal, and the concert began soon afterwards. During the intermission, as always, the maestro did not say much, just asked rather abruptly, "What actually is the elevation in Meran?" I had not the slightest notion that he might not be feeling well and simply replied, "I don't know, but I don't think it's very high." He said something about pressure on his chest, but because he is always so healthy, I didn't think anything of it and asked whether I could do something for him. "No, no; it's fine," he replied. The second part of the concert went well and without any problems. The next morning after breakfast we continued on by car to Turin. During the 270-mile drive, Mr. Blomstedt, as always, studied scores or slept a little; after all, the next concert was scheduled for that evening. After arriving in Turin, we checked into our hotel rooms, ate a little something, and Mr. Blomstedt suddenly said, "I think I need to call my brother Norman." As he described his symptoms to his brother on the phone, Norman told him to go and see a doctor immediately—Mr. Blomstedt obviously had heart problems. With the help of the hotel staff, we called a doctor who came very quickly and carried out an initial examination. His advice was to go to the hospital immediately because there was obviously an imminent risk there. Whether it was a heart attack, no one could say at that time because communication was difficult, with the doctor's broken English and German and our smattering

of Italian. An ambulance was called, and the medics took Mr. Blomstedt to a nearby university hospital. In the meantime, the orchestra had arrived, and the manager Andreas Schulz was informed. At that point in time, we did not yet know how it would all work out or whether Mr. Blomstedt's heart condition could be resolved and brought under control with some medication. Meanwhile, the local concert organizers did their utmost in helping us to communicate with the Italian doctors and to ensure the best medical care. It slowly became apparent that the problem could not be easily solved. Despite all the commotion, there were also a few amusing aspects, such as when Mr. Blomstedt lay in the emergency room, having a multilingual discussion with the Italian heart specialists who were trying to explain to him what was happening and what needed to be done. When Mr. Blomstedt argued, "But I have a concert tonight; can't you do the procedure tomorrow?" the physician flatly refused. So half the afternoon passed by. Meanwhile, attempts were made to find a substitute conductor for the concert. Even Mr. Chailly, who was in Milan, had been informed by this time and took the initiative to contact us. From his side, he did everything possible to support the speedy coordination of the medical procedure; indeed, all those involved made an incredible effort to help.

Because time was of the essence, Mr. Blomstedt had a cardiac catheterization done. The concert had to be canceled because they could not find a replacement conductor at such short notice. Thomas Dausgaard substituted for the remaining three concerts of the tour. The Turin concert was rescheduled for the following year.

I stayed in the hospital until I knew that everything was fine. The procedure went smoothly. Eventually, a doctor came out and said to me, "Your husband is doing well!" I said, "He is not my husband, but I am nonetheless very pleased." By this time, it was late in the evening. The orchestra continued on their travels in the morning, and I stayed in Turin for the next five days to check on things and to be at the hospital for one to two hours during visitor hours. One needed to explain to the hospital staff, for example, that Mr. Blomstedt is a strict vegetarian and did not like a few particular vegetables. Together we somehow succeeded with this, and we had some fun. Mr. Blomstedt recovered quickly, and in less than a week, we organized travel arrangements for him to return to his apartment in Lucerne. Mr. Schacke, who had arrived in the meantime, requested the [Red

Cross's help in transporting Mr. Blomstedt], and I could head home.

During all this time, I did not sense that Mr. Blomstedt was afraid. Although in general he reacts sensitively on the subject of disease and hospitalization in connection with other people, he behaved very composedly and responded matter-of-factly to the circumstances. Of course, there were the usual considerations, as to how this life-threatening narrowing of the arteries had come about. But given that the maestro lives an exemplarily healthy lifestyle, without the use of alcohol, tobacco, and other harmful substances, one could conclude that too much stress could have been the cause.[21]

After his forced break, Herbert Blomstedt celebrated his fiftieth stage anniversary on June 24, 2004, in Leipzig. He chose the same program that he performed for his debut in Stockholm: Bach's Suite No. 2 in B Minor, Beethoven's Piano Concerto No. 1, and Hindemith's symphony *Mathis der Maler*. The soloists were Katalin Kramarics, the first solo flautist of the Gewandhaus Orchestra, and Richard Goode on the piano.

Gewandhaus before and after the German reunification

Up until the reunification of Germany, the orchestra was made up almost exclusively of local musicians. The reason for this was that in GDR times the four conservatories in Leipzig, Dresden, Weimar, and Berlin were training for their respective catchment areas—and had employment guarantees for graduates! The best students were given the top positions in the local orchestras. In this way, the musicians of each orchestra were homogeneously shaped by their educational institutions, which in the case of the Gewandhaus Orchestra created a very specific sound, often described as "warm, dark, and saturated." The LGO kept to themselves and preserved its unique sound. There was, however, one drawback in that they were rather immune to external stimuli.

The young Israeli violist Nimrod Guez shares his experiences with the Gewandhaus Orchestra from 2005 to 2007:

It was very interesting for me as a young musician to begin in an orchestra with such tradition, where a certain playing style has been maintained for many years and a relatively closed group of people has known each other for many years. At first, one does not quite know how to behave and what to expect. Indeed, for a long time, the LGO had almost exclusively recruited musicians from their own locale, but when I joined, a new direction had already been taken so that there were already a few foreigners. I felt a strong sense of family and belonging in the orchestra, which can sometimes be constraining but can also be helpful and supportive once you belong.

I have been strongly influenced by Tabea Zimmermann, who represents a younger generation of musicians with a certain idea of how to engage with classical music. In this respect, it was particularly interesting for me to play under Mr. Blomstedt because he's been around for so long and conducts the most important orchestras in the world. One can see that he comes from a certain tradition but has learned and discovered new things because he's involved with music daily. It was incredibly inspiring to witness his legendary experience and tremendous dedication to development, his vast respect for music, which leads him to always ask how something is meant to be, and should be, understood and what new technical possibilities there are. Mr. Blomstedt seems so fresh and young in this respect. He is curious and is pronouncedly affectionate with music. I remember once when I was a section leader and had a question; he first of all expressed his delight with the question. His answer showed that he was bearing the whole score in mind and the role that our viola voice had in this whole was important to him. Of course, it shows that he is a trained violinist because one can only have his idea of sound if one has held the instrument under one's own chin and from his own practice understands something of bowing technique.

A natural friendship developed between us. After my audition, we had a brief conversation, and despite all his due reserve, I [thought], *I am warmly welcomed, and he is aware of the fact that I am young and standing at the beginning of my career, and he will help me.* We sat together and chatted a bit. He asked me where I came from, and so on. I really had the feeling that he wanted to get to know me as a person—he wasn't just being polite!

It was already his last season when I joined; everyone knew him well and knew where they stood with him. For many, this was fine; for others, less so. This is also normal. But I found it remarkable that the young people in the orchestra were very taken with him, and he appealed to them. And I had a good friend, close to retirement, who retained his interest in Blomstedt and loved the maestro above all. In the following seasons, the orchestra was always very joyful when HB came as a guest, and they were eager to learn new things. He is truly inspiring.[22]

The last season

"We are happy now that we are here where we belong—with you in Leipzig": with these words, Herbert Blomstedt, speaking for the entire orchestra, began the LGO's first home concert in early September 2004—his last season in Leipzig. One couldn't ignore the quiet melancholy.[23] Three concerts in Athens and Edinburgh had preceded this one, and in October, there would be a tour through the eastern part of the United States with a purely Brahms program. On Reformation Day, Blomstedt conducted the Berlin Philharmonic, performing Johannes Brahms's Symphony No. 2 and Symphony No. 4. In early December, he conducted a much-acclaimed performance of George Frideric Handel's *Messiah*, with the RIAS Chamber Choir and the soloists Johanna Stojkovic (soprano), Ingeborg Danz (alto), Christoph Genz (tenor), and Christian Gerhaher (baritone).

After the Indian Ocean tsunami in December 2004, the Gewandhaus Orchestra gave a benefit concert with their chief conductor in the St. Thomas Church, performing Johann Sebastian Bach's Suite No. 2 in B Minor and his Violin Concerto in A Minor.

In January 2005, Herbert Blomstedt made a late debut: he stepped into the orchestra pit of the Leipzig Opera House for the first time. He had chosen *Fidelio*, his favorite opera. On January 29, 2005, Georg-Friedrich Kühn from *Deutschlandradio Kultur* (a German culture-oriented radio station) praised Blomstedt for his "very streamlined, trim Beethoven, without any padding nor pathetic exaggeration." In the *Leipziger Almanach*, Sebastian Schmideler's article was headlined, "Brilliance of the Music, Misery of the Management." It alluded to the fact that heavy criticism and boos from the audience had been directed at the opera management. The reviewer highlighted the "inviolable integrity of this conductor" and stated, "With his steady equanimity and unrelenting discipline, he succeeds in credibly showing the high moral claims of this oratorio to the ensemble, the opera choir, and his formidable orchestra. For this unmistakable sincerity in successfully conveying the message, the audience applauded him. . . . Loud cheers and enthusiasm came from all the seats."[24]

During the second half of February, the LGO went on a final tour to Japan, with a stopover in Taiwan. In April, Herbert traveled to San Francisco, where he performed seven concerts with the SFS.

For the conclusion of the Leipzig Bach Festival in May, he, his orchestra, and the Gewandhaus Chamber Choir performed Johann Sebastian Bach's Mass in B Minor. The soloists were Ruth Ziesak (soprano), Anna

Larsson (contralto), Christoph Genz (tenor), and Dietrich Henschel (baritone). "Blomstedt reaches into the soul in the St. Thomas Church," wrote Peter Korfmacher of the *Leipziger Volkszeitung.* "The sound has lost none of its delicacy, or its brilliance."[25]

On their last tour with Blomstedt, the Gewandhaus Orchestra traveled first to Essen and Cologne, where Sibelius's and Tchaikovsky's sixth symphonies were on the program. Audiences and critics responded with great enthusiasm. Michael Stenger wrote the following in the German newspaper *Westdeutsche Allgemeine Zeitung* for the May 22, 2005, edition: "Another acclaimed evening with Blomstedt . . . a very special event, because everything vain is foreign to him, because he—one almost wants to say, in good German tradition—serves the music. . . . The orchestra, which Blomstedt . . . successfully led into the new millennium, loves their boss. One can feel it. . . . Blomstedt with his sincerity remains an exceptional phenomenon for me."[26] After this, they performed works by Grieg, Brahms, and Stenhammar in Oslo, and one week later they presented Bruckner's Symphony No. 8 in Zurich—almost as if in anticipation of the final concert.

Just a few weeks after the Mass in B Minor, another famous sacred work was on the Gewandhaus Orchestra's program: Brahms's *A German Requiem,* with Christiane Oelze and Christian Gerhaher as soloists. It was the last time that the Gewandhaus Choir and the Gewandhaus Chamber Choir performed with Blomstedt as the presiding music director.

Farewell and welcome

Herbert Blomstedt's contract in Leipzig was initially for a period of five years and was extended by two years in 2003. Now in 2005, it was time for active retirement. He had turned down many requests from the world's top orchestras in recent years due to time constraints. That could change now. Henceforth, Blomstedt wanted to be available for all top orchestras.

On July 1, 2005, the eighteenth Gewandhaus music director was bid farewell in the ballroom of the Old Town Hall. Herbert's successor, Riccardo Chailly, had arrived, and both maestri embraced each other at the finale to the thunderous applause of the audience. The following day MDR Figaro, a German radio station, ascertained that seldom had a change of office in the Gewandhaus taken place so calmly and without a hitch.[27]

The lord mayor, Wolfgang Tiefensee, referred to the departing Gewandhaus music director as "a godsend for Leipzig and the Gewandhaus

Orchestra." A portrait of the maestro, painted by Bernhard Heisig, was presented to Herbert by Mayor Tiefensee; Herbert immediately placed it at the disposal of the Museum of Fine Arts in Leipzig. Peter Pastreich, Blomstedt's manager from the time in San Francisco, gave the laudatory speech, which has now become legendary; the speech was filled with humor and stories, mainly about the Spartan lifestyle of his former music director. Much to the amusement of the invited guests, Blomstedt assured them that "most of it is true."[28] Herbert made it clear that this was not really a good-bye but rather a "see you later." Nevertheless, his calendar was already full of concert dates with famous orchestras for the next few years.

The eighteenth Gewandhaus music director had been inaugurated into his office with Bach and Bruckner. Both composers are connected to Leipzig in a special way: Bach through his work as cantor of the St. Thomas Church, and Bruckner since the premiere of his Symphony No. 7, with Arthur Nikisch conducting, at the end of 1884 in the Leipzig Stadttheater (city theater), which is considered the beginning of Leipzig's Bruckner tradition. Blomstedt noted in his speech that no other orchestra was so convincingly predestined to interpret Bruckner as the LGO. Consequently, the gala concert marking the end of their shared musical work featured Johann Sebastian Bach's Prelude and Fugue for Organ in E-flat Major, played by Michael Schönheit, as well as Anton Bruckner's Symphony No. 8, which later appeared as a live recording under the German label Querstand.

When, at the end of the concert, Blomstedt was appointed as the honorary conductor of the LGO, another performance of *Fidelio* was already scheduled in two months' time.

The Gewandhaus Orchestra has remained Herbert Blomstedt's home. He confirms with pleasure that he feels like he is coming home when he arrives in Leipzig again; this is usually repeated several times a year. It is apparent that the audience as well still welcomes Blomstedt as their old conductor. He is guaranteed standing ovations in Leipzig.

Sebastian Breuninger said that "the orchestra did not really want to bid him farewell but rather welcome him in the new position of honorary conductor. And since then, in rehearsals and concerts, I've seen an even freer, more relaxed Herbert Blomstedt, full of fresh energy and free from the burden of not always having to deal with the daily tasks of a principal conductor and only focused on what's really essential and enduring."[29]

Milestones and memories

On the occasion of his eightieth birthday, Herbert Blomstedt conducted three concerts with the Gewandhaus Orchestra, featuring Julian Rachlin as soloist. On the program were works by Jean Sibelius. After this, he went on tour in Germany.

On July 17, 2011, the former Gewandhaus music director received the Bach Medal of the city of Leipzig during the Bach Festival in the Alten Handelsbörse (old stock exchange). In their statement, the panel of judges identified him as "one of the few symphony orchestra conductors who have regularly included works by Johann Sebastian Bach in their programs." Professor Andreas Schulz stressed in his very heartfelt speech that by the 1950s Blomstedt already strove for purity in performance practice, calling the honoree not only an "exceptional conductor but also an exceptional man."

For his eighty-fifth birthday on July 11, 2012, the city of Leipzig planted a Kentucky coffeetree, which was grandly unveiled in his presence on September 26, 2012, for their honorary conductor in the park between the Gewandhaus and the Moritzbastei cultural center. A memorial stone with a golden plaque makes mention of Herbert Blomstedt and his accomplishments in Leipzig. In his speech, the Gewandhaus director Andreas Schulz pointed out that the tree grows not only particularly high—some seventy feet—but also has very deep roots, and in this way drew parallels to the work and the character of the honored maestro.

1. "True pleasure is a serious business." This quote from Seneca is inscribed on the organ in the concert hall of the Leipzig Gewandhaus Orchestra.

2. Hartmut Brauer and Peter Michael Borck, interview by UW, September 30, 2010, Leipzig. In this chapter, all quotations and information from both musicians are taken from this interview and later clarifying communications.

3. Jens F. Laurson, "Leipzig Gewandhaus Orchestra Brings Old World Tradition to US," Culture, *Deutsche Welle*, February 17, 2010, accessed October 7, 2016, http://www .dw.com/en/leipzig-gewandhaus-orchestra-brings-old-world-tradition-to-us/a-5255456.

4. See Johannes Forner, *Kurt Masur: Zeiten und Klänge,Biographie,* (Berlin: Propyläen, 2002), 330ff.

5. Ibid., 331ff.

6. "Schon zweihundert Jahre miteinander musiziert," review of concert performance by Leipzig Gewandhaus Orchestra, Herbert Blomstedt conducting, *Frankfurter Allgemeine Zeitung*, September 3, 1998; *Die Welt*, September 3, 1998.

7. Herbert Blomstedt to UW, personal communication, March 15, 2012.

8. Andreas Schulz, interview by UW, June 5, 2006; additional information added later.

9. *Historical performance practice* means "performing music with special attention to the technology and performance conventions that were present when a piece of music was composed." "What Is Historically Informed Performance?" Society for Historically Informed Performance, accessed October 7, 2016, https://sohipboston.squarespace.com /what-is-hip/.

10. *Live Concert From the Church of St. Nicolai, Leipzig: "Wir sind das Volk," Leipzig Commemorates 9th October 1989* (Victoria Mullova/Nancy Argenta/St. Thomas Boy's Choir/ Leipzig Gewandhaus Orchestra/Herbert Blomstedt) Arthaus DVD B00004W5WN, 2000.

11. "Pianist Jewgenij Kissin und Gewandhausorchester unter Blomstedt mit Beethoven und Bruckner," *Leipziger Volkszeitung*, February 12, 2000.

12. Herbert Blomstedt, quoted in *Leipziger Volkszeitung*, Christmas 2007.

13. Peter Korfmacher to Herbert Blomstedt, Christmas letter, December 2007. Printed with permission of the author.

14. Andrés Maupoint and Dr. Christoph Sramek, interview by UW, September 16, 2007, Leipzig. All quotations in this chapter from these two musicians are taken from this interview.

15. Herbert Blomstedt to UW, personal communication, July 29, 2012. At the time of Grieg's birth in 1843, Norway was still a part of Sweden.

16. Sebastian Breuninger wrote these words of appreciation for Herbert Blomstedt for this book.

17. Peter Korfmacher, "Sonnabend und gestern Abend: Oper und Gewandhaus im Leipziger Rosental," review of concert performance by the Leipzig Gewandhaus Orchestra, conducted by Herbert Blomstedt, *Leipziger Volkszeitung*, September 1, 2003.

18. Katrin Seidel, "Herbert Blomstedt dirigierte vor ausverkauftem Konzerthaus Werke von Johannes Brahms, Antonín Dvoràk," review of concert performance by Julia Fischer (violinist) and the Leipzig Gewandhaus Orchestra, conducted by Herbert Blomstedt, *Leipziger Volkszeitung*, October 4, 2003.

19. *Mendelssohn: Elias* (Sibylla Rubens/Nathalie Stutzmann/James Taylor/Christian Gerhaher/Leipzig Gewandhaus Orchestra/Gewandhaus Chamber Choir/Gewandhaus Choir/Herbert Blomstedt) RCA Red Seal double CD B0009W4M1W, 2005.

20. Tobias Wolf, "Felix-Mendelssohn-Bartholdy-Festtage 2003 / Glanzvoller Auftakt: 'Elias,'" *Leipziger Volkszeitung*, November 3, 2003.

21. Marie Theres Pless, interview by UW, July 17, 2011, Leipzig.

22. Nimrod Guez, interview by UW, May 20, 2010, Munich.

23. Peter Korfmacher, "Gestern Abend im großen Saal: Herbert Blomstedt, Gewandhausorchester und Jean-Yves Thibaudet eröffnen," *Leipziger Volkszeitung*, September 4, 2004.

24. Sebastian Schmideler, "Glanz der Musik, Elend der Regie: 'Fidelio' in Leipzig," *Leipzig Almanach*, January 31, 2005, http://www.leipzig-almanach.de/buehne_glanz _der_musik_elend_der_regie_fidelio_in_leipzig_sebastian_schmideler.html.

25. Peter Korfmacher, *Leipziger Volkszeitung*, May 10, 2005. Interested readers can decide for themselves whether the enthusiastic critic was correct in his impression, on the basis of the live recording released as a DVD by EuroArts (B000B6N5YG). In a bonus film, Herbert Blomstedt gives a short introduction to the work and talks about his special relationship with Bach. See *Bach: Mass in B Minor* (Ruth Ziesak/Anna Larsson/Christoph Genz/Dietrich Henschel/Leipzig Gewandhaus Orchestra/Gewandhaus Chamber Choir /Herbert Blomstedt) EuroArts DVD B000B6N5YG, 2005.

26. Michael Stenger, *Westdeutsche Allgemeine Zeitung*, May 22, 2005.

27. Dieter David Scholz, interview by MDR-Figaro, July 2, 2005.

28. Peter Pastreich's speech is quoted in Martin U. K. Lengemann, *Herbert Blomstedt. Eine Annäherung in Text und Bild* (Berlin: B&S Siebenhaar, 2007), 102ff.

29. Sebastian Breuninger to UW, personal communication, May 1, 2011.

Around the World as Honorary and Guest Conductor

Success, as I see it, is a result, not a goal.
—Gustave Flaubert

H ERBERT BLOMSTEDT LIKES TO describe himself as a freelance pensioner since his retirement from the position of music director of the Gewandhaus Orchestra. He has no lack of contracts—he is the honorary conductor of seven leading orchestras worldwide and regularly appears as a guest conductor with several others. This chapter outlines Blomstedt's collaboration with orchestras that have not been previously mentioned or only briefly alluded to.

Roy Branson said the following about Herbert:

> What impresses me very much about HB after all these years is that he is no different now than when he was a young man. What he is now, he was then. All of the basic characteristics were there. Since then, of course, he has had many experiences, very complex ones. His strengths, in my opinion, include consistency, focus, and all the elements of discipline. He sees through all kinds of artificiality, whether it's in church, in music, in community—he is going to be himself.
>
> I don't see a contradiction between his strictness on the one side and his open-mindedness on the other. The strictness is a focus on his efforts for what he has to do. You see it in people who produce great theology or great science. That does not mean that you have to be intolerant of different viewpoints.
>
> There is one other thing to mention: if you go backstage, there are a lot of people who come around, but eventually they leave. Then the conductor, especially a guest conductor, goes to a hotel or

an airplane. What a lonely life! I once asked him about it, and he said, "It's good to be lonely." You have to care a lot about your work and have to be very strong psychologically to live this sort of life.[1]

The NHK Symphony Orchestra in Japan

From October 19 to 26, 1973, the Staatskapelle Dresden took a long-planned trip to Japan, led by its then still secret boss. The country fascinated him straightaway. Representatives of the NHK Symphony Orchestra came to the concerts and were so impressed by Blomstedt that they immediately invited him for a guest appearance.

Yet, it wasn't until November 1981 that the first collaboration with Japan's most important orchestra occurred. To this day, Herbert Blomstedt remembers some striking details, such as the time he and Waltraud were picked up at the airport with two cars. A previous guest conductor, Lovro von Matačić, had brought thirteen suitcases, and the drivers were very puzzled that a music director plus his wife had only three suitcases!

When it came time for the first rehearsal, the orchestra sat reverently, as if they were in a church, all dressed up with white shirts and suits. What a contrast to the work clothes worn at European and American rehearsals! But on that day, there was also a special reason for the formal mood: a member of the orchestra had died shortly before and was to be buried according to Buddhist rituals. The conductor asked whether he could come along, and the musicians took this as a gesture of solidarity.

In this way, the maestro won the hearts of the Japanese, especially because the concerts soon thereafter were very successful and everyone was impressed. The manager, Takao Hase, was a huge admirer of German orchestras and even spoke German. He promptly told the guest conductor that they would prefer to keep him there. But this was out of the question for Blomstedt; he had to leave his young family alone often enough in Sweden because of the Staatskapelle Dresden.

Prior to this, the NHK Symphony Orchestra had worked with a number of honorary conductors from the German classical music scene. In 1986, Blomstedt, who at the time was also head of the Staatskapelle Dresden, was made the sixth honorary conductor after Joseph Rosenstock, Joseph Keilberth, Lovro von Matačić, Wolfgang Sawallisch, and Otmar Suitner. The Japanese thought very highly of the tradition from Dresden and Leipzig, as does Herbert Blomstedt.

To this day, Herbert connects orchestral culture and orchestral music inseparably with Germany and believes these to be represented best in Dresden's and Leipzig's orchestras.

I feel very connected to Germany! Orchestral music is Germany for me! Bach, Beethoven, Brahms, Schumann, Mendelssohn, Bruckner, Mahler—these are German territory for me! That is where my music comes from! French music is also nice. I like it very much, but it does not have the same meaning as the German classics and romantics.

The NHK is technically on par with the best orchestras in Europe. But they were sometimes missing something that can be hard to describe. It also depends on what kind of music they played. One can experience surprises. I performed Beethoven symphonies with the NHK, which were comparable to the intensity and understanding that one can achieve, for example, in America. But if I play the same symphony in Dresden or Leipzig, it is even more wonderful. This is their language! There are more timbres and articulate nuances. If one plays Bruckner with a very good American orchestra, they do it perfectly, but one can sense that it is foreign to them. As efficient as they are, it is not their own language. By contrast, with the Bamberg Symphony, the Bavarian Radio Symphony Orchestra, and the orchestras in Leipzig and Dresden, one feels that they are at home there.

This is completely normal: French orchestras perform French music best. There is something light and fragrant in their music, which people who are too serious may not be able to manage so easily. Charm is the main thing.

My approach to the NHK is the same as everywhere in the world, and I am confident that the musicians are so sensitive that they understand me. Otherwise, words would not help. Perhaps, in certain cases, one can give a few technical instructions: please not so loud here, less phrasing there, or make that voice a bit more pronounced. One can always work with these issues. But if they can't bring my body language together with the notes in front of them, then the only thing left for them is to just play the notes. The Japanese do possess a great deal of sensitivity, and one can experience very beautiful performances by Bruckner, Brahms, and Beethoven. A few years ago I performed a Sibelius program, and that was excellent! For a while, a few wind instruments in the orchestra were a weak point, but now they have new, young strong ones who play Sibelius's music with an understanding that is even rare in Germany. The first piece was an early tone poem from 1895, *The Swan of Tuonela*, with a big solo part for the English horn, a sort of alto oboe.

I had a few misgivings because of this piece, but I was assured that they now had an excellent young player. And indeed, I have never heard it played so beautifully as by this Japanese girl! She hardly looked up to me; she did not need to. She played wonderfully. The hall with four thousand seats was fuller than I had ever seen it. At the end, we played the popular Symphony No. 2. My secretary in Tokyo assured me that this music was her father's favorite symphony.

In Tokyo, there is even an amateur orchestra that plays Sibelius exclusively. The Japanese love and revere Sibelius and Finnish music as if they were their own. At the same time, they also have great affinity for German music and have a lot of "German" in them. They have a group mentality and obey willingly. In the orchestra, they follow a leader. In French orchestras, for example, I have experienced much more individualism.

Although Blomstedt could not be under contract to the NHK, he wanted to contribute to its qualitative development by regular guest appearances. As time passed, he also invited top musicians from the Staatskapelle Dresden to assist him. He noted, for example, that the timpanists needed new impulses; therefore, in November 1992, he brought the solo timpanist Peter Sondermann with him, who performed Beethoven's Symphony No. 5 among other works. In the end, Sondermann received special applause not only from the conductor but from the whole orchestra. Sondermann remained for three months as a visiting professor at the Kunitachi College of Music before he returned to Dresden.

Soon guest concertmasters came from Dresden in order to optimally influence the orchestra from the first chair. Peter Mirring from Dresden and Karl Suske from Leipzig, who both appreciate their former boss very much, came along regularly on these trips. The latter once said in an interview with Claudius Böhm for the Gewandhaus Orchestra's magazine: "In Japan, it has been said repeatedly that the orchestra sounded completely different when I sat in the first chair. . . . Perhaps it was simply that the violinists made a bit more of an effort for my sake."[2]

In an interview, Peter Mirring said,

Herbert Blomstedt initiated the collaboration with the NHK Symphony Orchestra. The first musician from the Staatskapelle to partner with the NHK was Peter Sondermann, our legendary solo timpanist. Then in the 1990s, I was asked whether I could come as a guest concertmaster. Since then, as far as possible, I go back every year. It's a wonderful experience! The NHK consists only of Japanese musicians. Many speak German very well, because they have studied in Germany. These musicians are fantastically disciplined. They do not chat with each other during rehearsals, and as soon as one changes a bow stroke, the whole group knows—I don't know how they do it! They are very sharp and incredibly well prepared.

A few years ago we performed *Tristan and Isolde* together. Since they are not an opera orchestra, I thought to myself, *How can these colleagues possibly want to manage Tristan? The second act is hard!* But it wasn't a problem. By the second rehearsal, it was perfect![3]

Since then, Herbert Blomstedt travels to Tokyo every second year for several weeks to collaborate with the NHK. The management there has even filmed a documentary about the maestro. They wanted to portray every aspect of his lifestyle and asked to be allowed to film him even during his personal devotional time of Bible reading and prayer. Herbert Blomstedt was, in his own words, "at first, a little hesitant whether this was a good idea. But then I thought if they want to do this and find it interesting, why not?" They also filmed him attending church at the Leipzig Seventh-day Adventist Church. "The Japanese found it interesting that I sat in the pew and sang songs. In Germany or anywhere else in the Western world, that would interest no one, but in Japan it was broadcast on national television!"

Blomstedt is full of praise for the abundant courtesy and appreciation shown him by the NHK. He has never encountered an issue with the Sabbath while working with the NHK. Once he wanted to go with his wife, who always felt welcomed in Japan, for the weekend to an Adventist school. The high school, which is located in the mountains on the outskirts of Hiroshima and has about five hundred students, had invited the maestro to give a short address during its church service. The manager of the orchestra insisted on picking up the couple from their hotel by car and personally taking them to the railway platform of the bullet train. He waved good-bye until the doors closed. When the Blomstedts returned two days later, he stood at the same spot to pick them up again!

Very special concertgoers

The writer Kenzaburō Ōe is almost a regular guest at Blomstedt's concerts in Tokyo. When Ōe was awarded the Nobel Prize for Literature in 1994, Blomstedt conducted a celebratory concert with the Royal Stockholm

A Great Song

Philharmonic Orchestra, which included Modest Mussorgsky's *Pictures at an Exhibition*. Ōe's wife and his eldest son, Hikari, who is severely mentally impaired since birth, accompanied him. The parents described the seventeen years they spoke to Hikari without getting a sound or a single syllable from him in response. And then, suddenly, one day as his father was out walking with him, they saw a flock of large birds flying overhead, and the son said his first word: "Cranes!"

With much dedication and encouragement—from the beginning, his parents treated him as if he were not impaired—he was able to progress, and over the years, it became apparent that he possessed great musical talent. He composes songs that are reminiscent of children's songs and are very popular with Japanese audiences. The Nobel Prize winner said that his son is more well known and famous in Japan than he is. While in Stockholm, Blomstedt invited the family to attend a rehearsal, and Ōe later told him that this was the most awesome experience for his son.

The following two letters come from other special concertgoers who hold the maestro and his music in their hearts. The first letter is from the assistant to the conductor in Tokyo, Kaori Takagi, on April 27, 2010:

Dear Maestro Blomstedt,

I thank you so much for the wonderful concerts you have performed with us. Your time with us was highly inspirational. We truly appreciated your assistance and your beautiful music-making. I shall tell you the message from Hiroshi Matsuzaki, who is our principal horn player, below:

"I am very happy and honored to play under your great conducting. I have been playing extra hard because the music is dedicated to God. The performances with you are precious memories. I will retire from the NSO this upcoming October. I would like to express to you my deepest gratitude for sharing your music with us."[4]

Letter from the Japanese concertgoer Shuichiro Nemoto on April 15, 2010:

Dear Maestro Herbert Blomstedt,

I'm writing this letter to express my sincere thanks to you. Your music has been enlightening to me since I listened to you during your first visit in Japan.

I began listening to classical music when I was a young teen and found that it's difficult to find opportunities in Japan to attend live concerts of first-class European orchestras, especially Middle-European ones. I tried to get the musical flavor through discs and/or broadcast programs. In that sense, those concerts first performed in Tokyo with Leipzig Gewandhaus and Staatskapelle Dresden provided me with the experience of hearing the real sound and, therefore, the real music.

My trip to Middle and Eastern European countries in the late '70s, when I was a college student, deepened my understanding of the background of the arts. After graduation, I joined the financial industry and spent more than thirty years in various cities, such as New York, Hong Kong, and Tokyo, which stimulated my eagerness to listen to real music created through integrity and sincerity. My job was not always clean and sometimes ugly, and I suspect that I was looking for some [spi]ritual activities to reflect on and keep myself on the right track. The music performed under your baton, without exception, moved me. I've enjoyed the various opportunities to listen to your music.

As for recent concerts, Bruckner's Seventh Symphony with the Gewandhaus Orchestra in '05, Sibelius's Second Symphony with the NHK Symphony Orchestra in '08, and Bruckner's Eighth Symphony with the Czech Philharmonic Orchestra are especially unforgettable, and the sounds are still alive in my brain.

The live recording of Brahms's Symphony No. 1 with the Staatskapelle Dresden and Bruckner's Eighth with the Gewandhaus at the farewell concert are my favorite CDs.

Though I could fill up your absence with CDs, I would really appreciate it if you would continue to share your precious time with Japan.

Last but not least, I fully respect you and your music, and I sincerely wish you and your family the best.[5]

Finally, the conductor's message for the benefit concert on September 28, 2011, in Tokyo:

[Victor Hugo said,] "Music expresses that which cannot be said and on which it is impossible to be silent."

Since the tragedy in March, the terrible tsunami, my thoughts have been with you constantly. I admire your courage and stamina and am convinced that they will be rewarded.

I was in San Francisco when it happened. We dedicated all four concerts that week to you who had been through so much. We opened each concert with the Japanese national anthem, "Kimigayo." And three thousand people stood at attention every night. A huge wave of sympathy rolled over to your shore.

And now we play for you here directly. It is music full of comfort and joy. But not without dark overtones and undertones, just as life is itself: Mozart, with his extremely touching mood, and Brahms, who builds up a huge drama surrounding islands of beauty and peace. And at the end is a triumphant victory over all hardship and pain.

God bless you all, listeners and musicians!

Bamberg Symphony

The Bamberg Symphony has its roots in Prague. The German Philharmonic Orchestra of Prague was founded in 1940 with Joseph Keilberth as the musical director. After the war, most of the musicians fled across the border to Bavaria, which was in the American occupation zone. Some met in Bamberg again and soon made plans to reestablish the orchestra. In March 1946, they appeared publicly for the first time in Bamberg's Central Hall. Critics hailed the evening dedicated to Beethoven as a great event, and the orchestra was ranked as equal to metropolitan orchestras. Three years later, after his debut in Bamberg, Keilberth wrote in his diary of a "poignant reunion with the people of Prague," and added, "Very good orchestra." The following year, he left the Staatskapelle Dresden to work full time with the very young Bamberg Symphony and led it to a growing national importance. Other formative conductors were Eugen Jochum and Horst Stein; since 2016, Jakub Hrůša has been the principal conductor.

In December 1982, Herbert Blomstedt made his debut with the Bamberg Symphony. The manager at the time was Rolf Beck, who invited Blomstedt after hearing of his successful work as the music director in Dresden. After the first rehearsals in the small Franconian town, Blomstedt was impressed by the awesome achievement of the young orchestra: "It was love at first sight! The orchestra still played in a Bohemian way— very folklorish and enormously musical."

In the absence of their own concert hall, the Bamberg Symphony performed in the medieval Dominikanerbau (a Dominican monastery), which had been refurbished for cultural events. The acoustics were good, but the orchestral seating was very unfavorable. The wind instruments sat in the choir area, which is invisible to many in the audience; the strings were in the transept. Herbert later said, "It was a little primitive, but there was a wonderful spirit. The audience was delightful; the orchestra outstanding. They offered me the position of principal conductor, but I could not say yes—I still belonged in Dresden!"

Of course, the Bamburgers were disappointed by the negative reply, especially since tragic events had led to a prolonged vacancy in the chief conductor's position. However, Blomstedt would collaborate frequently with the orchestra from that point on. On February 18, 2007, they celebrated their one hundredth joint concert.

Blomstedt attributes the current fine Bamberg Symphony concert hall, built in 1993, and the subscriber base of about six thousand listeners, which is nearly 9 percent of the population, to Rolf Beck's energy and wisdom. Blomstedt performs an almost exclusively German-Austrian repertoire with them: Beethoven, Brahms, Bruckner, Mendelssohn, and Mahler. At the end of January 2009, they performed the Piano Concerto No. 2 by Johannes Brahms, with Yefim Bronfman as the soloist. This internationally acclaimed pianist, who only performs with the best orchestras in the world, said afterwards, "Nowhere have I heard such a fine Brahms as here!"[6] Playing with the orchestra was perfect for him. After the intermission, Antonín Dvořák's Symphony No. 8 resounded; according to the Maestro himself, "That was an improvement on Brahms. Although there is no longer a Czech or a Bohemian sitting in the orchestra, there is still something Bohemian there. Oh, how they played! Very beautifully!"

In Dresden, Blomstedt became acquainted with and came to appreciate that which is characteristically "Bohemian"; he encountered it again in the Slavic "linden city" of Leipzig. According to Blomstedt, this Bohemian style became a part of Saxony as a result of migration influences long ago.

The Bohemians have something very spontaneous, while the Germans are more analytical and accurate, wanting to do everything properly and by the book. Order must prevail everywhere; that's part of the secret of the German cultural scene and its paramount significance in science, music, literature, and art. This is not possible without accuracy. But in the process, some spontaneity is lost. And spontaneity is something the Bohemians possess in abundance! So they sometimes come up a little too short on accuracy. The best combination is to be found in a city like Dresden, which is close to the border. Here both characteristics come together to form a blissful unity!

In March 2006, the orchestra awarded Herbert Blomstedt with the title of honorary conductor. In November 2010, the Friends of the Bamberg Symphony bestowed the orchestra's Golden Badge of Honor on Blomstedt. For him, the Bamberg Symphony is "an exceptional orchestra that one cannot help but admire and love. Its very existence is a miracle. . . . Every time I am surprised once again at the very wonderful music made in the enchantingly beautiful Bamberg: not only with grand technical perfection, but with a calmness, genuineness, and freshness that is increasingly rare today."

Bavarian Radio Symphony Orchestra

Since 2008, Herbert Blomstedt has collaborated regularly every year with the Bavarian Radio Symphony Orchestra (BRSO). Nimrod Guez was a solo violist in the orchestra from September 2007 to October 2011. He described what he especially liked about Herbert's musical and individual personality and his experiences with him at the BRSO:

> In this orchestra, everyone is focused. There is a great desire to play music beautifully and passionately. Herbert Blomstedt directs this energy so well.
>
> Conductors have different ways to get an orchestra with one hundred musicians and more to cooperate. With Mr. Blomstedt, it is his personality—what he knows about the music, how intensely he feels the music, and the incredible amount of experience he has internalized—as he interprets the music. One notices whether people with leadership skills have strong characters, perhaps they are very charismatic or, in certain circumstances, manipulative; but those who can truly lead others don't need to harp on it all the time because they believe in what they do. Mr. Blomstedt does not try to force the orchestra. Rather, he inspires us to go in a certain direction, in a way that lets us retain our identity. We don't just follow; we are happy to go along with him and do everything possible to create an unconstrained sound. When a person has such a profound understanding of musical compositions, it is impossible to explain it as if from a textbook or give theoretical instructions—one has to feel what the person means. Therefore, it is my goal to be as sensitive as possible, to give something of myself, and to render service to the music.
>
> At rehearsals, one immediately gets a sense of the respect Herbert has for the people with whom he works and for the music. He not

only contributes a lot but also listens attentively. For example, there are fantastic solo wind instrument players at the Bavarian Radio Symphony Orchestra who can offer him something. He perceives it, comments on it, and shares his ideas about it. There is a strong give and take. His body language does not force a certain interpretation. He gives many vivid introductions as an impetus, and then we have the chance to creatively make it happen. He never gets in the way of the music and yet never relinquishes his perspective of how it should be done. The rehearsals are generally not very different from the concert. Some conductors want it to explode at the performance so that the listeners fall off their chairs. Herbert Blomstedt simply loves music and *always* tries to make music as passionate as possible. In concert, it happens so naturally that it becomes something special!

Nowadays, because there are so many soloists, each must have his or her special trademark—have something unique to be successful. Herbert Blomstedt does not need to have a very special interpretation to move people. He is merely in it with his heart as much as he is with his head, proving that the emotional and intellectual worlds do not have to be so far apart. Such music one can listen to again and again!

He is very analytical in how he understands the text and keeps track of the whole score, which contributes to a stronger experience of the music.

He doesn't openly parade his religion, but one notices that he has found something for himself and is very balanced in his inner being.

As musicians in training, we were taught that there was a clear division between baroque and romantic music. But with Mr. Blomstedt one learns that a continuous development has taken place, even if the musical language in different periods is not the same and expresses distinctive things; the link exists![7]

Helmut Veihelmann was the principal cellist of the Bavarian Radio Symphony Orchestra for almost four decades. When he encountered Blomstedt as a conductor for the first time, he was

pleasantly stirred and surprised about a number of things. His physical and mental presence is admirable. He obviously never gets tired. One can only envy him for his freshness and vitality! His absolute sovereignty creates the impression that he's a man in the artistic zenith of his life and enjoying it. Not because he is satisfied with what he has achieved but because he knows how to do it. He knows the trade and the dramaturgy—with Bruckner, this is very important. So he can bring together a huge colossus without getting lost in the small details. He knows how to rehearse and possesses a good mix of exacting and giving. In the rehearsals, when he explains his understanding of the music—sometimes using figurative language and expressed so well, although German is not his mother tongue—then one sometimes wonders, *Now why didn't I think of that?* Herbert Blomstedt's sovereignty also means that he simply does not need to play the dictator, impatient and unfriendly.

I only have positive impressions of him! He works tirelessly but is never grim about it. One can feel his confidence in the musicians that the concert will be good. Because of this, the ice is instantly broken (if there ever was any), and one can work together quite naturally.

He is not a star, in the sense that people just melt when he steps on stage, but this is unessential because I know the musical and spiritual substance that he's made of.

Blomstedt never places his personal view of the music in the foreground but is faithful to the text, and one realizes that this works! One does not absolutely have to add something. He has no need of antics, and showmanship he can do without, because he trusts in the power of music. He acts very intellectually, thinks things through, and does not do anything from a gut feeling.

In dealing with Mr. Blomstedt, one feels this must be a cheerful, kind person! Although he obviously works very hard, I have always found him to be very jovial and relaxed. He does not give the impression of being driven, doesn't try to please the media, and doesn't do the popular thing. He remains true to himself—or to his faith—and makes music for its own sake, and doesn't aspire to becoming a big star. This is something extraordinary!

One can tell that Herbert Blomstedt has deeply analyzed performance practice. He emphasizes harmonic progressions and articulation, and he has adopted more recent insights in a manner that does not appear dogmatic but purely natural.[8]

The Gustav Mahler Jugendorchester

The Gustav Mahler Jugendorchester (GMJO) considers itself a talent factory for European orchestral musicians. It was founded in Vienna in

1986 through the initiative of Claudio Abbado, its former music director. The original goal was to promote the making of music between young Austrians and musicians from the former Eastern Bloc. Since 1992, the GMJO is open to musicians under the age of twenty-six from all over Europe. Every year the best musicians from a group of more than two thousand exceptionally talented young candidates are selected through a rigorous process to participate in the orchestra's projects. Prominent orchestra members supervise the young musicians in the rehearsal phase. Then two major tours occur during the semester break, which include appearances with very prominent conductors and soloists in prestigious concert halls and at major festivals. In this way, the young musicians are exposed to a wide range of different concert experiences.

The GMJO "is under the patronage of the Council of Europe" and is now considered the best international youth orchestra worldwide.[9] Artistically and organizationally, it is financially independent and solely obligated to promote young musicians.

In the second half of March 2008, Herbert Blomstedt led the GMJO for the first time. With Alban Berg's Violin Concerto, featuring soloist Leonidas Kavakos, Sibelius's Symphony No. 7, and Bruckner's Symphony No. 5 on the program, they went on the Easter tour to Austria, Germany, Luxembourg, Italy, and Spain, performing twelve concerts in ten cities. The audience, which includes many young people, responded enthusiastically to the combination of elite young musicians and a wise, old, and world-renowned conductor. And Blomstedt's encyclopedic understanding of music and his pedagogical and didactic skills impressed the young musicians during rehearsals.

In 2010, a second tour took place during the summer. Baritone Christian Gerhaher and violinist Hilary Hahn were the soloists for the different programs, which included *Songs of a Wayfarer* by Gustav Mahler, Johannes Brahms's Violin Concerto, Bruckner's Symphony No. 9, and Paul Hindemith's *Mathis der Maler*. They performed ten concerts in nine cities—including celebrated performances at the London Promenade concerts, in Dresden's Semperoper, and at the Salzburg Music Festival. It was particularly clear in London's Royal Albert Hall that there is still an interest in classical music when concerts are affordable and an enthusiastic young orchestra is performing.[10]

Alexander Meraviglia-Crivelli has been the secretary general of the Gustav Mahler Youth Orchestra since 1996. "With heart and soul" and "without looking at the clock," he and three other employees are "almost constantly busy with music: there's no other option when one has time-consuming projects. One just has to be exceptionally engaged and motivated," he notes succinctly. Of course, he knew Maestro Blomstedt long before the maestro's debut with the GMJO: through recordings and concerts that "afforded me with many wonderful moments, such as Bruckner's Fourth Symphony or Mozart's Piano Concerto No. 17 with the Vienna Symphony Orchestra—an excellent and unforgettable performance!"[11]

The cultural manager feels it is a "true privilege" that the GMJO collaborates with many significant artists. Pierre Boulez, the now-deceased Sir Colin Davis, Michael Gielen, Bernard Haitink, Herbert Blomstedt, and other conductors from Blomstedt's generation, at the zenith of their conducting careers, all shared their rich experience in concerts together with the GMJO. Meraviglia-Crivelli shares a paraphrased statement by Boulez: "That one treats young musicians as professionals, that one helps them to advance and needs to get the absolute best out of them. Enthusiasm and dedication have to be shown by example. The established artists who work with the young people have to do so at a highly professional level, and that is the challenge!" Claudio Abbado said of himself that in this way he learned a lot about his own manner of rehearsing and teaching music and also learned to analyze it more.

Herbert Blomstedt is known for his good rapport with young people. According to Meraviglia-Crivelli's observation, he impresses "by his serious, profound, devoted engagement with music. One has to live by one's convictions, and Herbert Blomstedt is especially convincing and builds a wonderful connection to the orchestra. This is an indication of the sincerity of a conductor—the orchestra notices exactly if one is serious about it or not."

The maestro and the secretary general of the GMJO met a few years earlier in Zurich at an event of the *Tonhalle* Association to plan the 2008 Easter tour. "Mr. Blomstedt was exceedingly cordial; his warmth is always wonderfully delightful and rarely to be encountered," Meraviglia-Crivelli remembers. He found the maestro was "completely unpretentious, being genuinely focused on what's essential and significant, with inexhaustible curiosity and openness towards other people. He exemplifies reaching out to others. But he does not flaunt his feelings. Many conduct for the camera, for the audience, but he is there to entirely serve the music. He doesn't stand above it or in its way."

He perceives the collaboration with Blomstedt as "stimulating and demanding. It makes one aware of the responsibility one has to a great artist in order to create the conditions so that he can flourish. At the same time, one is motivated to meet his expectations. This also eradicates any self-adulation because one has to question one's actions again and again! Anyway, working with Mr. Blomstedt broadens one's horizons. If one takes the opportunity to talk with him, it makes one think about one's own opinions and positions."

When pondering how one could most aptly describe Herbert Blomstedt, Alexander Meraviglia-Crivelli came up with the word *kindness*: a word that is used by many people to describe the maestro. "However, the best way to describe him is as a kind of mixture of Jacob Burckhardt, the leading Swiss cultural historian, and one of the great conductors, say Furtwängler; but he himself is one of the greats. He has a keen historical and cultural mind that thinks universally. He places an artistic creation within its overall context. He is engaged with the world and with people in such a way that this flows into his artistic work. One must be involved and well read to do this!"

Mr. Meraviglia-Crivelli also mentions another important term to describe Herbert Blomstedt's character: respect.

Respect for a creation means capturing its rich diversity and inquiring about all that pertains to its origin. Knowing about the person who created the work is the responsibility of the reproducing artist. Herbert Blomstedt lives out this aspect of an artistic creation to such an extent that one quickly begins to question one's own assumptions. And being compelled to do this can be more enriching than to always be in the right. In any case, Maestro Blomstedt sets standards that one would like to have in one's day-to-day environment. He is not ostentatious but leaves a lasting impression because he continues to deal with people, objects, and the arts in profound and open ways.

Orchestre de Paris

Every year or two Blomstedt performs with the Orchestre de Paris. The collaboration is appealing in part due to the very different mentality of the conductor and the orchestra. Yannick Launoy, one of the administrative staff at the Salle Pleyel (a concert hall) and a regular concertgoer, describes this difference after attending two performances of Stravinsky's Piano Concerto and Bruckner's Symphony No. 5 on March 24 and 25, 2010:

Until then, I only knew Herbert Blomstedt from his Beethoven recordings and a CD with Grieg/Chopin piano concertos, featuring

A Great Song

Olli Mustonen and the San Francisco Symphony. I decided to attend both concerts. For the first night, I chose a seat behind the stage so that I could see the conductor very well. And then he came: almost a young man who was beaming at the orchestra, as if they were all his friends. Throughout the Bruckner symphony, he smiled at them again and again! I had the impression that he took them to another level of reality. He is one of those conductors that one has to observe, even when his gestures are not emphatic. He looks sober and straightforward, but one has the feeling that music exudes from him. He was in charge of the orchestra, but at the same time, I felt that his control was the best way to give everyone the adequate space they needed to perform excellent music. Throughout the whole symphony, he maintained this connection! Despite the fact that listeners tend to eventually lose the thread during a Bruckner symphony, the ovations at the end of the concerts were really fantastic. The audience was just as overwhelmed as I was by the magic that we had just experienced. On the second night, I sat on the second balcony because I had heard enough rich sound the previous evening. Now I wanted to hear the music from above. I couldn't believe that I was going to listen to the same Bruckner symphony two days in a row. I really just wanted to find the magic of the previous evening again. I was able to convince two of my colleagues to come along with me. They are not really fans of the Orchestre de Paris; the orchestra is able to play wonderfully, but at times it has performed terribly. Herbert Blomstedt succeeded in conducting one of the finest concerts I've ever heard in my life by the Orchestre de Paris. I write this as someone who attends concerts at least a hundred times a year. The second time the magic was still there. The orchestra was still under the spell of the Nordic maestro. I even cried; I cannot pinpoint at what place in the symphony, because I am not a musician and cannot read music, but I know when grace and enchantment are present.

In the days following the concerts, I bought the recordings of Blomstedt's Nielsen and Sibelius symphonies and listened to them for many, many days. Recently, I found the YouTube video of Blomstedt performing Bruckner's Fifth with the NHK Symphony Orchestra in Tokyo. I was excited to see and hear that this man is able to obtain what he wants from each orchestra. One only has to look at his eyes during the last chord of this symphony. Everything was in his final look: modestly, without showing off, but so intensely that the whole orchestra followed him. And the best part? The orchestra was one with him and produced the music that he had taught them during the rehearsals.[12]

1. Roy Branson, interview by UW, August 3, 2007, Ekebyholm, Sweden.

2. Karl Suske, interview by Claudius Böhm, "Vielleicht war es einfach so" [Perhaps it was just like this], *Gewandhausmagazin* 61 (2008/2009).

3. Peter Mirring, interview by UW, October 1, 2009, Dresden.

4. Letter written in English.

5. Letter originally in English.

6. Herbert Blomstedt to UW, personal communication.

7. Nimrod Guez, conversation with UW, May 20, 2010, Munich.

8. Helmut Veihelmann, conversation with UW, May 18, 2009, Munich.

9. "Gustav Mahler Jugendorchester," Gustav Mahler Jugendorchester, accessed October 11, 2016, http://www.gmjo.at/Home/AbouttheGMJO/Biographie/tabid/70/language/en-US/Default.aspx.

10. A multipart documentary of the rehearsals and concerts across Europe from the GMJO's 2013 Easter tour with Herbert Blomstedt is well worth viewing. The episodes are available on YouTube: "The GMJO With Herbert Blomstedt at Gulbenkian: Episode 01," YouTube video, 6:45, posted by "Gustav Mahler Jugendorchester," April 12, 2013, https://www.youtube.com/watch?feature=player_embedded&v=hU5kwyC-FbM#at=40.

11. Alexander Meraviglia-Crivelli, interview by UW, February 17, 2011, Vienna.

12. Yannick Launoy to UW, personal communication, July 2 and 9, 2010.

Contributions by Herbert Blomstedt

My Collaboration With the Amsterdam Concertgebouw Orchestra, the Berlin and Vienna Philharmonics, and the Great American Symphony Orchestras

AMSTERDAM'S ROYAL CONCERTGEBOUW ORCHESTRA, the Berlin Philharmonic, and the Vienna Philharmonic are among the best orchestras in the world, and I consider myself fortunate that I can perform music with all three of them every year. At the same time, it is a challenge and an inspiration.

The Concertgebouw became world renowned through the firm discipline of its second principal conductor, Willem Mengelberg. Today the Concertgebouw captivates its audience by its elasticity, sensitivity, and sophistication more than by mere perfection. The warmth of its expression is also supported by the excellent acoustics of the hall. During many guest performances, I was able to get better acquainted with the soul of the orchestra; in 2004, we went on a wonderful tour together to America, because Riccardo Chailly, their chief conductor, was preparing for his new office as my successor at the Gewandhaus. Since then, we perform together every year.

I sporadically conducted the Berlin Philharmonic during the Herbert von Karajan era. Since standing in for Nikolaus Harnoncourt during a performance of Bruckner's Symphony No. 5 in 2008, I also guest conduct this wonderful orchestra annually. In many ways, they are the opposite of Amsterdam. For example, they are made up of musicians from twenty or more nations. Because of this, they have perhaps the most skillful musicians in the world—each, as it were, an Olympic champion. Each musician also has a very individual, strong personality. They are all tremendously committed to the musical work. Nothing is impossible for them. If it is possible to inspire them with a work or an interpretation, they are unstoppable.

A Great Song

I had a late debut with the Vienna Philharmonic in January 2011, once again standing in for Nikolaus Harnoncourt, for a concert in Salzburg celebrating Mozart's birthday. The Viennese are considered a difficult orchestra. They have high expectations—and rightly so. But I had a wonderful connection with these gifted musicians. We could immediately make music at a high level, and we look forward to continuing to work together in Vienna and elsewhere. In 2012, we went on a cruise together in the Mediterranean, performing three programs from the Viennese classics. The Strauss encore received the biggest applause again and again. The philharmonic is known worldwide especially for this repertoire because of the New Year's concerts. And they play this music with incomparable charm. In sound, style, and temperament, these musicians are very remarkable. This is also due to the fact that they are a private association; they play every day in the Vienna State Opera and only in the philharmonic in their spare time. This is a colossal amount of work and can only be accomplished with particularly high discipline. They also administrate themselves and have no principal conductor or manager. They set their own standards and are proud about it. The world can be grateful.

For more than thirty years now, I have also regularly conducted the leading American orchestras with great pleasure. What sparked this friendly relationship was certainly my first extended trip to America with the Staatskapelle Dresden. The so-called Big Five are all fantastic: the Boston Symphony Orchestra, Chicago Symphony Orchestra, Cleveland Orchestra, New York Philharmonic, and Philadelphia Orchestra. They compete constantly with each other, and one always thinks the latest performance is impossible to supersede. They also all present their concert series in New York, mostly in Carnegie Hall, so a direct comparison is easily possible. They are all highly dependent on European tradition; they were also influenced by European chief conductors of different natures until Leonard Bernstein became the first American music director of the New York Philharmonic in 1958.

However, the orchestral landscape of the "Next Five" is impressive, and the quality of a performance on a good evening is quite comparable with the Big Five: Detroit Symphony Orchestra, Los Angeles Philharmonic, Montreal Symphony Orchestra, Pittsburgh Symphony Orchestra, San Francisco Symphony. They were also strongly influenced by their European chief conductors, such as the French Paul Paray in Detroit and Pierre Monteux in San Francisco or the German William Steinberg in Pittsburgh. In Pittsburgh, the deep and warm German sound that

Contributions by Herbert Blomstedt

Steinberg had consistently cultivated for twenty-four years, from 1952 to 1976, was still clearly present even five years after his departure when I conducted Brahms and Bruckner there. I was amazed that even Max Reger's Hiller Variations were performed at their best. I discovered one reason for this in the orchestral score: there I found annotations of the previous performance—conducted by Paul Hindemith! When the orchestra asked me to be their music director, I was almost inclined to say yes. Only factors that had nothing to do with the orchestra deterred me. But in San Francisco, everything came together, and I joyfully accepted. The rest is history.

What I Learned From My Teachers— Esteemed Role Models

Lars Fermæus

Lars Fermæus was my violin teacher in Gothenburg from 1941 to 1945. I owe more to him than to any other teacher. Under his leadership, the door to the wondrous world of music opened wide for me. Even his studio was a world unto itself: books and music scores lined all the walls from the floor to the ceiling; in the center of the room, there were two music stands anchored on the floor, with built-in lighting for playing quartets. He was a very challenging and inspiring teacher. Every lesson began with scale and bow exercises according to Otakar Ševčik, followed by a progressive étude, then a concerto movement for the main study, and to end, a piece of chamber music in order to get to know the literature and to practice sight-reading. He directed a private music school, and it was always possible to find two or three other students for the chamber music. If not, I just played violin duets with my teacher. What bliss!

Lars Fermæus was a born musician and a student of Carl Flesch in Berlin. He was the third concertmaster in the Gothenburg Symphony Orchestra. He also possessed incredible energy and seemed to be more excited about music than any other members of the orchestra. He was good looking, with his blue-black hair and his noble, aquiline nose. I was thirteen when I started lessons with him, and he always called me by my first name: "*Snälla Herbert!*" ("dear little Herbert"; only later on did he leave the "little" out.) He smiled so charmingly when he said it that one just had to love him. His behavior was a bit theatrical, and his face was always finely powdered. Still, I admired him endlessly, and his musical instructions were to me as if spoken by God Himself. He always told me that I needed to go to high school, complete school, and then continue on to a university. "Otherwise, you will not be a real musician."

He had a sense of humor! When he played with skilled amateurs in the Sundberg Quartet Society and he wanted to correct a mistake, he said without any irony, "Is it really written like that?" When the loud screeching of a colleague was too much for him, he used to say, "Please, please, Carl, not so much material!"

He died childless in 1976, leaving behind many grateful students. Fifteen years later I met his niece, Lilleba Aagesen, in San Francisco. She was on a cruise with her husband and introduced herself to me after a concert in Davies Symphony Hall. I had never seen her before, but I hugged her spontaneously as an ambassador of my beloved teacher. A few months later I got a letter from her, containing something very special: her uncle's cufflinks made of pure gold and engraved with his initials, L. F. To me, they are priceless.

Gottfried Boon

The violin has always been my first instrument. Later, while attending the Royal College of Music, I had Gottfried Boon as a piano teacher and learned my second instrument. He was the most famous piano teacher in all of Scandinavia, and he had trained first-class pianists, such as Hans Leygraf and Hilda Waldeland. Boon was a spirited gentleman and a brilliant teacher and was a former pupil of Artur Schnabel. He elegantly solved the problem of addressing the students—with the informal "*Du*" (you) or the formal "*Sie*" (you)—by just omitting the pronoun: "Have practiced a lot this week?" "Were at the concert yesterday?" He always hummed when I played and was always feeling my shoulders to see if I was loose enough. But the essence of what I learned from him was this: "First, think of the sound, and feel it in your fingertips—only then play." Playing music was not something mechanical but spiritual. Just pressing the right key at the right moment was a great sin to him, and he was furious when there was a lack of true music. Once he shouted to me, "It is not at all music!" Another time he went to the window, said nothing, but pointed, as if to say, "Here—jump!" It was not pleasant, but it was useful. The next moment he was again positive and loving. I was incredibly fond of him. I knew that he believed in me, and this inspired me even more.

I became especially aware of how right he was in his "first think of the sound" belief when I made music with orchestras. To discover how the music sounds only when one begins does not lead to any sound culture. Only when the sound already exists in the mind can one convey it to the orchestra. The orchestra responds so differently that the smallest change in tempo produces a different nuance. Gottfried Boon was right, and I am eternally grateful.

Tor Mann

Tor Mann was a central figure of Nordic culture for almost forty years, an important bearer of tradition, and at the same time a pioneer for the future. His teacher Conrad Nordqvist had been a pupil of Franz Berwald, and he personally knew the three Nordic giants Carl Nielsen, Jean Sibelius, and Wilhelm Stenhammar, whose music he tirelessly promoted throughout his life. He came from the orchestra and played cello in both the Stockholm Philharmonic Orchestra and the opera. As a chamber musician, he traveled all over Sweden. He was a man of much experience!

He was the professor of orchestral conducting at the Royal College of Music in Stockholm for twenty-two years, until 1961 when I became his successor. So I was able to learn from him and was inspired by his skill, his go-getting spirit, and his humor. He belonged to the generation of conductors that knew the scores accurately but also felt obliged to "improve" on them. There were three students in his class when he explained to us the works of Sibelius and Nielsen. At times, we felt that he sometimes went a bit too far and had strained the score. Precision in playing technique, natural arrangement, and a balanced orchestral sound were his main objectives—good points of departure for any musician.

In rehearsals, his humor was priceless. The double basses he affectionately described as "wheelbarrows." But if someone was lacking a sense of humor, he could be sharp. In a letter dated October 29, 1952, he wrote to me about a world-renowned conductor: "[S]oon he will no longer be able to show his face in Stockholm. . . . The orchestra detests him, and I must say that in the long run, he is awful. Dry and heartless and without a sense of humor, and you know, that those who have to play under him don't think much of his baton technique. Pure wood chopping, without a fixed point. His Beethoven VII . . . sloppy and vulgar."

Although a little envy might be at play here, his judgment is typical. As a musician, he was very rigid and would not tolerate any excesses. His comments on the symphonies of Sibelius and Berwald had been published, and I feel fortunate to own some of his Nielsen scores, which were kind gifts from his widow.

In Tor Mann's youth, the orchestra sat in the classic seating arrangement, with the first violins on the left and the second violins on the right. After the Second World War when the modern, or American, seating whereby the second violins were placed behind the first violins was also adopted in Europe, one naturally lost the special stereo or dialogue effect between the violins. Tor Mann accepted this new development, like most conductors, as progress. It was clear to him that the precision was thus better, but it was a loss musically and in this way one could not do justice to the compositions. Nevertheless, he retained the American formation. Here he thought like a practical musician and not as an advocate of the composer. In a radio interview with Nils Castegren on February 6, 1967, he responded to the question of the classic seating: "I do not think one can do it with a modern symphony orchestra. . . . It's the worst thing for the musicians when foreign conductors come and move the [instruments] around. Their ears turn around." Unfortunately, I had also "learned" this view from him. It was not his fault, but mine. It took almost fifty years before I dared to consistently introduce the classic seating again and was able to determine that a modern symphony orchestra mastered the inter-action in the classic arrangement very well and, at the same time, was able to restore the desired stereo effect. Orchestras today are much more open and willing to experiment than they were fifty years ago.

Igor Markevitch

Today, as I write these lines, on August 23, 2012, an exhibition opens in Montreux commemorating this *compositeur et chef d'orchestre* (composer and conductor), who was born one hundred years ago and lived for a long time on the Swiss Riviera. I met Igor Markevitch for the first time in 1950 when he taught a summer course at the Mozarteum, a university in Salzburg. There were a dozen students in his class with very different qualifications. For example, there was Alexander Gibson from Scotland and Eifred Eckart-Hansen from Denmark, who had conducting experi-ence, and Wolfgang Sawallisch, who was the music director in Augsburg. For them, Markevitch's class was perhaps too elementary: Sawallisch soon traveled home again. But for me, this kind of training came just at the right time. I came to Salzburg as a university graduate with enormous curiosity but without any practical experience and deliberate artistic discipline. Markevitch demanded that we conduct the rehearsals from memory, resulting in endless studying of the scores, day and night. The intention was to virtually force us into the most profound interaction with the score so that we could devote all our attention to the music and the orchestra when directing.

Eleven-year-old Daniel Barenboim, inexperienced as I was the first time, came to the summer school in 1954. We had much in common.

He, too, benefited greatly from this class, and I think if one takes a closer look, one can recognize our common role model in us today. So, very different students could benefit from one and the same teacher.

Igor Markevitch was of the opinion that the art of conducting can be learned, just as violin technique or playing the piano, which have been defined for about three hundred years and are described in textbooks. However, conducting is a much later genre of music making, and it had not yet been so well described. Markevitch's technical role models were especially Arturo Toscanini and Hermann Scherchen: the utmost clarity, not only in rhythm, but also in the expression, coupled with the greatest economy, which means eliminating everything superfluous. I liked this almost scientific approach, and it motivated me to work hard. Artistically, the rehearsals were prepared with in-depth analyses of the musical structure and the resulting interpretative intentions. We realized then how the sound of the orchestra changed from one conductor to another and had to convince ourselves of what is good and desirable and what was to be avoided and how it could be avoided. Everything was very instructive and enlightening. At the time, we didn't think much about the fact that Markevitch himself was a highly significant composer. This is what gave his analyses a particular depth and sharpness.

As a teacher, Markevitch was a very strict observer, but he never humiliated a student in front of the orchestra. He always remained calm but sharp. He said patience was his best quality and impatience his worst. At times, he could be like a Russian tsar who never admitted a mistake, but he could also show great sympathy, warmth, and humor. I experienced this most plainly and embarrassingly at a rehearsal for the Brandenburg Concerto No. 5. Markevitch stood, invisible to me, right behind me. And suddenly, with one outward beat, I hit him on his mouth. Dead silence in the orchestra. I was crushed. He was silent and put his hand to his mouth. He was bleeding! Then he said very quietly, "I told you; you should be more flexible." A brilliant teacher!

The following summer I was back in Salzburg with him; later on, when his health was ailing, I even helped him teach courses in Santiago de Compostela, Spain, and in Monte Carlo. He had special trust in me and described himself as my "Papa Igor." When I hesitated for various reasons to accept the position of music director for the Staatskapelle Dresden, he advised me to say yes. He was right.

Today I can only thank him. I cannot compare myself with him—we are too different—but I regret that, with his extraordinary talent, he never had the opportunity to direct leading orchestras like I did. The reasons for this are manifold. But perhaps he could not adequately assert his best qualities.

Jean Morel

In the spring of 1953, I was able to study at the Juilliard School of Music in New York because of a scholarship from the Sweden-America Foundation. I still remember my fellow students: Samuel Krachmalnick, Bob Mandell, and Jorge Mester. Our conducting teacher was Jean Morel, a French musician and conductor who came to North and South America during the Second World War. He conducted opera in New York, taught conducting at Juilliard, and led the Juilliard Orchestra. In these short months, we studied mostly French solfège, a kind of ear training, which is very effective. The exercises usually consisted of dictations of short movements with multiple parts. Jean Morel conducted the orchestra himself and maintained a very high level. He was considered a great specialist of French repertoire. As a percussionist, he had played *L'Histoire du soldat*, a virtuoso solo part, under the direction of the composer Igor Stravinsky.

Apart from the intense exercises in solfège, I benefited most from the score analyses with Morel. I have partially adopted his system of denoting scores; maybe it was a typical French system: all woodwinds were marked in red, also the trumpets and trombones, but horns, harps, and strings in blue.

However, I learned the most from the rehearsals that I watched in Carnegie Hall. I could slip through an unguarded door into the rehearsals of Toscanini, Walter, and Mitropoulos. It was of course forbidden, but I had accomplices. We hid in the bottom of the first-tier boxes. But once when Guido Cantelli rehearsed Mendelssohn's *Italian Symphony*, I ventured down to the parquet and sat in the third row so that I could listen to the conductor's instructions. A tall old man, leaning on a walking stick, came and sat down beside me. One side of his mouth drooped; obviously he was suffering from ill health. He wanted to look at the scores together with me. It was Otto Klemperer. Truly, you never stop learning.

Leonard Bernstein

At that time, Leonard Bernstein, the great hope of American music, was living opposite Carnegie Hall, on 57th Street. I had learned that he would be teaching a conducting class at Tanglewood in the summer of 1953. I went to see him at his home and asked whether I could still take his course, even if registration had closed long ago. Generous as he always was, I was accepted into the course. Up until his last breath, he always gave everything he could. We actually rarely saw him in Tanglewood, for he was involved in everything, everywhere, including his own compositions, symphonies, and musicals. The class was mostly taught by his assistant Lukas Foss and consisted mainly of score analysis at the piano. Foss was a virtuoso pianist. It was quite an experience to listen to him play and then expound on Mozart's "Gran Partita" for thirteen wind instruments.

But when "Lenny" himself taught us, we were in high spirits. He was the complete opposite of Markevitch: we learned little about conducting itself; that did not seem to interest him so much, but we learned even more about music. He was music personified: spontaneous, warm, surprising, visionary, unfathomable, enchanting, yet highly intellectual, and unconditionally emotional—qualities that are each singly admirable but are rarely found in combination. Europeans could easily perceive him as showy; however, with him it was all quite natural. It's who he was. His teaching was not especially memorable to me, but his thirty-fifth birthday was, as we were able to celebrate together with him and his family on August 25. He had become a father and was bursting with happiness.

The most beautiful thing that happened during the summer at Tanglewood was a telegram from Johannes Norrby, the manager of the Stockholm Philharmonic Orchestra, offering me a debut concert on February 3, 1954. That was a catapult launch. When I told Leonard Bernstein of the success of this concert, he wrote a letter full of warmth and charm to me by return mail. "I am simply delighted at your news. The criticisms are extraordinary, and I am as proud as I can be of you." He concluded by asking, "Will you be coming to America?"

That would, as is characteristic of me, take quite a while, but thirty years later I became the music director of the San Francisco Symphony. A few months before his death, Leonard Bernstein guest conducted the Vienna Philharmonic in "my" concert hall in San Francisco. Even though he was only seventy-one years old, he was fatigued and ill. His assistant was standing backstage with a lit cigarette and a glass of whiskey ready. Afterward we sat in my room and reminisced gratefully about old times. Some of his cigarette ash fell on my tie; he was very unhappy about that. He was a man who wanted everything and could do anything. There was only one thing he could not do: say no. That was fortunate for us, his students, his musicians, and his audience; but in the end, it was his misfortune. He meant a lot to me, but I wish I had learned more of his spontaneity, openness, warmth, and foresight.

What I Learned From My Orchestras

The Gothenburg Symphony Orchestra

The Gothenburg Symphony Orchestra was never really "my orchestra"; I have only been their guest conductor. But they were my first love when I went to school in Gothenburg. I adored them and listened to them twice a week for five years. I knew every musician by name, and I still know their names today: Endre Wolf, the young, quite phenomenal concertmaster from Hungary; Guido Vecchi, the noble solo cellist who gave lessons to my brother, Norman; Thore Jansson, the magnificent solo clarinetist—when he played, the soul widened like the blue expanse of the sky; and Lohengrin Cremonese, the bass trombonist with the fairy tale name. How could one ever forget such personalities? They were my idols.

And the new concert hall! It had almost the best acoustics in the world. The sound was like an embrace from head to foot and struck at my heart. A miracle. The intermissions were discoveries. The audience—always a full house of thirteen hundred people—did not lounge around in any smoking areas, mutually poisoning each other, but moved slowly around the hall as if on a beltway. Here one could admire the celebrities of the city: the well-built and widely popular composer and painter Gösta Nystroem and the musicologist and radio director Julius Rabe, who was a wise man and the musical conscience of the whole country. Here one could meet the music critics Carl Tillius and Knut Bäck; both were sought-after piano teachers. Tillius was always friendly and positive. Bäck was small like Edvard Grieg and not unlike him but with a goatee—and a sharp pen. He was actually our neighbor. One had to be careful.

In this ideal environment, while Europe sank around us in ruins, I was privileged to make my first symphonic discoveries in peace but with great excitement. I discovered the sheer size and beauty of classical music. I learned to love music: Bach, Beethoven, Brahms, and Bruckner. Was it a coincidence that they started all with a *B*? Anyway, they were part of the best in music. Anything that was not of this level was, for the time being, left undiscovered.

In 2006, I was elected an honorary member of the orchestra.

The Stockholm Philharmonic Orchestra

The Stockholm Philharmonic Orchestra was also never really "my orchestra," even if I have performed more than two hundred concerts with them. As a young conductor, I learned a lot from these outstanding musicians, who had much more experience than I did. I learned to have respect for the orchestra. They were not there for my personal pleasure. The musicians had great expectations and challenged me progressively. I worked like a madman to live up to all of this. Sometimes it was possible; at other times, it was not.

One embarrassing episode is unforgettable. We tried Symphony No. 4 by Tchaikovsky. The finale is very fast and played with virtuosity and I had just successfully played it with my little orchestra in Norrköping. Now, with a really big symphony orchestra, I wanted to make it even better; following the Russian model, I set a rapid pace. That was too much and too boisterous for my colleagues. I countered that I had found it to be very doable with less skillful orchestras. Then the principal violist, Lince Berglund, shot back at me with irritation: "I can assure you that we have also played this work with much better conductors than you." Sometimes one has to learn important lessons the hard way.

As a student at the Royal College of Music, I visited countless rehearsals, and so I knew the orchestra. We lived near the Konserthuset (concert hall), and the orchestra generously allowed me to listen in to all rehearsals for seven years. In this way, I was able to observe many of the greatest conductors of the time at work: Fritz Busch, Wilhelm Furtwängler, Joseph Keilberth, Rudolf Kempe, Erich Kleiber, Victor de Sabata, Bruno Walter, and many others. That was tremendously instructive. From others, I learned how I absolutely did not want to conduct.

The moment came on February 3, 1954, when I was invited to conduct my debut concert in Stockholm—a miracle! God, the orchestra, the audience, and even the critics (at that time, there were seven newspapers in Stockholm!)—all were gracious to me. The orchestra was absolutely wonderful. They willingly played the second orchestral suite by Bach with an unfamiliar baroque articulation. For Hindemith's then very modern *Mathis der Maler* symphony, they placed their whole virtuosity at my disposal. I learned that one cannot do anything without a willing orchestra. One has to prove oneself reasonably worthy of the musicians' trust. Everything depends on good preparation and on God's help. Truly, Solomon said, "Unless the LORD builds the house, they labor in vain who build it" (Psalm 127:1).

I played a lot of New Music with the Stockholm Philharmonic Orchestra. Major classical works are not assigned so often to young guest conductors. But the local premieres—that was our own territory. But we had a dilemma: the orchestras, especially in the '60s and '70s, were not very enthusiastic about this type of music. That was understandable because many new works from this period were increasingly intellectual, and the equally important emotional element was not easily heard. I, however, felt it was part of my responsibility to support young composers, and I enthusiastically went about each new work, hoping to break the ice with the musicians. Only if one deals with each new work as a masterpiece does it have a chance. I stood up eagerly for Lars-Erik Larsson, Ingvar Lidholm, Siegfried Naumann, Bengt Hambraeus, Hilding Rosenberg, Karl-Erik Welin, Dag Wirén, and many others. I never regretted it, and I learned a lot from them.

Once, however, I was really pushed to my limits. We premiered a new symphony by a young Swedish composer. But the music had neither flesh nor blood, only hard granite. I was as frustrated as the musicians but didn't show it and performed it as if it were Brahms. I reaped the consequences after the intermission. Following the second movement of Haydn's Symphony No. 102, I broke down and had to leave the stage. After vomiting and drinking a few cups of tea, I was fit again, and the concert went on. The next day there was a review by Teddy Nyblom in the *Aftonbladet* with the headline "Double Nausea."

I am infinitely grateful that the Stockholm Philharmonic Orchestra and its manager at the time, kind Johannes Norrby, gave me such a wonderful start. They trusted me more and more with great works and accompanied me faithfully during a very important phase of my career. For example, we tackled the difficult *Rite of Spring* together and then enjoyed it and combined it with Ingvar Lidholm's *Poesis* (which fifty years later was an international success)[1] in performances while on tour. During a reception at the Swedish embassy in Copenhagen, the orchestra's accomplishments were recognized with typical Danish humor: "Yes, we must confess that everything is better in Sweden. They have the better currency, the better cars, the better composers, the better orchestras—and the better neighbors." So I learned, in all modesty, to be a little proud of the fact that I was a Swede and still am today.

The Norrköping Symphony Orchestra

This was my first "real" orchestra. It is a pure miracle that I became the chief conductor of the orchestra. In 1954, when I became the principal conductor, Norrköping was the fourth largest city in Sweden. Back then, the orchestra was small, consisting of only thirty members, and was thus actually only a chamber orchestra. But it was very professional, and the musicians had a healthy self-confidence. After two auditioning concerts, they were convinced that they could move forward under my leadership.

The crux of the matter was that I refused to rehearse on Saturday. And on Saturday, they had their dress rehearsal for the weekly concert on Sunday. How I wish I knew what was thought and said in the orchestra's meetings at that time! But the orchestra agreed to completely restructure its usual weekly schedule. During the seven years of my tenure, Saturdays were always kept free during my concert weeks with the orchestra, and the dress rehearsal was held at 11:00 A.M. on Sunday morning. It is almost unbelievable that the musicians and their labor union accepted this. But I never heard a word of protest, although the musicians could no longer attend the usual soccer matches or maybe a desired Sunday mass.

That had to mean that I was really wanted—that making music with me was worth this great sacrifice! This experience strengthened my self-confidence and inspired me tremendously. Becoming a conductor was a slow and sometimes tedious process for me. But the long preparation had paid off. Later, during my time in Dresden, I learned once again from my musicians that good things come to those who wait.

The Norrköping Symphony Orchestra was marked by a rare optimism and extraordinary enthusiasm. They willingly ate everything out of my hand, even though much of it was certainly still half baked. Their confidence in me was my greatest asset. In my mind, I can still see their faces in front of me: there was the principal bassoonist Harry Axelsson with his big eyes that sometimes threatened to pop out because of his sheer enjoyment at making music; the fine, cultured concertmaster Georges Raymond, coming from the best Belgian violin tradition; the principal double bass Hille Johansson, a unique character, who recommended thought-provoking literature to me and gave me Sven Lindqvist's first book. He must have realized that I was about to turn into a music nerd. Or he saw me as a kindred spirit. Not to be forgotten are the Russian nobleman Georgi Kuguscheff and the three refugees from Latvia: Berzins,

Vestens, and Zarins. What fates lay behind these names! And there was still the old Swede John Hake. What a spirited musician he must have surely been in the prime of his life! Then he was old and could barely do vibrato. I loved him anyway. How happy he made me one day in concert when his left hand actually began to vibrate! It was as if someone had risen from the dead—a miracle! Music is able to move mountains!

In Norrköping, I not only learned many symphonies but also learned out of gratitude to show respect and love to all of my musicians without exception. They made my life all the richer.

The Oslo Philharmonic

I learned some decisive things from the wonderful Oslo orchestra, long before I became their chief conductor. I also learned something special: patience.

In the early 1960s, I was offered the position of music director for the symphony in the old Hanseatic city of Bergen. While I was happy in Norrköping, this was like a gift from heaven because I longed for a full symphony orchestra so that I could also play the great symphonic works. I met with the three leading men of the orchestra, including the composer Harald Sæverud, at Holmenkollen (a residential area and ski-jumping hill) in Oslo. We negotiated very specifically and also discussed remuneration. I was in constant contact with my manager, Per Gottschalk. He had instructed me not to accept an offer without first informing him. He repeatedly demanded more money, higher honoraria—until the three men withdrew their offer and left for Bergen.

I was in despair. I had missed a great opportunity for the wrong reason: money. That is not my style. That one is paid at all is only an added bonus to the joy of making music. Back in Stockholm, my musical father, the composer Hilding Rosenberg, consoled me and said, "Don't be sad. This has happened to me often. You'll see that it is a blessing in disguise."

He was right. Only a few weeks later Per Gottschalk phoned me from Oslo: "Come quickly; the Oslo Philharmonic wants you as their music director!" This orchestra was, of course, even better than the one in Bergen. My manager probably already knew that the orchestra was interested in me and therefore wanted to prevent me from committing to Bergen.

One has to learn to wait. It is like getting an audience with the king. One must not babble on but must wait patiently until one is addressed. The dignitary takes the initiative.

My first concert with the Oslo Philharmonic was on May 12, 1960. It was a special program in the New Music series, with works by Fartein

Valen, Béla Bartók, and Igor Stravinsky, and featured the first performance in Norway of *The Rite of Spring*. The orchestra shrank from nothing. The musicians were, like most Norwegians, full of optimism and possessed a healthy self-confidence. Life in Norway can be dangerous at sea and in the mountains. One has to be brave to be able to live there, but it's worth it. The country is attractive and rich in resources. The language is beautiful and melodic. Each sentence ends with an upward movement. It sounds like a friendly invitation.

I have benefited from this fundamentally positive attitude. It is not enough to play brilliantly; it is the spirit that elates music making. The spirit of Norrköping lived on here to an even greater degree, and I felt at home. There, right in the front, sat the first concertmaster, Ernst Glaser. He was the soul of the orchestra, reserved yet friendly, but having great authority, respected and loved by all. Recently, I was very touched when I met his son Ernst Simon Glaser, a solo cellist in Gothenburg, who has the same seriousness, depth, and warmth.

Ernst Glaser sat in the second chair. He let his student Bjarne Larsen sit in the first chair to perform the great solos. Something like this is also a sign of greatness and sets the standard for the entire orchestra. In the first flutist's chair sat Ørnulf Gulbransen, a master student of Marcel Moyse from the Marlboro Music Festival in Vermont, who looked almost like the "king of the mountains." His performances had something unforgettably charming about them. Frøydis Ree Wekre played horn like a star and spent twenty-five years as principal horn. Among the violas, I found Sven Nyhus, who turned out to be a great specialist in folk music and who provided many stimulating suggestions. His daughter Åshild is the principal viola of the philharmonic today and is also an excellent player of the Hardanger fiddle. It's wonderful how music lives on within a family.

The Danish National Symphony Orchestra

In Copenhagen, a whole new situation awaited me. Before, I had always had a positive reception, but here the atmosphere was rather cautious and characterized by doubt. This was because of old tensions between the orchestra and its administration.

The orchestra, then perhaps the largest and best-equipped symphony orchestra in Scandinavia, belonged to the Danish Broadcasting Corporation and was thus a part of the music department of the corporation. At the same time, the symphony's regular concerts on Thursdays formed the backbone of the philharmonic life in Denmark. Together with a second in-house orchestra, the entertainment orchestra, and the excellent radio choir, very large scale works, such as Mahler's Symphony No. 8 or Arnold Schoenberg's *Gurre-Lieder*, could easily be performed with all our own resources. The expectations were exceedingly high, and they had had excellent conductors in Nikolai Malko and Fritz Busch. The orchestra was founded in 1925 as one of the first broadcasting orchestras in the world. The great man behind it all was the singer Emil Holm, the corporation's first director. A musician as head of the entire broadcasting corporation! Through his vision, energy, and contacts, the strings were equipped with outstanding Italian master instruments in one sweep: eighteen violins, six violas, and six cellos by masters such as Amati, Guarneri, Gagliano, Ruggieri, and so on. These were a priceless addition to the orchestra.

But now Emil Holm had passed away, as well as Nikolai Malko and Fritz Busch. The orchestra was at an impasse, and in general, there were complaints about the level of the playing technique. Mogens Andersen, the new head of the music department, was small in stature but big in vision and drive. But he was primarily an avid champion of New Music, which didn't sit well with the orchestra. The tensions between him and Waldemar Wolsing, the orchestra board chairman, were legendary. One morning Mogens Andersen told me that he bumped into Waldemar Wolsing in the hallway. "Good morning," the orchestra board chairman greeted him in a friendly manner. *What did he mean by that?* the head of the music department wondered. While under an aura of calmness, the air was heavy with suspicion. The orchestra saw me as Mogens Andersen's ally. And I was. After all, he had hired me. But I saw myself equally as an ally of the orchestra. We needed an artistic uplift.

I had to slowly earn the confidence of the musicians, but in the end, we never had conflicts. The recipe for getting along consisted of diligence and humor. The atmosphere at rehearsals and concerts was always quiet and respectful; gradually, more warmth, passion, and excitement came. For the first time, I conducted all the symphonies and other orchestral works by Carl Nielsen. The musicians' familiarity with this repertoire benefited me greatly. It was the basis for my interaction with this great symphonic composer, which still continues until today.

Nielsen's Symphony No. 2, known as "The Four Temperaments," was inspired by four paintings that Nielsen had seen in a bar. The delightful Danish sense of humor could be seen again in the orchestra's music foyer where they had hung up four identical photos of me. The caption underneath read, "The Four Temperaments."

The orchestra was rich in colorful personalities. Two concertmasters,

Leo Hansen and Charles Senderowitz, occupied the first violinist chair. Two musicians could hardly be more different. One was aristocratic, restrained, always friendly, at peace with himself, and at the same time, serious and elegant—an ideal concertmaster. He played an Amati instrument. His colleague, however, was lively and tremendously quick to reply. His family came from Ukraine, but he was born in Copenhagen, and his humor was original Danish. When he told of a stereotypical virtuoso, he pointed with his index finger to his temple and said with a smile, "He is lacking a director."

The woodwinds had brilliant players in Frantz Lemsser, Jørgen Hammergaard, and Ib Eriksson, continuing the great tradition of Gilbert Jespersen, Svend Christian Felumb, and Aage Oxenvad.

A problem gradually developed in the bass register. The performance of the principal bassoonist, Leo Lipschitz, regressed for some reason, and so, as the principal conductor, I had to make some changes. This is one of the most difficult tasks of an orchestral conductor. I think I did this with the utmost sensitivity. He reacted calmly and moved to third place in the group. Only later, when we were on a tour of Denmark and sitting alone in a train compartment, did he tell me how stressful this experience had been for him. He had even had suicidal thoughts. He gave me this advice, should similar circumstances come up again, to deal even more considerately with the person concerned. He spoke with such calmness and maturity that he impressed me deeply. We became best friends. I was a guest in his home several times, which was like a museum, with modern Danish art galore. Only through this incident did I really discover what a great man he was—a profound cultural personality. Later on, he accomplished much as the secretary and head of the Malko Competition in conducting. His wife, Aase Zacharias, was a cellist in the same orchestra. Later, I got to know her better and found the same warmth in her. Both were wonderful people.

Today, as honorary conductor of the orchestra, a wave of friendliness flows towards me from the whole orchestra. I would wish the same for all who come into contact with the orchestra.

The Staatskapelle Dresden

The fifteen years during which I was at first the "secret" and then the official music director of the Staatskapelle were probably the most formative of my life. For the first time, I stood in front of an orchestra that was among the best in the world.

I was forty-two years old when I heard the orchestra live for the first time, and on April 17, 1969, I conducted them for the first time in concert. It was a far-reaching experience for me.

As a schoolboy, I had often listened to the orchestra on the radio; while in Sweden, we listened to the symphony's concerts on the German radio station at 11:00 A.M. on Sunday mornings. The Staatskapelle was regularly broadcast under the direction of Karl Böhm. We sat spellbound in front of the small Bakelite radio by Telefunken. I never dreamed I would one day hear the orchestra live (at that time, the world was at war), much less imagined I would conduct this orchestra one day in the far future. I was just a music-obsessed student. Never did I dream of one day standing in front of this "miracle harp" as its music director. Yet, now all this came true but slowly, *poco a poco*.

By December 1969, I was back for further concerts, and the orchestra began vigorously trying to recruit me. I had made my concerns clear about being the music director of an orchestra under communist rule; however, the orchestra persevered. I like to think of myself as having endurance. But the orchestra surpassed me in this regard! They showed me all their sacred art heritage sites, art galleries, the Zwinger, the Silbermann organs, Saxon Switzerland National Park, Pillnitz Castle, and Moritzburg Castle. They assured me that even in the opera, everything would be just fine: "We will carry you through this." When I finally said yes, the orchestra still had to convince the state that it would only accept this Christian "from a capitalist country" and would under no circumstances be content with any "GDR world-class conductor." This took a few more years.

It is difficult to describe in detail what I learned from this experience. Those who were members of the orchestra at the time can understand it better. The orchestra was characterized by complete commitment. In the GDR, the inner imagination was the only alternative for people who were longing for meaning and truth. One created another world, in which beauty was absolute. This world became real through music. The concerts were always sold out—an island of the blessed. There were hardly any available evening tickets. If one was lucky, one could perhaps inherit a subscription from a relative (called an entitlement). One came in one's best clothes, arrived early, and stayed late to make the most of the uniqueness of the experience.

And the orchestra members? Already driven by the pursuit of absolute beauty and truth, they rose to ever-new heights because of their earnest audience. The orchestra members had tremendous inner strength and self-purifying wills, which could be all consuming and were only endured because of the grandeur of the music. The reward was also considerable. Gratitude flowed from the audience. Despite all their self-criticism, the musicians were thankful that they were allowed to play with such unique colleagues. During my fifteen years of working in Dresden, no one defected to the West. The orchestra was worth more to them than anything else.

Value? In one of my first rehearsals with the orchestra, I was rehearsing a part for the trombones. "Please, only the trombones," I said. And they played the part wonderfully. During the break, the second trombone player, Hans Kästner, came to me and said, "Professor, when one speaks of the trombones, one never says 'only.' " A delightful sense of humor, worth more than anything!

A dozen strong personalities in the orchestra were spiritual and musical examples: The first concertmaster, Peter Mirring, was originally from Berlin, but he had become *Dresdner assoluto* (the proverbial Dresdner). The small-statured Rudolf Ulbrich, sitting next to him, enjoyed so much respect from his colleagues that when he sank down less than half an inch in his chair, the whole orchestra immediately played twice as quietly. The concertmaster of the second violins, Reinhard Ulbricht, sat bolt upright on the front edge of his chair; he was a role model for his numerous students and all other colleagues. The highly cultured principal viola, Jochim Ulbricht, exemplified the spirit of the whole orchestra—and was one big inspiration for everyone. The woodwinds Johannes Walter, Kurt Mahn, Manfred Weise, and Wolfgang Liebscher were already striking personalities as wind soloists, but together they had a fantastic homogeneity. Later a special solo flutist, Eckart Haupt, distinguished himself as a musicologist and graduated with a doctoral degree before his retirement. Everything the principal horn, Peter Damm, did was the best and was unattainable by others. Every tone from Hans-Peter Sondermann's ("Specialman"; yes, that was his name) Dresdner timpani sounded as if it had been carefully weighed in gold. His secret has been buried with him. Finally, the harpist Jutta Zoff: how did she as a child prodigy manage to perform with seven different instruments? But even more, how did she manage to present such a rich inner world with her harp? In *A Hero's Life* by Richard Strauss, there is a point at the end of the great love scene where the harp plays a simple G-flat major chord, softly and dreamily. How she prepared this chord and then finally played it made this place the highlight of the whole work for me.

Ah, these wonderful people! Their total devotion is dear to me.

The Swedish Radio Symphony Orchestra

The Swedish Radio Symphony Orchestra became the culmination of my Swedish experience. At the same time as I was directing one of the oldest orchestras in Western culture (more than 425 years old) in Dresden, I became the chief conductor of the youngest orchestra (about fifteen years old) that I had ever directed. Built up through intensive training under its conductor Sergiu Celibidache, the orchestra had already reached a considerable technical level. Sergiu Celibidache could be proud of it, but he did not want to take full artistic responsibility. And so I became the orchestra's first chief conductor. A strong triumvirate in the music department managed the orchestra with vigor and prudence: Magnus Enhörning, Allan Stångberg, and Ingvar Lidholm.

Since 1962, I had lived with my family in Danderyd, near Stockholm, and there my home remained while working in Oslo, Copenhagen, and Dresden. I did not want to uproot my family again and again but rather provide the stability that I had missed as a child. For that reason, the invitation of the Swedish Radio Symphony Orchestra was a godsend for my wife and myself. I could spend more time at home with my loved ones. I was hired in 1977. Our four girls were then twenty, eighteen, eight, and six years old. It was a wonderful time.

In 1979, our new concert hall, the Berwald Hall, was inaugurated. The acoustics were good, especially for the radio, but a bit direct and lacking in tone color. Its size also proved to be a bit small for really large-scale works. I added to my repertoire, especially from Swedish music. There were a lot of good, pioneering spirits, and the quality of the musicians was outstanding. The radio had established its own training institute for musicians in Edsberg Castle, north of Stockholm, with the best possible teachers in order to secure a pool of young musicians for the orchestra. The visions of the triumvirate proved to be correct and bore good fruit. Great talent was there, fostered by a conducive environment.

However, some tradition and a healthy, well-balanced self-confidence were lacking. The contrast with Dresden, where the orchestra was in full bloom and highly esteemed by the audience, was very large. I dreamed of similar conditions for the orchestra in my homeland, but four hundred years of growth cannot be condensed into just ten years. In addition, we had the new *Mitbestimmungsgesetz* (MBL Act—the acronym for the Co-determination Act), a well-intentioned but somewhat clumsy outgrowth of a democratic idea.[2] I remember a meeting with my musicians where I suggested a few reforms. My old classmate from the College of Music, the excellent timpanist Bengt Arsenius, did not agree: "Perhaps this works in the GDR but not here." He probably meant that the musicians under GDR rule were not sufficiently democratically minded. But that was not true: the discipline of the orchestra came from within, was an expression of artistic control, not out of obedience to a higher authority. Yet, Bengt Arsenius expressed the crux of the matter: every orchestra is different, every situation is different, and every problem has to be solved individually. As the Swedish poet Gustaf Fröding says, "What constitutes truth in Berlin and Jena is just a bad joke in Heidelberg." Adding to this is Henrik Ibsen's insight in his play *An Enemy of the People*: "A normally constituted truth lives, . . . at most twenty years—seldom longer."[3]

With the renewal of the MBL Act, even the triumvirate that had hired me had to step down. I realized that the basic conditions for my work no longer existed, and I resigned. Even today I do not know whether I did the right thing. But I did learn how delicately the threads are spun in the orchestral organism and how helpful a long tradition can be.

The musical standard of the Swedish Radio Symphony Orchestra is admirable in every respect, and I enjoy it every time that I come back as its honorary conductor. The musicians not only have virtuosic fingers and lips but also open ears and warm hearts. I wish that the great, wide world would know more about how high the quality of the playing is in Sweden. But even more than that, I wish that the musicians themselves could be proud of the fact that they are musicians. This has nothing to do with pride or arrogance; a real musician is always humble. That music has such a high value that it can become the center of a life with even the highest ethical standards and not just remain a delicate ornament, a nice conversation, or an exciting circus—of that one may justly be proud. Artists should be the pioneers of the whole nation. Through their extraordinary sensitivity, they draw their sustenance from deeper sources, feel the present tides more intensely, and look further into the future than the average person. In this way, they help to give life more meaning and thus have a vital mission to fulfill, which is also a commitment. This mission ennobles the artist.

However, one can only achieve this self-confident artistry if a large audience supports the musicians. We are still a long way off from this in Sweden; but we are working on it. The audience is very good but too small. It would have to be a grass-roots movement, by which the musicians could feel supported, just as it is the case in Dresden and Leipzig. We look forward to the future with complete confidence.

The San Francisco Symphony

My experience in San Francisco was again something completely new. Since 1970, I had traveled to the United States every year for a few weeks for concerts and master classes. Therefore, America was not new territory for me. The people lived a very different lifestyle than I did, but I found them to be open and sympathetic. The circles in which I moved were cultured, and the people admirably easygoing.

When I conducted the San Francisco Symphony for the first time in June 1984, I was impressed by their high technical and musical standard. The musicians were really in no way inferior to "my" Dresden family. They only lacked the four hundred years of tradition, with that infallible instinct of how to articulate every note and how to shape every phrase so that it can sound very authentic. They were aware of this—that's why they brought me from Dresden and not some charismatic "shooting star." This, of course, gave me great joy. But at the same time, I applauded the orchestra and its manager, Peter Pastreich, for the fact that they did not, like some other orchestras, regard short-term success as more important. At the signing of the contract, Peter Pastreich gave me a beautiful volume with aerial photographs of San Francisco, titled *Above San Francisco*. His dedication sounds almost prophetic today:

For Herbert Blomstedt,

   Looking forward to you taking the San Francisco Symphony above—and beyond—San Francisco.

With admiration and affection,
Peter Pastreich
31 July 1984

Success came fast enough though. Peter Pastreich's recipe proved to be correct; it was a wonderful partnership. The music sometimes rose into the ethereal. The orchestra changed without being aware of it. I also did. There was an interaction similar to Dresden—a constant give-and-take.

I maintained my obsession with detail but always kept the whole picture in view. And following my habit in Dresden, I always addressed the musicians as "Mr. So-and-so." This was unusual and perhaps took some getting used to in America, but I believe no one perceived it as formal and distant. Before the concerts, I sometimes gave the soloists some final instructions on small slips of paper. Some of them kept all these slips and turned them into a juicy collection. Nevertheless, I became more easygoing. Though I was not aware of it myself, my colleagues noticed it gratefully. I opened myself more and more to American music and learned and performed new scores galore. I even received the Ditson Conductor's Award for distinguished service to American music from Columbia University in New York. Unfortunately, I never made it to a work by George Gershwin.

In San Francisco, I learned to respect and follow the very strict rules of the American labor unions. An official armed with a stopwatch comes on stage a few minutes before the rehearsal concludes. At that exact second, one has to stop, otherwise overtime must be paid. Merciless.

I actually made an exercise out of it. I managed now and then to finish a work or a movement on the exact second—and then I was rewarded with applause. Basically, it is a rule that developed out of respect for the individual. Who knows if a musician must make a telephone call, pick up a child on time, or needs to catch a bus?

However, I could not learn everything—for example, dancing. At my first annual banquet for the main sponsors, I sat with Mrs. Davies to my right. She had donated millions of dollars for the concert hall, which was named after her—Louise M. Davies Symphony Hall. After dinner, she invited me to dance with her. To my shame, I had to confess that I had never learned to dance. "Something is missing in your education," she said. Nonetheless, I was allowed to stay for ten years.

During my time in San Francisco, I only needed to hire one new solo player. Thanks to my predecessor, Edo de Waart, all other instruments were already superbly employed upon my arrival. The principal flutist was Paul Renzi, who had played under Toscanini as a teenager. His father had been an organist at St. Peter's Basilica in Rome and also a friend of Verdi's.

The first oboist was Marc Lifschey, a legendary musician who had been a solo oboist under George Szell in Cleveland but preferred the freer air in San Francisco. The principal clarinet was David Breeden, a perfect wind player and a quiet anchor, in addition. And the bassoon! Three of them shared the same first name, Stephen, and they were all world champions: Stephen Paulsen, Steven Dibner, and Steven Braunstein. Sometimes tears came to my eyes when they played. That the fourth was named Rob Weir was an anomaly. But everyone loved him also. The list is getting long; but how could I leave them out? Arthur Krehbiel, the principal horn with the incredibly beautiful tone, assured me, "When the mood is right, everything will be right." His "mood" was almost always right. All the wonderful characteristics of a solo trumpet were brought together in Glenn Fischthal; Mark Lawrence with his colleagues Paul Welcomer and John Engelkes were a wonderful trombone section.

So who exactly was the solo player that I had to hire? Marc Lifschey still played beautifully, but his tone was becoming increasingly small and remained *mezzo forte* (moderately loud). A new man was hard to find after such a predecessor. The young man who was finally chosen was Bill Bennett. His tone was perhaps not as "sweet" as Marc Lifschey's, but he had other characteristics that were irreplaceable: flexibility, charm, modesty, an in-depth education, and a sense of humor. He became a favorite of us all. In 1992, he premiered (from memory!) the oboe concerto composed for him by John Harbison and recorded a CD. We were all devastated when he was diagnosed with a brain tumor a few years ago. He survived, but the question of whether he would ever be able to play again remained. With iron discipline, he succeeded. On February 23, 2013, he joined again as a soloist, this time in playing the Oboe Concerto by Richard Strauss. After the first fifty-seven bars, he collapsed on stage, and four days later he died.

It was very moving and instructive to watch as the musicians, the administration, and the audience mourned for him. As one big family, they held together. This is another example of how music can make connections and how one hundred very different people can grow together into a single organism—the orchestra. After almost thirty years, I am happy to still be connected with the orchestra as conductor laureate. We play together annually; the learning continues.

The Norddeutscher Rundfunk (NDR; North German Radio) Symphony Orchestra

The fact that I was elected as music director of the NDR Symphony Orchestra was in a sense a homecoming. And that made me very happy. For one, my wife was a native of Hamburg. Second, I had a vague feeling that the founder and longtime music director of the orchestra, Hans Schmidt-Isserstedt, would have liked to have me as his successor. And now it was so, more than twenty years after his death.

I knew the manager of the orchestra, Rolf Beck, through my regular guest conducting of the Bamberg Symphony Orchestra, where he had presided very successfully for a long time. He was an able musician (a choral conductor) himself and also a trained lawyer—skills he could use well as a manager. We got along well, and the orchestra was very good. Everything was just perfect until the Gewandhaus Orchestra in Leipzig needed a new music director and offered me the position. This placed me in a very difficult situation.

There was no question that the Gewandhaus Orchestra was the more famous, tradition-rich orchestra. But they were in a delicate transition. At the time, the Hamburg-based orchestra was perhaps even better than the one in Leipzig as far as pure playing technique is concerned, but I saw more opportunities in Leipzig. What should I do now? Here I had to learn something unprecedented.

I decided to say yes to the Gewandhaus, but first I wanted to fulfill my three-year contract with Hamburg. Mr. Beck and his orchestra in Hamburg were not enthusiastic about this development, to put it mildly. They had all, like me, looked forward to a long and happy collaboration, and no sooner had I begun than I spoke of an early end. I could very well understand the disappointment in Hamburg and accepted Mr. Beck's proposal to stay for only two years so that he could begin looking for a new music director that would hopefully lead to a more permanent relationship.

But they were still two good years. We had an excellent working relationship and performed many wonderful concerts together. In 1997, the orchestra's Brahms program was nominated as the best concert of the year in Tokyo. No wonder—the double bass originally owned by Brahms's father was played in the orchestra! A trip to South America during the same year was also memorable. There we performed even more Brahms.

I had to learn to make music as beautifully as possible while facing some opposition. My colleagues in the orchestra helped me unreservedly. We became real friends. And after the two years were over, I was happy to accept the invitation for the annual guest concerts. I think I have to make up something in Hamburg for what I owe the orchestra and the city. Since Günter Wand, the most widely revered of all former chief conductors, died, I've also been asked to direct Bruckner symphonies, which he had conducted so brilliantly. These concerts were and are always of particular excitement and emotion for all of us. Somehow everything has come full circle, and we all feel happy and grateful.

The Leipzig Gewandhaus Orchestra

The task in Leipzig was enormous, sometimes thankless, and endlessly stimulating. In the communist era, the orchestra was favored by those in power, which my predecessor, Kurt Masur, took advantage of. Through his good contacts and his unflagging energy, he managed to build the new Gewandhaus concert hall—to my knowledge, it was the only newly built concert hall in the GDR. It opened in 1981 and is an ideal building in many respects, especially acoustically and in terms of the space for the musicians and the administration.

But the musicians had also suffered much under the regime. Once a sanctuary for a freely developing musical initiative, the Gewandhaus became an institution of musical production to, effectively as possible, improve the image of the GDR in the outside world and earn foreign exchange. For example, toward the end of the communist era, the orchestra was suddenly augmented by fifteen musicians to a total of two hundred members so that they could travel even more and bring the much-needed Western currency home. In this way, a lot of the quality was lost. By effectively focusing on a big-hit repertoire that was repeatedly in demand, many of the finer nuances of playing were neglected.

So, lots and lots of work awaited me. Without the joy that music brings, without the help of 185 great musicians, who also took as much pleasure in pure music, it would not have been possible. Simply put my strategy was the following:

1. To reintroduce the position of the Gewandhaus director who should take over the entire administration of the orchestra. I found the right man for the job in Andreas Schulz.
2. As the music director, I would concentrate on the purely musical tasks.
3. To play again more early classical music (Haydn, Mozart, etc.) where articulation and phrasing are in the foreground.
4. To play more baroque music, also with specialized guest conductors. This would also benefit the weekly motets and Bach cantatas in the St. Thomas Church.
5. To streamline the sound in the romantic repertoire, without a loss of strength and while retaining the traditional dark "colors" of the orchestra.
6. In favor of greater transparency, to introduce the classic German orchestral seating—with the second violins on the right.
7. To play interesting new pieces, partly from my own repertoire (Nielsen, Sibelius), as well as some others.

To my great delight, everyone collaborated wonderfully, including the city fathers, under the leadership of the lord mayor and the head of cultural affairs. The second violins had not made music in the "right" place since the golden times under Franz Konwitschny (who died in 1962).

For them, particularly the older colleagues, it was very unusual, and many initially felt lost when far from their collaborators in the first violin section. But it was well worth it.

My successor, Riccardo Chailly, continued this work in his own way and gave the orchestra new impulses, which are very successful. And so the orchestra is now in a wonderful condition. Once again it is there where is belongs—at the top.

The audience also assisted. It was only possible with their support. In Leipzig, music takes an unusually special place. The annual survey in the *Bild-Zeitung* (*Picture newspaper*) is significant in regard to this. A randomly selected group of citizens from Leipzig selects the one hundred most important people of the city. The results appear in the newspaper, and everyone is curious. During the time I was in Leipzig, the lord mayor was number one; number two was the Gewandhaus music director! Number three was the former Gewandhaus music director! Number four was the cantor of St. Thomas Church! Because the two lord mayors during my tenure were amateur musicians (viola and cello, respectively), the four most important people of the city were musicians! This would be difficult to match in Berlin, Munich, and Vienna.

Thus, the Leipzig Gewandhaus Orchestra music director has an enormous task. The expectations are huge. Only if we are willing to keep learning anew can we accomplish the task. I am grateful that as honorary conductor of the Gewandhaus Orchestra I can still contribute something to the musical life of this unique city. I admire these musicians, who with enormous diligence and devotion have become what they are today. They are a gift from God.

* * * * *

Finally, a few thoughts about two orchestras that were never "my" orchestras but that later appointed me as a honorary conductor and with whom I have played music for a long time with much enjoyment.

The Bamberg Symphony

I already admired the Bamberg Symphony as a student in Stockholm when it gave a guest performance there under its first chief conductor, Joseph Keilberth. I think the final work was Schubert's *Great C Major Symphony*; after this tremendous accomplishment, the symphony played a fifteen-minute encore: *Till Eulenspiegel's Merry Pranks* by Richard Strauss! I admired the orchestra beyond measure, and I succeeded in going backstage and seeing the maestro six feet away from me. But I didn't dare speak with him or ask for an autograph.

Now I have conducted more than one hundred concerts with the orchestra myself, and the admiration has grown into love. They have a very sensuous sound, performing music with ease, while concentrating like no other orchestra. This is probably something they inherited from their history: their origins are in Prague. The beautiful, relatively small city of Bamberg, which was never destroyed during the war, and its thousand-year-old culture has helped to preserve this sound. Here one rides to rehearsals on a bicycle. Here one can learn to live simply again, without hurriedness, and then pass on the musical message to the whole world. The orchestra travels more than any other German orchestra, partly because it is so popular but also because the city of Bamberg is too small to exclusively employ it. Nevertheless, almost one in ten residents of Bamberg is a subscriber to the symphony. No other city has achieved this!

The NHK Symphony Orchestra in Tokyo

This amazing orchestra, probably the best in all of Asia, was the first orchestra to award me the title of honorary conductor. Since 1981, when we first performed together, we have performed more than one hundred concerts. Takao Hase, the manager at the time, quipped after the last concert that he would take my passport away so that I would have to stay in Japan forever. He kindly refrained from doing it. Instead, in 1986, I was appointed honorary conductor for life.

Kindness and respect are very important throughout Japan. We could learn much from them—if we wanted to. At the airport, the manager himself met us, not an unidentified driver with a name plaque. Two limousines were available for us and our luggage. The limousine, which arrived every morning to take me to rehearsals, had headrests covered with white lace, and the driver wore white gloves. When I got to the rehearsal hall, three men from the administration were already waiting for me on the stairs, and they bowed as if by command.

The orchestra is highly focused; nobody says a word. All listen intently. Although their English is very rudimentary, they react very quickly to any instruction. There are no technical problems. Everyone knows his or her part perfectly. One can immediately go in depth, to expression, to articulation, and to balance. It's no wonder they have become so good. They also play with much emotion when they get the chance.

And the audience! The Nippon Hōsō Kyōkai (Japan Broadcasting Corporation) broadcasts *every* concert on television, forty or more programs a year, in addition to several preparation programs. Afterward post-event programs are aired, in which the performance is discussed—a gigantic conservatory for more than 125 million people!

Even here we Europeans could learn something. Music is not subject to a quota; music creates the quota!

Great order prevails on the streets. Everything is meticulously clean. There are no discarded bottles, no graffiti, no fighting, and no theft; crime happens only on a big scale. How did they manage this? They are simply well educated—also through music. Once again, we have something to learn.

---

1. The composer dedicated the 2011 revised version to Herbert Blomstedt, "A great conductor and a dear friend."

2. The Codetermination Act "is a German law which requires companies of over 2000 employees to have half the supervisory board of directors as representatives of workers." *Wikipedia*, s.v. *"Mitbestimmungsgesetz,"* accessed October 14, 2016, https://en.wikipedia .org/wiki/Mitbestimmungsgesetz.

3. Henrik Ibsen, *An Enemy of the People*, trans. R. Farquharson Sharp, act 4.

"Why I Am a Christian"

THE LECTURE SERIES "WHY I AM (Not) a Christian" has included many notable German politicians, such as Helmut Schmidt, the former German chancellor; Gerhard Stoltenberg, the former minister of Defense; Peter Schulz, Hamburg's former lord mayor; and Sabine Leutheusser-Schnarrenberger, a federal minister of Justice[1] Before Herbert Blomstedt gave the following speech for the lecture series, Johann Sebastian Bach's Prelude in A Minor for organ was played as a tribute to the speaker.

* * * * *

As far as I'm concerned, this music could go on much longer, but I am happy to be able to talk to you here. For a musician, I can assure you, it is a peculiar feeling. These walls have heard Johann Sebastian Bach himself . . . and these walls have heard Philipp Nicolai and his mighty voice. "Wachet auf, ruft uns die Stimme" [in English, the hymn is known as "Wake, Awake for Night Is Flying"], "Wie schön leuchtet der Morgenstern" ["How Lovely Shines the Morning Star"], and so on, are known to every musician and touch our hearts.

The question today is, Why? Why am I a Christian? Why am I here anyway? This is a strange story. Pastor Denecke[2] already mentioned that I agreed to speak without hesitation. This is not typical for me. But in this case, I did not hesitate for a moment, and I'll tell you why. On August 30, I was here in Hamburg. That was a Saturday which meant no rehearsal. In the morning, I went to church, as I like to do, and the sermon preached that day was about the parable of the good Samaritan.

A Great Song

I was very moved by the message. Of course, we often think about this parable, especially in a city like Hamburg, where we still see poor people begging for some attention, money, and love on almost every street. I rarely give something and so have a bit of a guilty conscience about it.

After the service, I went for a walk and thought, *I cannot help everyone, but let me help someone.* But whom? I decided to walk in the direction of St. Catherine because this church is something special for a musician. As I was on my way, a young man approached me and asked in broken German, "Excuse me, where is the Brahms Museum?" I told him that there was no Brahms museum in Hamburg as far as I knew. But I told him that there is a Johannes Brahms-Platz [Brahms square], there by the concert hall. I was curious. The man was very thin and looked hungry. I asked, "Are you a musician?" "Yes," he said, "I'm an organist from Moscow." That is unusual! In all of Moscow, there may be five organs. The Orthodox Church has no organs. And here is a young organist from Moscow, and he meets another musician! I did not tell him who I was, but instead I said, "If you are an organist, you might want to go with me to St. Catherine's Church; that's the church where Johann Sebastian Bach once played in his youth."

Once Bach walked all the way from Lüneburg, where he was studying with Georg Böhm. He wanted to hear Johann Adam Reincken in St. Catherine's Church, because Reincken was famous. But Bach surely had an ulterior motive because Reincken was so old; perhaps Bach thought he could have Reinckn's place if he could play for him. And there, the two of them sat. Bach played, and Reincken listened with astonishment. And then Reincken wanted to give Bach a big test and gave him a theme, a Dutch folk song, since he came from Holland. From this folk song, Bach should make a fugue. And the young Bach improvised a fugue—the great Fugue in G Minor. That happened here.

I wanted to invite the young man to dinner, but the restaurants around here were closed, and I told him that sometimes music might be more important than food. Although he had not eaten properly in several days, he agreed. So we entered the church, and suddenly we heard the organ begin to play. The young man said, "I have to go up there." So we climbed up to the organ balcony. There was the organist, Mr. Adamski, just wrapping up. I spoke to him, "Sorry, I have met a young friend who wants to try out the organ. Would that be possible?" Mr. Adamski agreed, and the young man began to play. Now it was our turn to be astounded, and Mr. Adamski suggested we go down to the nave and listen from there. So we sat there while the young musician played for about an hour, one piece after another—without a score. Mr. Adamski said that he played the most difficult piece one can play: Trio Sonatas by Bach. Then the young man improvised a bit, and I said, "Isn't it strange? I met him by chance in the street, but actually I don't think it was by accident. I do not believe in coincidences. I think it was an act of Providence."

Mr. Adamski said nothing, just looked at me, and encouraged by his willingness to listen, I went on. Finally, Mr. Adamski mentioned this lecture series and said, "You need to speak [about this] in this church for the lecture series." And he asked me if I would be willing to do this. He would then coordinate with the senior pastor, Denecke.

When I got back to my hotel, I looked at my schedule, and on the given day, I was available. When Pastor Denecke sent me a fax in São Paulo, where I had just traveled with the symphony orchestra, I immediately said yes. Because with a prologue like this, one cannot say no, correct?

Why am I a Christian? Perhaps the question why is not easy to answer. There are so many whys in the Bible. A few months ago I was fortunate to conduct an a cappella concert. There is this beautiful motet by Brahms, "*Whyyy* [sung, then a great pause], *whyyy?*" [sung again]. The text is from the book of Job: why are humans born if they still need to go through so many trials? This is Job himself who is speaking, and he accuses God. Too often these whys preoccupy us.

I cannot solve the big whys; neither can the Bible. It can only ask the questions and guide us to think.

But why I am a Christian is easy to answer. I was baptized when I was thirteen years old and have never looked back. It was not always easy. I have made mistakes, sometimes doubted; but that was good—it makes one stronger. One needs difficult experiences in order to strengthen one's spiritual muscles.

Why am I a Christian?

1. It gives me dignity. I think that many of the difficulties we go through come from the fact that we no longer appreciate our own worth. We believe we are broken and not worth anything and that we can do what we want with ourselves. It does not matter. I remember an experience when I went to Leningrad for the first time with the Staatskapelle Dresden. We had a German tour guide who lived in Leningrad, Dr. Schäff—an old surgeon who lived in Russia before the revolution and had been through a lot. He was not trained as a museum guide. I noticed that he did not describe the old icons as an art historian but as a believer. He knew exactly how the icons illustrated the biblical stories. We started conversing and came to stand in front of a window, looking at a church. I asked him for the name of the church (it was Saint Isaac's Cathedral), but he did not know it himself and went to ask the museum guard. She had dozed off, and he tapped her lightly on the shoulder. "Sorry; can you tell us which church is over there?" She was startled and said, "I don't know that! And anyway, what do you mean 'church'? We come from apes." To which Dr. Schäff replied, "You perhaps, but not me!" He subsequently told me this, because I do not understand Russian.

How true! Despite all the theories about evolution and creation, he recognized that he was created. And that gave him a sense of self-worth that cannot be taken away. One can do stupid things, and then one is worthless in one's own eyes, but the basic idea that I am created in God's image creates a point of departure, which is quite different than if we think we have evolved over billions of years from amphibians. One can talk a lot about the theory of evolution, but this is not the time and the place. However, the certainty that we are created beings gives us dignity. We sometimes need this very much.

2. *It creates a perspective for one's life.* The Bible is clear: God is the Lord of creation. And this gives us a vision and hope: The same Jesus who died will also return. In this way, one receives a global perspective on life, which we often need when the hustle and bustle of our daily lives sometimes threatens to overwhelm us.

3. *The following is perhaps especially important for a musician or an artist: the Christian faith helps to save us from hubris.* As artists, we are so busy with ourselves; that is the nature of our work. We are our own material; we need to work with ourselves: as a singer, one needs to study one's throat well. Our art must develop with the help of our imagination, but we easily forget that which can be interesting outside of ourselves and around us and that we are not alone. Christians, Jews, or Muslims—all those who believe in one God—know that in relation to this God we are small. Whatever you are doing, you are small. You are indeed created in God's image, but you are not God. This is sometimes very good to know. I have an American colleague who has often conducted in Europe. He is a very good conductor and very well known. I met him once at a restaurant and was happy to see him, but he spoke only of himself, and I soon lost interest. Later I heard that he does the same thing in the circle of his admirers: "Did you notice how I did this part? Wasn't that nice? Here, in this bar, all my colleagues do such and such. But that's totally wrong; it must be so-and-so. I did it like that for the first time today.

Wasn't that wonderful? This is how it is correct." After talking like this for fifteen minutes, he says, "Now let's talk about something else. What do you think about my performance?" This is very human, especially if one is an artist. But the one-God religion tells us that we are always small in relation to our Creator.

4. Christianity shows us where we can receive forgiveness—a big problem for people at any time. I sometimes feel like all people, including myself, carry a huge load. In our relationship with God, this debt can be eliminated immediately. Forgiveness is necessary to lead a healthy life. I noticed the following when I worked in the GDR: how impossible it was to practice forgiveness under socialism. If someone had done something against the state, it was never forgiven. Never! The person could have sat in prison for years. They were never accepted again; they remained under suspicion forever. Even after the reunification, it's like this. Whoever has done something wrong in the GDR will not be forgiven. Christianity gives forgiveness and joy and brings emotional and physical health.

Christianity brings us near to the source of creation. We're all artists somehow, right? In the kitchen, in every workplace, one creates something, and the Creator is the primary reason for all of this.

There are angel drawings by Paul Klee that he drew in the last year of his life, while he was very ill. He was an avowed atheist, but he was a seeker. In 1920, he wrote his book *Creative Confession*. A few lines from the book are on his gravestone. The last part is, "My dwelling place is . . . slightly closer to the heart of creation than usual, and still not close enough."

In these lines, I sense a deep yearning for the Source of creation. I also feel this desire. This connects me, a Christian, with Paul Klee, the atheist: wanting to go back to the Source, to our origins. Perhaps it takes a lifetime to get there. As a Christian, I believe our Source is God.

---

1. This chapter is an excerpt from Herbert Blomstedt's unscripted speech, given on October 20, 1997, in St. Catherine's Church in Hamburg. A tape recording served as a template for the text, and all presentations from the lecture series in St. Catherine's Church were published. This speech was edited for this biography in consultation with Herbert Blomstedt.

2. Pastor Axel Denecke was the lead pastor of St. Catherine's Church in Hamburg at the time of the speech.

Appendix A

Biographical Information, Honors and Awards, Discography (Selection)

Life

Herbert Blomstedt was born on July 11, 1927, in Springfield, Massachusetts, United States, the son of Swedish parents: father Adolf Blomstedt (October 8, 1898–January 28, 1981), a pastor of the Seventh-day Adventist Church; and mother Alida, née Thorson (February 1, 1899–October 23, 1957), a concert pianist. Herbert's parents were married in 1922.

Herbert Blomstedt's siblings: Norman (April 30, 1924–September 15, 2005), a physician; and Marita (June 16, 1938), a nurse.

Herbert Blomstedt's wife: Waltraud, née Petersen (December 2, 1928–February 8, 2003), a French, German, and English teacher. They were married on May 29, 1955, at Ekebyholm Castle in Sweden.

Herbert Blomstedt's daughters: Cecilia (May 29, 1957), a doctor; Maria (February 6, 1959), a doctor; Elisabet (December 27, 1969), a physiotherapist and librarian; Kristina (October 10, 1971), a businesswoman.

Herbert Blomstedt's grandchildren: Alexander (1994), Oscar (1994), Christian (1996), Anastasia (1996), Moa (1998), Ida (2001), Magnus (2002).

Education

1945–1950: Royal College of Music in Stockholm (Conducting inter alia with Tor Mann)
1948–1952: Uppsala University (Musicology inter alia with Carl-Allan Moberg)

1949, 1956: Summer courses at the Kranichstein Music Institute in Darmstadt (Contemporary Music inter alia with John Cage, Maurits Frank, and Heinrich Strobel)

1950–1955: Several courses at the Mozarteum in Salzburg (Conducting with Igor Markevitch)

1952: Training at the New England Conservatory of Music in Boston, Massachusetts

1953: Juilliard School of Music in New York (Conducting inter alia with Jean Morel)

1953: Tanglewood Music Center in Lenox, Massachusetts (Conducting with Leonard Bernstein and Lukas Foss)

1956: Summer course at the Schola Cantorum Basiliensis in Basel (Renaissance and Baroque Performance Practice with Ina Lohr and August Wenzinger)

Professional activities

February 3, 1954: Debut concert at the Stockholm Concert Hall with the Stockholm Philharmonic Orchestra

1961–1971: Professor of Conducting at the Royal College of Music in Stockholm

Appointments as chief conductor

1954–1961: Norrköping Symphony Orchestra

1962–1968: Oslo Philharmonic

1968–1977: Danish National Symphony Orchestra

1975–1985: Staatskapelle Dresden

1977–1982: Swedish Radio Symphony Orchestra

1985–1995: San Francisco Symphony

1996–1998: NDR Symphony Orchestra

1998–2005: Leipzig Gewandhaus Orchestra

Honorary conductor

1986: NHK Symphony Orchestra

1995: San Francisco Symphony

2005: Leipzig Gewandhaus Orchestra

2006: Bamberg Symphony

2006: Swedish Radio Symphony Orchestra

2006: Danish National Symphony Orchestra

2016: Staatskapelle Dresden

List of honors and awards

1965: Member of the Royal Swedish Academy of Music

1971: Knight of the Order of the North Star, awarded by the king of Sweden

1978: Honorary doctorate, Andrews University

1978: Knight of the Order of the Dannebrog, awarded by the queen of Denmark

1979: Litteris et Artibus—gold medal of the Royal Swedish Music Academy

1992: Ditson Conductor's Award for distinguished service to American Music, Columbia University

1993: Honorary doctorate, Southwestern Adventist University

1997: Honorary doctorate, Pacific Union College

1998: För Tonkonstens Främjande, a medal of the Royal Swedish Academy of Music

1999: Honorary doctorate, University of Gothenburg

2001: Anton Bruckner Award of the Bertil-Östbo Bruckner Foundation, Linz, Austria

2003: Commander's Cross of the Order of Merit of the Federal Republic of Germany, awarded by the German president, Johannes Rau

2007: Max Rudolf Award of the American Conductors Guild for outstanding achievements as a conductor and teacher

2007: Golden Badge of Honor of the Staatskapelle Dresden

2008: Johann Walter Plaque of the *Sächsischen Musikrats* (Saxon music council)

2008: Prize of Honor of the Carl Nielsen Society, Denmark

2010: Golden Badge of Honor of the Friends of the Bamberg Symphony

2011: Bach Medal of the city of Leipzig

2012: Charles E. Weniger Award for Excellence, Loma Linda University, Loma Linda, California

2012: Seraphim Medal of the Swedish royal family

2012: Kilenyi Medal of Honor, Bruckner Society of America

2013: International Classical Music Award, for the complete Bruckner symphonies box set

2013: Award of Excellence, Associated Church Press, for the article, "Present Truth in Music," in the *Adventist Review*

2013: "Best Audio Bruckner Recording," Bruckner Society of America

2013: Socii et Amici Medal, University of Gothenburg

2014: Honorary Gold Medal, Stockholm Concert Hall Foundation

2014: "Visiting Professor Emeritus," Senzoku Gakuen College of Music, Tokyo

2014: Wilhelm Hansen Prize of Honor, Copenhagen
2014: Rolf Schock Prize, Stockholm
2016: NHK Broadcasting Cultural Award, Tokyo
2016: Léonie Sonning Music Prize, Copenhagen
2017: Brahms Prize, *Brahms-Gesellschaft* (Brahms society), Schleswig-Holstein

Honorary position
2001–2008: President of the *Stiftung Musikforschung Zentralschweiz* (a foundation for music research in central Switzerland)

Discography (selection)
Bach: Mass in B Minor (Larsson/Ziesak/Genz/Henschel/Leipzig Gewandhaus Orchestra/Leipzig Gewandhaus Chamber Choir), EuroArts Bluray B007WB5D66, 2012.

Bartók: Concerto for Orchestra/Kossuth (San Francisco Symphony), Decca CD B00000424P, 1995.

Beethoven: Complete Symphonies (Staatskapelle Dresden), Brilliant Classics CD B007NCP86E, 2012.

Beethoven: Leonore (Moser/Cassilly/Donath/Büchner/Ridderbusch/Adam/Polster/Staatskapelle Dresden/Leipzig Radio Choir), Berlin Classics CD B0000035N6, 1996.

Beethoven: Missa Solemnis (Schneider/Romberger/Kupfer/Croft/Leipzig Gewandhaus Orchestra/MDR Radio Choir), Querstand CD B00A6K-GDEG, 2013.

Beethoven: Symphonies 1–9 (Leipzig Gewandhaus Orchestra), Accentus CD, release June 2017.

Beethoven: Symphonies No. 9 (Saturova/Fujimura/Elsner/Gerhaher/Leipzig Gewandhaus Orchestra/MDR Radio Choir/Leipzig Fewandhaus Childrens Choir), Accentus DVD B01L32LU16, 2016.

Berwald: Symphony No. 1 in G Minor, "Sinfonie Sérieuse"/Symphony No. 4 (San Francisco Symphony), Decca CD B00000E54X, 1993.

Brahms: Ein Deutsches Requiem (Norberg-Schulz/Holzmair/San Francisco Symphony Chorus/San Francisco Symphony), London/Decca CD B00000424O, 1995. (This recording won a Grammy Award.)

Brahms: Symphony No. 4/Choruses a Cappella, op. 74, no. 1, 109, 110 (Leipzig Gewandhaus Orchestra/MDR Radio Choir), Decca CD 455510, 1998.

Bruckner: The Complete Symphonies (Leipzig Gewandhaus Orchestra), Allegro Hybrid SACD B0094BDO9A, 2013. (This set of recordings won an International Classical Music Award in 2013 for the category "Best Collection" and a prize for the best Bruckner audio recording in 2012 from the Bruckner Society of America.)

Bruckner: Symphony No. 4, "Romantic" (San Francisco Symphony), London CD B00000423L, 1995.

Bruckner: Symphony No. 6/ Wagner: Siegfried Idyll (San Francisco Symphony), Decca CD B00000E544, 1993.

Bruckner: Sinfonie Nr. 9/Adagio für Streichorchester (Leipzig Gewandhaus Orchestra), Decca CD B000026CRE, 2009 (import).

Grieg: Peer Gynt (Malmberg/Haeggander/Hoffman/White/Lisi/Rapp/ Myksvoll/Meyer/San Francisco Symphony Choir/San Francisco Symphony), Decca CD B0000041VN, 1990. (This concert was the top-award winner for "Critics' First Choice.")

Grieg: Piano Concerto/Chopin: Piano Concerto No. 1 (Mustonen/San Francisco Symphony), London CD B000004275, 1996.

Hindemith: Orchestral Works (San Francisco Symphony/Leipzig Gewandhaus Orchestra), Decca CD B0000C6IW2, 2004.

Hindemith: Symphonia Serena/Die Harmonie der Welt (Leipzig Gewandhaus Orchestra), Decca CD B00004T762, 2000.

Hindemith: Mathis der Mahler/Symphonic Metamorphosis (Walther/San Francisco Symphony), Decca CD B0041TRFPE, 1997.

Mahler: Symphony No. 2 (Ziesak/Hellekant/San Francisco Symphony Choir/San Francisco Symphony), London CD B00000423M, 1994.

Mendelssohn Bartholdy: Elijah (Rubens/Stutzmann/Taylor/Gerhaher/ Leipzig Gewandhaus Choir/Leipzig Gewandhaus Chamber Choir/ Leipzig Gewandhaus Orchestra), RCA Red Seal CD B0009W4M1W, 2005.

Mendelssohn: Piano Concertos 1 and 2 (Thibaudet/Leipzig Gewandhaus Orchestra), Decca CD B00005Q673, 2001. (This was another top award winner "Critics' First Choice.")

Mendelssohn: Symphony No. 3, "Scottish"/Symphony No. 4, "Italian" (San Francisco Symphony), Decca CD B00000E4YP, 1993.

Mozart: Konzertarien (Moser/Staatskapelle Dresden), Berlin Classics CD 0184072, 2006.

Nielsen: The Symphonies Nos. 1–3 (San Francisco Symphony), Decca CD B00001X5A0, 1999.

Nielsen: The Symphonies 4–6 (San Francisco Symphony), Decca CD B0015T2GIO, 1999.

Orff: Carmina Burana (Dawson/Daniecki/McMillan/San Francisco Symphony Choir/San Francisco Symphony), Decca CD B0000041YC,

1991. (This won a Grammy Award.)

Sandström: The High Mass/Lidholm: *Kontakion* (Schönheit/Barainsky/Olsson/Torjesen/Arman/Ernman/Paasikivi/MDR Radio Choir/Leipzig Gewandhaus Orchestra), Deutsche Grammophon CD B0006VXF2I, 2005.

Schubert: Symphonies 5 and 8 (San Francisco Symphony), Decca CD, 1992.

Schubert: The Symphonies (Staatskapelle Dresden), Berlin Classics CD B0036ULAXM, 2010.

Sibelius: The Symphonies (San Francisco Symphony), Decca CD B000FO-Q1EA, Collector's Edition 2006.

Strauss: Also Sprach Zarathustra/Till Eulenspiegel/Tod und Verklärung (San Francisco Symphony), Decca CD B000007OTP, 1998.

Richard Strauss: Rosenkavalier Waltzes/Burleske/Capriccio Sextet (Thibaudet/Leipzig Gewandhaus Orchestra), Decca CD B0009AM5FY, 2005.

Appendix B

Example Concert and Work Schedule for the 2013/2014 Season

JULY 12–14, 2013 (THREE concerts)
Munich, Germany
Munich Philharmonic
Ludwig van Beethoven: Symphony No. 4; Hector Berlioz: *Symphonie fantastique*

August 16, 2013
Hamburg, Germany
NDR Symphony Orchestra/Frank Peter Zimmermann, violin
Johannes Brahms: Violin Concerto in D Major, op. 77; and Symphony No. 4 in E Minor, op. 98

August 17, 2013
Sønderborg, Denmark
NDR Symphony Orchestra/Frank Peter Zimmermann, violin
Johannes Brahms: Violin Concerto in D Major, op. 77; and Symphony No. 4 in E Minor, op. 98

September 11–28, 2013 (eight concerts)
Tokyo, Osaka, and Nagano, Japan
NHK Symphony Orchestra
Johannes Brahms: Symphonies No. 1–4, Violin Concerto in D Major, op. 77; *Academic Festival Overture*; Variations on a Theme by Joseph Haydn, op. 56a; Symphony No. 1 in C Minor, op. 68

October 12–13, 2013
Vienna, Austria
Vienna Philharmonic Orchestra
Anton Bruckner: Symphony No. 5 in B-flat Major

A Great Song

October 16–18, 2013 (three concerts)
Prague, Czech Republic
Czech Philharmonic
Ludwig van Beethoven: Symphony No. 7 and Symphony No. 8

October 24, 2013
Copenhagen, Denmark
Danish National Symphony Orchestra
Anton Bruckner: Symphony No. 5 in B-flat Major

October 26, 2013
Ribe, Denmark
Danish National Symphony Orchestra
Anton Bruckner: Symphony No. 5 in B-flat Major

November 2–4, 2013 (three concerts)
Dresden, Germany
Staatskapelle Dresden/Frank Peter Zimmermann, violin
Antonín Dvořák: Violin Concerto in A Minor, op. 53; Jean Sibelius:
Symphony No. 2 in D Major, op. 43

November 16–17, 2013
Bamberg, Germany
Bamberg Symphony/Till Fellner, piano
Ludwig van Beethoven: Piano Concerto in G Major, op. 58; Wilhelm
Stenhammar: Symphony No. 2 in G Minor, op. 34

November 21–22, 24, 2013
Hamburg and Lübeck, Germany
NDR Symphony Orchestra/Piotr Anderszewski, piano
Wolfgang Amadeus Mozart: Piano Concerto No. 25 in C Major, KV
503; Wilhelm Stenhammar: Symphony No. 2 in G Minor, op. 34

December 5–6, 2013
Leipzig, Germany
Gewandhaus Orchestra/Piotr Anderszewski, piano
Wolfgang Amadeus Mozart: Piano Concerto No. 25 in C Major, KV
503; Pyotr Tchaikovsky: Symphony No. 5 in E Minor, op. 64

Appendix B

December 12–13, 2013
Stockholm, Sweden
Swedish Radio Symphony Orchestra
Works by Richard Wagner, Ingvar Lidholm, and Antonín Dvořák

December 18–20, 2013 (three concerts)
Gothenburg, Sweden
Gothenburg Symphony Orchestra
Works by Ludwig van Beethoven and Wilhelm Stenhammar

January 8–10, 2014 (three concerts)
Zurich, Switzerland
Tonhalle-Orchestra Zürich
Works by Wolfgang Amadeus Mozart and Pyotr Tchaikovsky

January 15–19, 2014 (four concerts)
Amsterdam, the Netherlands
Royal Concertgebouw Orchestra
Works by Johannes Brahms

January 22–23, 2014
Paris, France
Orchestre de Paris
Works by Johannes Brahms

February 20, 22, 2014
Stockholm, Sweden
Royal Stockholm Philharmonic Orchestra/Garrick Ohlsson, piano
Works by Johann Sebastian Bach, Ludwig van Beethoven, and Paul Hindemith

February 27–28, 2014
Oslo, Norway
Oslo Philharmonic/Janine Jansen, violin
Works by Sergei Prokofiev and Hector Berlioz

March 20–22, 2014 (three concerts)
Philadelphia, Pennsylvania, United States
Philadelphia Orchestra
Works by Wolfgang Amadeus Mozart and Johannes Brahms

A Great Song

April 3–6, 2014 (four concerts)
San Francisco, California, United States
San Francisco Symphony/Carey Bell, clarinet
Works by Carl Nielsen and Franz Schubert

April 7–13, 2014 (three concerts)
San Francisco, California, United States
San Francisco Symphony/Garrick Ohlsson, piano
Works by Wolfgang Amadeus Mozart and Anton Bruckner

April 17–19, 2014 (three concerts)
Cleveland, Ohio, United States
Cleveland Orchestra/Mark Kosower, cello
Works by Antonín Dvořák and Pyotr Tchaikovsky

May 2–03, 2014
Vienna, Austria
Vienna Symphony/Christiane Karg, soprano/Peter Mattei, baritone
Johannes Brahms: *A German Requiem*, op. 45

May 9–11, 2014 (three concerts)
Bamberg, Germany
Bamberg Symphony
Works by Richard Wagner, Ingvar Lidholm, and Antonín Dvořák

May 15–17, 2014 (three concerts)
Leipzig, Germany
Gewandhaus Orchestra
Ludwig van Beethoven: Symphony No. 8 in F Major, op. 93; Wilhelm
Stenhammar: Symphony No. 2 in G Minor, op. 34

June 7–8, 2014
Berlin, Germany
Deutsches Symphony-Orchester Berlin
Works by Wolfgang Amadeus Mozart and Anton Bruckner

May 12–19, 2014 (five concerts)
Gothenburg, Jönköping, and Umeå, Sweden
Gothenburg Symphony
Wilhelm Stenhammar: *Serenade for Orchestra* in F Major, op. 31; Ludwig

Appendix B

van Beethoven: Symphony No. 3 in E-flat Major, op. 55, *Sinfonia Eroica*

May 26–27, 2014
Leipzig, Germany
Gewandhaus Orchestra/Michael Schönheit, organ
Paul Hindemith: Organ Concerto; Franz Schubert: Symphony No. 9 in C Major, D. 944

Appendix C

The Herbert Blomstedt Collection in Gothenburg

IN NOVEMBER 2010, HERBERT Blomstedt signed a contract to donate his library to the University of Gothenburg: books, notes, scores, recordings, and archive material. At that time, the collection included thirty-thousand volumes, more than fifteen-hundred feet in length. About half of the collection, more than three hundred boxes, was immediately taken to Gothenburg. The maestro still needs his remaining musical library for his ongoing work.

The collection is still growing: a complete old music library with music theory works from 1550 to 1850 has been added, as well as the sheet music of the Fredenheim Collection from 1780 to 1830.

Photos

With Waltraud, lifelong love and constant companion on our wedding day, May 29, 1955.

My father married us at Ekebyhom, Sweden, an old castle, now the site of an Adventist college. She was born in Germany, of Adventist parents, a Danish father and a Swedish mother. She was a teacher of French and loved classical music passionately. When I was on tour, I wrote her a postcard every day. When we traveled together, she heard every concert. She was a deeply pious person, devoted to God, to her family, and to her friends. She died after a long illness in 2003.

*Rehersing the Dresden Staatskepelle in the
"Kulturpalash," Dresden, ca. 1975.*

I was their music director 1975–1985, after a five-year period as an
unofficial leader. It was a fantastic experience with one of the world's
finest symphony orchestras. It was like being born again, and shaped
me musically for the rest of my life. We toured America for the first time
in 1979. This was the beginning of my American career.

As music director of the Oslo Philharmonic, ca. 1963.

Photo for my first Artist's brochure. Stockholm, ca. 1955.

After my debut with the Strockhom Philharmonic in 1954, my musical activities were managed by the concert agency "Konsertbolaget" in Stockhom.

In the park "Friedensblick." Dresden, ca. 1980.

Studying a new score in my apartment in Dresden, ca. 1980.

During my 15 years with the Dresden orchestra I remained living with my family in Stockhom. But it was practical to have a small apartment also in Dresden for my weeks with the orchestra.

This photo and the one following by René Larsson during my holidays in August 2015 showing me working in my study preparing a new score for performance later in the season.

After the performance of Brahms' Requiem in Gewandhaus, Leipzig, June 23, 2005.

I think this picture shows some of the joy and gratitude I feel towards my orchestra and my public after a concert where everybody has given their utmost. When everything has been as perfect as humanly possible, musicians use to say: "Tonight God was in the Hall." But I know He is always there, and we play to His glory. He is the ultimate reason for all our efforts.

Brahms: "Ein deutsches Requiem" / Gewandhaus, Leipzig / June 23, 2005.

This was my next to last concert as "Gewandhauskapellmeister," a typically modest title for the music director of one of the world's oldest and most prestigious philharmonic orchestras. Felix Mendelssohn, Arthur Nikisch, Wilhelm Furtwängler, and Bruno Walter were some of my most famous predecessors.

Photos by Kerstin Schindelhauer. Dortmund, ca. 2009.

Photos by Kerstin Schindelhauer. Dortmund, ca. 2009.